WASHED IN BLOOD

WASHED IN BLOOD

Male Sacrifice, Trauma, and the Cinema

CLAIRE SISCO KING

RUTGERS UNIVERSITY PRESS
NEW BRUNSWICK, NEW JERSEY, AND LONDON

Library of Congress Cataloging-in-Publication Data

King, Claire Sisco.

Washed in blood : male sacrifice, trauma, and the cinema / Claire Sisco King.

p. cm.

Includes bibliographical references and index.

ISBN 978-0-8135-5159-3 (hardcover : alk. paper) — ISBN 978-0-8135-5160-9 (pbk. : alk. paper)

1. Heroes in motion pictures. 2. Death in motion pictures. 3. Sacrifice in motion pictures. 4. Psychic trauma in motion pictures. I. Title.

PN1995.9.H44K56 2011

791.43'652—dc22 2011004715

A British Cataloging-in-Publication record for this book is available from the British Library.

Visit our Web site: http://rutgerspress.rutgers.edu

Manufactured in the United States of America

For Matt, MP, and Lo

CONTENTS

ACKNOWLEDGMENTS

I want first to thank the members of the "New Directions in Trauma Studies" seminar at the Robert Penn Warren Center for the Humanities at Vanderbilt University. Although a year spent thinking, writing, and talking about trauma should not really be called a "good time," this experience was amazing. I owe a great deal to each of the seminar participants: Laura Carpenter, Kate Daniels, Jon Ebert, Vivien Fryd, Christina Karageorgou-Bastea, Linda Manning, Charlotte Pierce-Baker, and Maurice Stevens. I also thank the center's executive director, Mona Frederick, and the center's staff for facilitating such a tremendous year.

I owe many thanks to my colleagues in Communication Studies at Vanderbilt University: Vanessa Beasley, Bonnie Dow, Kass Kovalcheck, John Sloop, and Paul Stob. I could not ask for a better place to work or for a better community among which to spend my days. I also extend great thanks to Paul Young, my colleague in Film Studies, who gave me a gracious welcome at Vanderbilt.

I heartily thank the American Association of University Women, whose generous fellowship allowed me to complete graduate school. Without their help many years ago, this project would not exist. I also thank Vanderbilt University for a pre-tenure research leave, which allowed me to finish this book.

An earlier version of portions of chapter 4 and the epilogue originally appeared as "Rogue Waves, Remakes, and Resurrections: Allegorical Displacement and Screen Memories in *Poseidon*," *Quarterly Journal of Speech* 94 (2008): 430–454. Permission to use this material is courtesy of the National Communication Association.

I am grateful for the faculty at Indiana University who shaped this work (and me) for the better. Joan Hawkins earns special thanks for never judging my caffeine habits or bad taste in movies and for being an incomparable advisor. I also thank Barbara Klinger, Beverly Stoeltje, Constance Furey, John

Lucaites, and Roopali Mukherjee for their willingness to challenge *and* support my work. I am so lucky to have found a group of colleagues and friends who are unfailing in their commitment to ideas, activism, and good times. These include Jeff Bennett, Isaac West, Chris Dumas, Jamie Skerski, Cara Buckley, Suzanne Enck-Wanzer, Darrel Enck-Wanzer, David Moscowitz, and Jeff Motter. Thanks especially to Jeff and Isaac, who have read many versions of this project (and several others). I also owe thanks to Erin Rand for her generosity and general cleverness as a reader.

I thank Leslie Mitchner, Katie Keeran, Kate Babbitt, and all of those at Rutgers University Press with whom I worked. Their support, thoughtful guidance, and quick response times made the publishing experience delightful.

I also owe so much to my parents, Ralph and Evelyn Sisco, who have supported me beyond measure for my entire life. I'm sure there were times when they desperately wanted to ask me to stop talking or thinking out loud for even just one moment, but they never did. I thank them for enabling me to develop my voice. Thanks also to my brother, Kirk Sisco, for putting up with me all these years.

Finally, I want to express my gratitude and love for Matt King, my best friend and constant sounding board. We may not speak exactly the same language, but I can always count on his attention and compassion. His effervescent spirit and tireless energy (despite his own formidable schedule and tremendous responsibilities) have lifted me out of my darkest moments. Whenever I take myself too seriously, he and our beautiful daughters remind me of the joy of the everyday.

WASHED IN BLOOD

INTRODUCTION

Mel Gibson's *The Passion of the Christ* (2004) succeeds at being a hard film to watch. Like the devotional art of the Middle Ages, it focuses intently on the psychological and physical torment Jesus endured during the hours before his death, graphically depicting scenes of torture and fixating on Jesus's bloody lacerations. Its gore has led some critics to call *The Passion* a traumatic film: a film not only *about* traumatic suffering but also one that is traumatizing to viewers.[1] For instance, Owen Gleiberman's review for *Entertainment Weekly* locates *The Passion* within "the cinema of cruelty." Citing the "voyeuristic brutality" of the film, Gleiberman suggests that while it is possible to write Gibson off as a "glorified pain freak," his "torture-racked" film might be better understood as a "sacred form of *shock therapy*" fixated on the alleged "link between pain and what lies on the other side of pain—between horror and awe."[2] Lisa Schwarzbaum's adjacent review in *Entertainment Weekly* derides the film as producing little more than "shock and awe" and worries that viewers may be "traumatized by something they shouldn't need to see."[3]

Reviewers typically attributed *The Passion*'s fixation on trauma to the perceived singularity of Gibson as a star, filmmaker, and public figure.[4] Some celebrated Gibson as a religious devotee with a unique artistic vision and determination to offer an "accurate" portrayal of the gospels; others positioned Gibson as an anti-Semitic fundamentalist obsessed with the Christ story. In each case, however, Gibson's high-profile and divisive persona operated as the particularized lens through which most discussions of *The Passion* were filtered. Of special interest were the extreme personal and financial efforts Gibson undertook to get this film made and the risks such endeavors posed to his career. Some reviewers (and fans) even suggested parallels between the suffering of the film's protagonist and the sacrifices made by its director, framing Gibson as a modern-day martyr.[5]

Unfortunately, this focus on Gibson and the apparent singularity of his film obscures the larger historical, cultural, and cinematic context from which *The Passion* emerged. This film can be described as a striking cinematic event, and certainly Gibson's personal and financial dedication to the project exceeds the norm. *The Passion of the Christ* is not, however, as singular or peculiar a text as many might have believed. This film is only one of many Hollywood films to frame the sacrificial death of a male protagonist as a ritual of redemption. While Gibson's overt focus on the figure of Jesus Christ is somewhat unique, the intersecting discourses of trauma and sacrifice at work within *The Passion* operate as organizing frameworks through which Hollywood cinema has articulated, negotiated, and regulated hegemonic expectations about masculinity, national identity, and civic duty for decades.

So pervasive is Hollywood's fixation on the traumatic suffering and ritualized destruction of (mostly) white male bodies that *The Passion* represents an example of an overlooked body of American films: the sacrificial film. These films—in which a beloved but psychologically wounded male protagonist gives his life to save others and find redemption for himself—demonstrate the American investment in the rhetoric and iconography of trauma as embodied chiefly by a significant, yet largely unnoticed, character type in Hollywood cinema, the sacrificial victim-hero.[6] Exemplifying Kirby Farrell's notion of "traumatic heroism," sacrificial victim-heroes pervade U.S. films; yet almost no scholarship attends to the cultural and symbolic imbrication of trauma, sacrifice, and the cinema.[7]

A great deal of scholarly work does address sacrificial death and Christological themes in Hollywood movies, seeking out, for instance, "Christ figures" in film.[8] Often written from a theological perspective, this scholarship typically measures the accuracy or authenticity of cinematic Christ figures in relation to historical and/or biblical source texts. This literature also frequently constructs or deploys typologies for finding what are deemed "Christ-like" attributes in cinematic characters, for whom sacrificial death operates as one among many defining traits. These accounts, however, typically lack attention to the ideological and cultural work done by Christological narratives and iconography.[9] While theological film criticism considers how effectively cinematic Christ figures re-create their origin stories, such scholarship often stops short of considering the implications of the Christ story as a formative and influential logic in U.S. culture.

As such, *Washed in Blood* does not search for "Christ figures" in film, and it is not positioned within the field of film theology. Rather, this project addresses how, why, and to what ends the logic of traumatic heroism, as embodied famously but not exclusively by the Christ story, circulates in a number of discursive fields throughout U.S. public culture in ways that are both historically specific and ideologically driven. While I read many of the films addressed in this book in relation to Christological narratives and iconography, I also understand the cinematic depiction of traumatic heroism as participating in discursive formations specific to the historical and cultural contexts in which each film was released. Sacrificial films illustrate a particular instantiation of American trauma culture, and, revealing the overlapping logics that instruct both sacrificial films and trauma discourse, I argue that signifiers of trauma and sacrifice play significant roles in managing U.S. cultural memory.

This book draws from scholarship on the subjects of trauma and cinema, including the work of Farrell, E. Ann Kaplan, Janet Walker, and Adam Lowenstein, but also offers a new perspective for understanding how trauma works within U.S. film culture in relation to the logic of sacrifice, or noble death. Central to this interrogation of the intersections of trauma and sacrifice is the work of Georges Bataille, whose writings offer a productive (but frequently neglected) framework for understanding American cinema's reverent fascination with male bodies in pain. Understanding Bataille's writings and U.S. film culture as sites similarly enthralled with traumatic self-loss and sacrificial mutilation, I argue that Hollywood films advocate (whether consciously or not) a sacrificial economy in which traumatic heroism becomes a paramount marker of the (male) citizen-subject's worth. Although sacrifice might seem like an archaic—or even extinct—practice, it is frequently, if not compulsively, reenacted in American films.

Rites of Sacrifice

Similar to Jacinda Read's figuration of rape-revenge as a "narrative structure" that "has produced a historically specific but generically diverse cycle of films," sacrifice structures films across a variety of genres and subgenres, including war, action, horror, science fiction, and disaster films—the last of which this book addresses most specifically.[10] Given the importance of violence to sacrifice as a ritualized praxis, the figure of the sacrificial victim-hero occurs most frequently in films emphasizing onscreen violence and special effects. In each sacrificial film, the death of the victim-hero occurs in one of the final scenes and is the act on which the narrative's resolution (often quite literally) hangs.

Examples of sacrificial films include *Omega Man* (Boris Sagal, 1971), a science fiction/disaster film in which a military scientist offers up his blood to stop a global plague; *Poseidon Adventure* (Ronald Neame, 1972), a disaster film about a minister who gives his life to save passengers on a sinking ship; *The Exorcist* (William Friedkin, 1973), a horror film in which a priest dies to rescue a possessed young girl; *The Omen* (Richard Donner, 1976), a horror film in which a father sacrifices himself to stop the anti-Christ; *Terminator 2: Judgment Day* (James Cameron, 1991), an action film about a surrogate father who dies in order to save a young boy; *Braveheart* (Mel Gibson, 1995), a historical epic in which a military leader gives his life for national independence; *Titanic* (James Cameron, 1997), a melodramatic disaster film in which a young man trades his life for his lover's; *Armageddon* (Michael Bay, 1998), a disaster film about a father who gives his life to stop an asteroid attack; *Saving Private Ryan* (Steven Spielberg, 1998), a war film in which a decorated military leader dies to save a young soldier; and *Ladder 49* (Jay Russell, 2004), a drama centered on a firefighter who dies to save his friends. A number of more recent sacrificial films are remakes of prior sacrificial texts, including *The Omen: 6/6/06* (John Moore, 2006); *Poseidon* (Wolfgang Petersen, 2006), a remake of *The Poseidon Adventure*; and *I Am Legend* (Francis Lawrence, 2007), a remake of *Omega Man*.

Consonant with most ritualized sacrificial practices, sacrificial films depend on male victim-heroes—for much of what is at stake in sacrificial rites is the negotiation and redefinition of the masculine norms of the social body.[11] Sacrificial films typically deploy sacrifice as a strategy for managing the male victim-hero's positions of privilege and authority *within* the narrative *and* in relation to the larger cultural context from which the film emerges. Such films position the victim-hero as an embattled leader and patriarch—often literally as a biological father and sometimes figuratively as a paternal surrogate or member of the clergy. In all of these films, the sacrificial victim-hero weathers crises both public and personal; having lost his positions of institutional authority and/or suffered private losses, he begins his narrative arc in a place of peril and uncertainty.

So wounded is this victim-hero that he often bears the symptoms of trauma or what might be called post-traumatic stress disorder (PTSD), including flashbacks, nightmares, and repetition compulsions due to prior experiences of extreme terror or loss. After having labored in vain to overcome his own anxious doubt and emotional disquietude and to save his (literal and/or metaphorical) children, the sacrificial victim-hero ultimately realizes that his salvific potential and obligation to others require resignation to noble death—a final act of self-loss that, paradoxically, resolves his earlier traumas and restores his imagined sense of selfhood. In fact, trauma and sacrifice enable the victim-hero to earn transcendent authority, or what Bataille calls "sovereignty."

Such narratives operate as allegories in which the victim-hero's story of trauma and sacrificial recovery simultaneously *displaces and enables* a gendered rewriting of cultural memory about national identity and civic duty. Using Read's "cyclic model," I argue that, despite their generic variability, sacrificial films tend to be historically specific, recurring more prominently at certain moments in American history than at others.[12] Especially since the 1970s, for reasons to be discussed throughout this book, sacrificial films have emerged in correspondence with cycles of trauma culture, understood here as moments in which "trauma" operates as an organizing discourse for constructing and managing cultural memory. In such contexts, metaphors of wounds, pain, and crisis burgeon in public rhetoric and migrate across a number of discursive fields and the term "trauma" carries great currency, being used to describe a diverse and diffuse range of experiences including war, natural disasters, terrorism, child abuse, cultural change, and social unrest.[13]

This book considers cycles of sacrificial films from three distinct yet "tangled" historical moments in the United States during which representations of and public discourse about both the nation and its masculinity are "clothed in the language of crisis" and deploy a "vocabulary of pain and urgency": the early-to-mid 1970s, during which trauma discourse related primarily to the Vietnam War; the mid- to late 1990s, during which much public rhetoric framed white heterosexual masculinity as traumatized or "in crisis"; and the mid- to late 2000s, during which trauma discourse posited the nation itself as wounded by 9/11 and its aftereffects.[14] If, as Sally Robinson suggests, U.S. culture consistently and cyclically redefines itself in "waves of crisis and resolution," sacrificial films represent a significant tide that correspondingly rises and falls in cinematic culture, managing and making use of such perceived crises and traumas.[15]

One could point to innumerable films throughout the history of Hollywood cinema that take up the theme of "sacrifice," loosely defined. Films across many genres, from the western to the war film to the melodrama, feature characters that are forced to "sacrifice," or give up, things of great importance—romantic love, family, career opportunities, personal happiness, to name a few. Such films define sacrifice as a difficult choice that involves relinquishing a culturally cherished object or value. People most often talk or think about sacrifice in this sense, for example in discussions of the "sacrifices" a hero, a soldier, or a mother must make. This vernacular use of the word, however, obscures the specific and religious origins of sacrifice as a ritual process that offers up an object or person before witnesses as an act of atonement, expiation, and redemption. This generalized notion of sacrifice also obscures the extent to which sacrificial death as a salvific act remains primarily a male rite/right, both historically and within Hollywood cinema. Attending to this specific model of sacrificial praxis, therefore, makes visible America's investment in and dependence on the (allegedly) noble death of men—whether symbolically in cinema or literally on battlefields.

When considered in this way, sacrifice as a ritualized practice occupies a more specific and historically defined (but nonetheless prominent and recurrent) space in Hollywood cinema. To be fair, this is not to say no films outside of the three historical periods considered here feature sacrificial victim-heroes. Individual examples of this narrative structure exist throughout the whole of American cinema; but within particular moments in U.S. history, traumatic heroism becomes pronounced as a narrative trope in popular films: in the historical periods mentioned above, a series of sacrificial films appears in rather rapid succession, achieves prominence, and then wanes. Many sacrificial films, significantly, constitute some of the most well-known successes in recent cinematic history, including a host of films that rank in the 100 all-time top-grossing films: *Titanic* (1997), *Star Wars: Episode IV* (George Lucas, 1977), *The Passion of the Christ* (2004), *I Am Legend* (2007), *Armageddon* (1998), *Terminator 2: Judgment Day* (1991), *Saving Private Ryan* (1996), *Gladiator* (Ridley Scott, 2000), *300* (Zack Snyder, 2006), and *The Exorcist* (1973).[16]

Given that so many American films take up male sacrificial death as a narrative trope and given the popularity this narrative device has with American audiences, this book asks, "Why?" What historical and/or cultural conditions enable the retelling of this violent tale of male self-sacrifice again and again? Why are citizenship, nationalism, and heroism so frequently defined in terms of male suffering and death? How do sacrificial constructions of masculinity respond and contribute to cultural memory and fantasies about trauma and national identity? This book posits U.S. collective memory and fantasies about national identity as inextricably bound to cultural figurations of masculinity, arguing, as have Susan Jeffords and Barbara Biesecker, that cinematic constructions of male bodies frequently function as tools for thinking about and rescripting the nation's past.[17]

Sacrifice recurs as a narrative structure that constructs and makes use of perceived disruptions to prevailing public narratives about the national masculine, or the perceived masculinity of the United States as a national body. In particular, sacrificial films demonstrate and contribute to a larger trauma culture that deploys images of and narratives about male suffering, death, and redemption as strategies for reconstituting dominant notions of the subject, the nation, and the masculine. Steeped in trauma discourse, sacrificial films simultaneously construct and disavow cultural anxieties about the national masculine as both injured and injurious. On the one hand, sacrificial films construct "evidence" of national trauma, framing the suffering and violent death of the victim-hero as the most significant indicators of such trauma; but on the other hand, they imagine sacrifice as a regenerative and salvific ritual aimed at healing perceived wounds both within the diegetic worlds of the films and within their cultural contexts. Sacrificial films work to transform an allegedly traumatized (social) body into one that is *post*-traumatic, restaging traumatic loss so that catastrophe may be refigured as redemption, renewal, and rebirth.

Trauma Discourse

What is the discourse of trauma? Or, more precisely, what are the discourses of trauma? In the United States, many distinct but interrelated levels of discourse attend to questions of what trauma is or does. Three such levels will be discussed here. First, clinical discourse addresses traumatic experiences from medical, scientific, and/or therapeutic perspectives. Such work includes, for example, studies of the body's neurobiological responses to traumatic experience and treatment protocols and therapy regimens for survivors. Second, humanists (and some social scientists) address cultural representations of and responses to trauma. Much humanistic work draws directly from medical-scientific discussions of trauma. For instance, it is not unusual to find significant amounts of neurobiology cited in works of literary or film studies. Third, the concept of "trauma" circulates through public culture, appearing in sites as disparate as presidential rhetoric and popular cinema (sacrificial films in particular). This level of discourse, often dubbed "trauma culture," frequently appropriates and arguably exploits the logic and rhetoric of both medical-scientific and humanistic trauma discourses—as illustrated, for instance, by Gleiberman's and Schwarzbaum's descriptions of Gibson's *The Passion of the Christ* as a kind of cinematic shock therapy capable of traumatizing spectators.

While each of these levels of trauma discourse should be understood as distinct and as having decidedly different aims, significant (and perhaps surprising) areas of overlap do exist. For example, Bataille's work illustrates the imbrication of humanistic trauma theory and trauma culture. Cited and anthologized by humanistic scholars as a theorist of trauma, Bataille also demonstrates an attraction toward suffering characteristic of the trauma culture so often critiqued by humanists. Likewise, argues Roger Luckhurst, the technologies of the cinema—most notably flashback editing—have helped construct the terms with which the symptoms of trauma and PTSD, in particular, are defined. Luckhurst posits, "If the modern flashback [in film] seems uncannily mimetic of the psychology of trauma, then it is probably because films . . . were instrumental in helping formulate the psychological symptoms of mental illness linked with traumatic origins."[18]

The levels of trauma discourse also share assumptions, tropes, and images regarding what trauma does to human subjectivity. In *Trauma: A Genealogy*, Ruth Leys summarizes the canonical figuration of trauma in both medical and humanistic contexts. Describing diagnoses of PTSD, Leys explains, "The idea is that, owing to the emotions of terror and surprise caused by certain events, the mind is split or dissociated: it is unable to register the wound to the psyche because the ordinary mechanisms of awareness and cognition are destroyed."[19] The traumatized person, according to this theoretical and diagnostic paradigm, is "haunted or possessed by intrusive traumatic memories," rendering traumatic experience "fixed or frozen in time" and "perpetually reexperienced in a painful, dissociated traumatic present."[20]

Calling trauma a "black hole," psychiatrists Bessel van der Kolk and Alexander McFarlane illustrate this perspective, positing trauma as a "tyranny of the past" that takes the survivor hostage. They argue that in trauma the "memory of one particular event comes to taint all other experiences, spoiling appreciation of the present."[21] This construction of trauma also resonates in the popular press; journalist Patricia Cohen asserts in the *New York Times*, "Exposure to terrifying events can overwhelm and break down the body's natural system of self-defense. Traumatic memories continually bulldoze their way into the present."[22] This definition of trauma reverberates throughout humanistic trauma theory, including Cathy Caruth's figuration of trauma as a "breach in the mind's experience of time, self, and the world."[23] It also mirrors Dominick LaCapra's understanding of trauma as a "disruptive experience that disarticulates the self and creates holes in existence."[24] These canonical constructions of trauma share an understanding of trauma as creating a rupture, or break, in the subject's psyche.

The multiple levels of trauma discourse also characterize traumatic experience as outside of representation. Caruth argues that the injury of trauma owes to "its very unassimilated nature—the way it was precisely not known in the first instance"; it is "not available to consciousness" and thus exceeds the grasp of the survivor.[25] Psychiatrist Judith Herman similarly argues that "the ordinary response to atrocities is to banish them from consciousness. Certain violations of the social compact are too terrible to utter aloud: this is the meaning of the word *unspeakable*."[26] Bataille wrote of the survivors of the atomic bombing in Hiroshima during World War II that "those who were its witnesses, enduring the effect without dying, no longer had the strength necessary to form an intelligible representation of their misfortune"; when the "possibilities of human suffering" confront representation, "those possibilities exceed it infinitely."[27]

In response to unassimilated, unspeakable, or unintelligible trauma, therapeutic discourse typically links recovery to the survivor's ability to use testimony to reconstruct his/her "trauma story" and to "speak the unspeakable."[28] Psychiatrist Dori Laub argues that "it is essential for this narrative that *could not be articulated* to be *told*, to be *transmitted*, to be *heard*"; without such narrativization of trauma, the survivor risks becoming stuck, as the "'not telling' of the story serves as a perpetuation of [trauma's] tyranny."[29] Using cinematic metaphors, Herman posits that if trauma is "a series of still snapshots or a silent movie," then "the role of therapy is to provide the music and the words" in the hopes that reconstruction of the trauma and its "integration" into the life of the survivor will help to rebuild and renew his/her subjectivity.[30]

Therapeutic trauma discourse encourages the survivor to move on and leave behind injury so that "traumatic experience truly belongs to the past."[31] The hope is that by assimilating the trauma story into his/her personal narrative, the trauma survivor can become (again) a unified and integrated subject—no longer breached or disarticulated but repaired and sutured back together. Laub contends that "the testimony is, therefore, the process by which the narrator (the survivor) reclaims his position as a witness: reconstitutes the internal 'thou' and thus the possibility of a witness or a listener inside himself."[32] Laub's description of witnessing, interestingly, figures the survivor as not unlike a spectator: safely removed from and able to take in a traumatic scene. As I argue throughout this book, sacrificial films become a key site in popular culture for such narrativization, dramatizing the moving-on process in hyperbolic cinematic registers.

At stake in (and reinforced by) these various levels of trauma discourse are prevailing fictions of the subject as coherent, whole, and seamless. To posit a subject that has been shattered or broken by trauma is to imagine (and assert) that a complete and finished subject existed in the first place. Claiming a "before" and an "after" in relationship to perceived injury, trauma rhetoric reinscribes a fiction of subjectivity as a thing itself, discounting (if not disavowing) the extent to which subjectivity is a fraught, incomplete, and contingent *process of becoming*. The imagined timeline of traumatogenic injury, thus, implies that the unified subject imagined to have existed before trauma can be retrieved and made whole again. Although the experience of trauma itself is typically described as having "no beginning, no ending, no before, no during and no after" because of its recurrent and intrusive nature, the logic of traumatogenic injury fixates on a moment that *creates* such pathologic "timelessness," breaking what is otherwise understood as the subject's linear and coherent experience of him/herself in history.[33]

Maurice Stevens argues that within trauma discourse the canonical construction of a "past and complete un-representable trauma supports claims about the coherent subject of history."[34] The rhetoric of trauma, argues Stevens, does work to prop up ideological fantasies about what it means to be human.

> It says, "You see, there once was a whole, seamless and modern subject. Our effort to repair it, by making legible its injury, is proof enough of its having been there at one time, whole (read: vulnerable), pure (read: violable) and mature. Trauma has rendered this particular example of proper subjectivity damaged, where once, in a moment of innocent possibility, it was not.[35]

Like Stevens, Hal Foster notes that the circulation of "trauma discourse" in popular culture deploys injuries as key signifiers of intact subjectivity. He writes, "In popular culture, trauma is treated as an event that guarantees the subject, and in this psychological register the subject, however disturbed, rushes back as witness, testifier, survivor."[36]

Such an insistence on the possibility of the unified, autonomous, and volitional subject can be seen, for instance, in Laub's description of the relationship between trauma, testimony, and recovery. Laub explains, "There is, in each survivor, an imperative need to tell and thus to come to know *one*'s story, unimpeded by ghosts from the past against which *one* has to protect *oneself*.

One has to know *one*'s buried truth in order to be able to live *one*'s life."[37] Notice, then, the rhetorical emphasis on the singularity of the subject (the one), the assumption that there is a "truth" that such a unitary subject can "know," and the assertion that the individual can indeed have ownership over his/her identity and narrative.

While not denying the possibility that a painful or terrifying event can radically alter a person's physical, mental, and emotional senses of self and not denigrating an individual's choice to seek therapeutic assistance for suffering, I do wish to consider how trauma discourse might contribute to hegemonic fictions about the nature of the subject. The version of "the self" constructed and privileged by the rhetoric of trauma, particularly as it operates within popular culture and as it intersects with sacrifice, reinforces masculinist norms. Stevens argues that trauma discourse may unwittingly obscure the extent to which the purported "wholeness, purity and propriety of this subject have been built on the very particular ways it has always already been gendered, sexed, and, of course, raced."[38] The model of intact, coherent subjectivity illustrates a masculinist paradigm celebrating rationality, hierarchy, and individualism. Further, the intersection of discourses of trauma and with the rhetoric of sacrifice valorizes the white male body in pain as the exemplar of the citizen-subject and the most honorable form of heroism.

Assertions of self-shattering traumatic injury not only reaffirm masculinist notions of the unified subject, they also mark and privilege a particular kind of subject: the survivor of or witness to suffering. Foster continues, "Here is indeed a traumatic subject, and it has absolute authority, for one cannot challenge the trauma of another: one can only believe it, even identify with it, or not." What results is a paradox in which "*the subject is evacuated and elevated all at once*."[39] The concurrent evacuation and elevation of the subject via cinematic rites of sacrifice venerate white male bodies as humanity's most authoritative and vital victims, whose stories of suffering, loss, and redemption are said to matter above all others.

By privileging a certain subject whose experiential and testimonial authority is imagined to be unassailable, the discourse of trauma also risks becoming a kind of directive that enjoins the subject to *prove* its worth—for instance, to the collective or the nation-state—through its willingness to be sacrificed. Such is the work of wartime discourse about the "ultimate sacrifice," as exemplified by Horace's claim that "*dulce et decorum est pro patria mori*" ("it is sweet and fitting to die for one's country"). That is, when the authority assigned to the victim by trauma culture meets with the rhetoric of sacrifice, the resulting discourse marks death as the most noble offering a subject can make and therefore risks defining traumatic suffering as a social good or even a civic obligation. Such figurations of trauma may reinscribe trauma culture and perpetuate trauma's currency within American culture. Paradoxically, then, the work of scholars and clinicians devoted to the eradication of human suffering may become fodder for trauma culture—as embodied, for instance, by Hollywood's love affair with films about psychologically wounded characters who find redemption in traumatic experiences.

In this interrogation of trauma discourse and its cinematic articulations, I do not intend to prove the "truth" or "reality" of any particular traumas, nor do I adopt a literalist perspective in which sacrificial films are understood as belatedly responding to or registering a "real" trauma. This is not to say that there was not "real" terror and crisis experienced in the historical periods addressed in this book; each of the three decades discussed here is assuredly marked by experiences of fear, loss, and suffering that unsettled people's understanding of identity, culture, and history. Catastrophic events and collective suffering do impact how people think about themselves, the nation, and the human condition and therefore also impact mass-mediated texts (and vice versa). Given the elusive and variable nature of traumatic experience, however, locating the "real" of any historical trauma or social crisis is largely impossible.

Instead, I interrogate how sacrificial films participate in the discourses of trauma, affirming and deploying prevailing assumptions about what trauma is and does. How and why have certain events (or moments) been publicly framed as "traumatic" in public culture? How do sacrificial films contribute to such constructions? How does trauma rhetoric implicate Western fantasies about the subject, the nation, and the masculine? As Robinson advises, rather than seeking "hard evidence of actual social trauma," I address the "power of language, of metaphors and images, to convincingly represent that sense of trauma and turning point."[40] This investigation considers the myriad ways that clinical, humanistic, and popular discourses of trauma intersect and collectively, if unintentionally, reinforce America's dependence on the sacrificial economy.

Through focus on the discursive work of trauma I hope to avoid what Susannah Radstone describes as the all-too-common construction of trauma as something that happens to a "passive, acted-upon victim or culture." Radstone argues that "events do not come out of nowhere, and neither do they leave their mark on a previously blank page. The 'problem' with trauma is that the subject it proposes—the victim—is too absolutely passive."[41] Instead, by interrogating the "cultural process that weaves events into preexisting fantasy scenes," I understand "trauma" as constructed in and by culture and as inseparable from assumptions about what it means to be a subject, a citizen, and a nation.[42] Aiming to uncover the investment that American culture has in trauma discourse and the uses to which trauma so often gets put, this book shifts our focus: rather than imagining what trauma *does to* victims, it asks what trauma *does for* the imagined U.S. community.

To trace constructions of traumatic injury and recovery, I look toward symptoms of trauma culture scattered throughout public discourse. Juxtaposing clinical and therapeutic language, humanistic theory, public rhetoric, and popular film, I explore moments of American trauma culture that construct the national masculine as in crisis and consequently make recourse to trauma and sacrifice as overlapping frames that enable the "interpretation of injury" and offer promises of regeneration. Farrell argues that particular moments of Western culture take on a "post-traumatic coloration," producing a "cultural environment in which post-traumatic themes flouris[h]."[43]

Like Farrell, Herman notes that the history of "trauma" as a concept has been marked by periods of rise and fall, of great publicity and relative obscurity. For instance, she observes that "episodic amnesia" marks the study of trauma within psychiatric and/or psychological communities, in which cycles of "active investigation" of and attention to trauma "have alternated with periods of oblivion."[44] In the contexts I consider, clinical attention to trauma mirrors and helps guarantee its circulation in both the academy and popular discourse as a tool for understanding not only the psychological experiences of individuals but also U.S. culture and national identity. In each of the historical periods discussed here, "trauma" as a concept achieves new levels of prominence in clinical, academic, and/or popular contexts.

In the 1970s, Freudian theories of trauma emerged within psychiatric discourse as a way of understanding Vietnam veterans' postwar struggles and became an interpretive frame for describing the wartime and postwar nation. In the 1990s, this language became even more mainstreamed; for instance, such phrases as "recovered memory syndrome" and post-traumatic stress disorder became well known within public vernacular discourse. Also at this time, scholars in the humanities, including Caruth and LaCapra, turned to trauma theory, making trauma something of a cottage industry in academia.[45] In the first decade of the twentieth century, trauma reemerged in both popular and academic rhetoric as a frame for constructing America's experiences of 9/11 and the "War on Terror." Each of these periods also exhibits an apparent cultural interest in catastrophe, as exemplified by the popularity and prevalence of the disaster film within each of these historical timeframes.[46] It is no accident that disaster films and sacrificial films often appear coterminously—in fact, many disaster films are also sacrificial films, as will be examined in this book—because the cultural currency of trauma animates the depiction of disaster and the recourse to sacrifice within recent U.S. film culture.

Cycles of trauma culture also characteristically emphasize the experiences of male bodies and subjectivities. For Laura S. Brown, this masculinist inflection reflects the tendency to mark an event as "traumatic" for a culture only when it disrupts what is presumed to be the norm or affects the group occupying the greatest positions of privilege within that social body. It is for this reason that public rhetoric most often identifies trauma (not unlike sacrifice) as "things that can and do happen to men."[47] Events gain public recognition as *social, cultural,* or *national* traumas—as opposed to experiences, such as rape or incest, that get marked as personal, private, or individual traumas and that are most often associated with women—when they are understood to affect male bodies and to disrupt the master narratives that instruct and are instructed by hegemonic assumptions about the masculine. Hence, the "cyclical nature of crises in white masculinity," as demonstrated by such scholars as Robinson and Tania Modleski, itself derives from, corresponds to, and embodies a larger cultural tendency to deploy trauma as an interpretive lens, affective sensibility, and rhetorical frame.[48]

Furthermore, prevailing constructs of the subject get mapped onto larger social bodies, positing collectives or culture as subject to trauma—as exemplified by van der Kolk's claim that "societies that have been massively traumatized" follow "patterns of adaptation and disintegration" similar to those identified within individuals. The alleged wounds of the collective may then become a rationale for the nation-state's reliance on (often violent) defenses for restoring the imagined wholeness, purity, and security of the body politic.[49] That is, a common response to national or cultural trauma is the initiation of acts of violence and terror, such as war, that will yield more trauma. By naturalizing masculinist constructions of the subject and privileging male bodies as both most vulnerable to trauma *and* most able to resolve its effects, sacrificial films reify the perceived importance of both violence and male subjects to the sustained life of the nation-state and affirm the value of the "ultimate sacrifice" as the greatest and gravest performance of civic duty.[50]

Sacrificial films make use of the language of trauma and crisis as an "enabling fiction" that constructs and manages cultural memory about the national masculine toward hegemonic ends. When narrativized, trauma may (paradoxically) function as a coping strategy for the culture that imagines itself to be wounded or under attack. Farrell argues, "As a trope, trauma has adapted to frame the experience of individuals and nations. It can be formulated to relieve suffering and to adjust the scales of justice, but it can also rationalize dependence or aggression."[51] That is, trauma may be "claimed" or "asserted" when it seems politically or ideologically expedient; not merely a symptom of social anxiety, trauma culture acts a rhetorical response aimed at assuaging such anxiety. As Farrell suggests, Hollywood is a crucial (even if unwitting) site at which "trauma" gets used toward ideological ends, and perhaps no clearer example of Hollywood's "ideological use of trauma" exists than the sacrificial film.[52]

Allegorical Displacements

At the uncanny intersection of sacrificial logic and trauma discourse are stories that laud victim-heroes not for their ability to avoid or overcome suffering but for having been utterly undone; sacrificial films elevate the victim-hero as one ("the one") with experience beyond reproach and sacrosanct authority. Sacrificial films operate at an allegorical register, using tales of the individual victim-hero's trauma and recovery as synecdoches for dramatizing the nation's imagined suffering and salvation. Offering a textual mode of displacement, substitution, and, as Robert Hariman argues, a "necessarily imperfect translation" of history, allegories are uniquely positioned to manage what are perceived to be the nation's traumatic memories.[53]

According to a central strain of trauma discourse, as exemplified by Caruth's canonical work, a characteristic of traumatic memory is the "exactness" of trauma's return.[54] Caruth describes traumatic memory as neither shrouded by symbols nor contextualized by narrative but as the "literal return of the event against the will of the one it inhabits," rendering past, present, and future inextricably bound.[55] If trauma is thought to revisit survivors exactly, allegorical displacement provides a screen against such "overwhelming immediacy."[56] As Hariman demonstrates, allegories place past and present "side by side" so that their incongruities might be reconciled, offering a "defense mechanism" against the vicissitudes of human experience without risking a confrontation with history that might be perceived as too close, too open, or too traumatic. In sacrificial allegories, the past does not return to the text openly or exactly but becomes an absent presence whose memory is refigured through "dynamic juxtaposition" with the imagined present.[57]

Hariman understands allegory as the predominant mode of the postmodern condition, in which temporality is understood as fragmented and "semiotic excess" is the norm.[58] Allegory may also be understood as the master form of posttraumatic culture, which is marked by an imagined "breach" in constructions of "time, self, world" and to which allegory can effectively respond.[59] Hence it is that allegory has a history of "eternal recurrence at periods of loss and fragmentation." As a "twice-told-tale" hinging on the "restatement" of history, allegory performs a symptomatic act of repetition, but there is also a double movement within allegorical modalities—both *toward and away from* history and memory.[60]

Because much of its meaning lies outside of the narrative itself, allegory "carries a sense of loss regarding what it depicts."[61] Similar to understandings of traumatic memory as marked by gaps, fissures, and silences, allegory is structured by an absent presence—what is *almost* but not *quite* there in the text. This attachment to what is lost or left out—the insistence that something is missing, hidden, absent—can be understood as a rather melancholic gesture, akin to what LaCapra calls "acting out."[62] At the same time, allegorical displacement also resembles what Freud calls a "screen memory." Freud defines screen memories as childhood memories that displace repressed memories of later events that are too painful or shocking to be experienced directly. He argues that "painful experience is screened or covered" by the recollection of "something less significant."[63] Allegorical displacement also signals a defensive, or protective, gesture marked by an impulse toward "regeneration" and the assertion that from the rubble, or "ruins" of the past a (somewhat) new narrative can be reborn.[64] Allegory, thus, remains ambivalent, holding onto the past (if only indirectly) at the same time that it insists on moving on and beginning anew.

The ambivalence—which Bataille describes as the inherent simultaneity of attraction and repulsion—at the heart of allegory also characterizes the traumatic logic of sacrifice. LaCapra argues that if "the response to extreme, traumatizing events" tends to be "ambivalent and often combines attraction and repulsion," then sacrificial practice "maintains the ambivalence of victimization and is in this sense extramoral or 'beyond good and evil.'" Specifically, sacrifice "compounds ambivalence" by transforming the "victim" into a "gift to a divinity or divinelike being." In sacrifice there is loss: the ruination of the sacrificial object, which is itself understood to repair a greater loss, or breach, within the social body. In fact, sacrificial ritual itself might be understood as a compulsive form of repetition, "performatively reenacting traumatic scenes" of loss and victimization.[65] And yet sacrifice also promises regeneration for the object that is made holy through its destruction *and* for the collection of witnesses that is said to be reborn through such noble death.

Both sacrifice and allegory manage ambivalence by a substitutory offering. Allegory substitutes a new story for consideration of an old one so that anxious fascination with the past can buffered by its safe and distant representation; sacrifice redresses a crisis or breach within a community through expiatory substitution wherein the sacrificial object takes on and atones for the imperfections of the larger social body. Both allegory and sacrifice depend upon a kind of *stand-in*, and in the cinematic allegories considered here, this stand-in is the sacrificial victim-hero whose suffering and noble death allow for synecdochic figurations of the nation as traumatized and then recovered, lost and then found, ruined and then repaired.

In Hollywood sacrificial films, the allegorical work of trauma gets done on a number of levels. To briefly sketch the nature of this work, consider *The Exorcist*, a sacrificial film notable for its multiple appearances within cycles of sacrificial cinema: released in 1973, *The Exorcist* represents the Vietnam-era cycle of sacrificial films; re-released (or resurrected) in 1999, *The Exorcist* also embodies the repetitive character of both trauma and sacrificial praxis. Just as trauma is imagined to return again and again, ritual sacrifice is a practice whose work is never fully done but must be ritually reenacted, as in Bataille's suggestion that "each day, once again, we crucify," at least symbolically.[66] Although not typically classified as a disaster movie like the films analyzed closely in this book, *The Exorcist* typifies the defining characteristics of sacrificial cinema and offers a useful point of entry for considering this body of films.

First, sacrificial films feature communities in the grips of catastrophic loss or terror. In *The Exorcist*, demonic possession threatens to destroy a young girl, a troubled family, and the Georgetown community. *The Exorcist* devotes much of its screen time and special effects to graphic violence, including the laceration of bodies, the breaking of bones, and the spilling of blood. Despite the startling proportions of loss and destruction *The Exorcist* depicts, its narrative resolution asserts the possibility of recovery. Suggesting that in the end, most survivors are better off for having experienced suffering and endured (as in Nietzsche's claim that "what does not destroy me makes me stronger"), *The Exorcist* dramatizes the moving-on process of those directly affected by the traumas of the narrative—a process enacted quite literally in the final frames of the film as the main characters drive or walk away from the site of violent traumatic terror and loss.

Second, these films not only depict the trauma of intense physical and psychological suffering, they also center on men that overcome an identity crisis or a disruption of subjectivity. In their depiction of masculine triumph over crisis, these films make use of the protagonist's woundedness as a tool for reasserting masculine authority. In *The Exorcist*, sacrificial victim-hero Father Karras begins his narrative arc unsure of his identity and place in the world; Karras feels dislocated from his ordinary existence, unsure of his purpose, bereft of meaning. He has lost faith in himself, the Church, and God. If trauma is typically imagined as an interruption or disarticulation, this sacrificial victim-hero begins as the epitome of the traumatized subject. In fact, Karras exhibits clinical symptoms of PTSD. *The Exorcist* concurrently endows its protagonist

Figure 1. Regan MacNeill looking hopeful as she and her mother leave the scene of her traumatic possession behind. *The Exorcist* (Warner Bros.)

with a mythical, if not mystical, aura attributable to his personal experiences of loss. Further, Karras, like his sacrificial brethren, generates even greater meaning and authority for himself when he willingly accepts his own noble death, recuperating his identity, redeeming countless others, and effecting narrative closure—quite literally suturing up the "holes" in his story.

Life-affirming death "cures" Karras of his trauma. Granting redemption to himself and others, the sacrificial victim-hero allegedly achieves the coherence and purity that undergird fantasies of the modern subject. Although the act of sacrificial death is itself a traumatic one, this act affords its victim new meaning and new life, offering a posthumous narrative that resonates closure and redemption. While sacrificial films posit the victim-hero's crisis and recovery as symptomatic of historical trauma (his "falling apart" as synecdoche for that of the larger culture), his redemptive death also signals a consequent attempt to master what is perceived as traumatic history: redressing past loss not as senseless and meaningless but as productive and salvific. Like trauma discourse, then, sacrifice works simultaneously to evacuate and elevate the subject—the subject that gives up his life so that he may become sacred and others may be saved.

Third, in films of sacrifice, the language of trauma also shapes understanding of national experience. These films reconstitute history through the trope of injury by marking events, such as the Vietnam War and 9/11, as *national* traumas. To demonstrate, in *The Exorcist*, references to the Vietnam War and student protest movements create an interpretive frame for the film's narrative and its troubled hero.[67] By fetishizing historical events as wounds to a victimized nation, sacrificial films may foreclose critical attention to national history or cultural memory—disavowing, for instance, the possibility that the actions of the nation-state may have been a complicit participant in the terror, pain, and loss from which it is imagined to suffer.

What is more, sacrificial films also frequently fixate on spectular(ized) and catastrophic suffering, as embodied chiefly by *The Exorcist*'s special-effects matrix and its fascination with the ravaged and mutilated body. Such emphasis risks conflating the concepts of "trauma" and "disaster," obscuring the extent to which suffering is often felt commonly and quietly in the everyday and asserting that certain events (and therefore certain victims) matter more (read: are more traumatic/traumatized) than others. These narratives, thus, privilege certain kinds of suffering as more remarkable or extraordinary than others, echoing Brown's point that public determination of what gets called "trauma" is often guided by ideology.

The ambivalence that characterizes sacrificial allegories allows these films to give voice to anxiety and vulnerability at the same time that they "manage" trauma, demonstrating Kaplan's claim that the cinema may "translate" history, "unconsciously colluding with dominant forces" in order to repair

Figure 2. Actors in the film-within-the film dramatizing a student protest against military violence and evoking Vietnam-era iconography. *The Exorcist* (Warner Bros.)

perceived damage done to "public narratives."[68] In this light, sacrificial films replay conventional understandings of narrative, or testimony, as the antidote to traumatic experience. Paradoxically, this understanding of trauma insists that for a wound to be repaired it must first be reopened and represented. Alleging that cultures and nations, like individuals, can be wounded, sacrificial films produce evidence of such injury in order to offer up themselves as a cure for cultural traumas, claiming to heal and piece back together a community imagined as once whole, innocent, and seamless but now fragmented, injured, and suffering.

As Farrell argues, trauma's ambivalence invites interpretation. He writes, "Trauma destabilizes the ground of experience, and therefore it is always supercharged with significance and always profoundly equivocal in its interpretative possibilities. Like a traditional religious-conversion experience, it can signify rebirth and promise transcendence, or it can open onto an abyss."[69] This book argues that the logics of trauma and sacrifice engage these interpretive possibilities in ways that can *simultaneously* "open onto an abyss" *and* "promise transcendence," figuring self-loss as both an end and a beginning. The sacrificial film's insistent return to the trope of traumatic heroism enacts the repetition and stasis said to characterize traumatic memory *at the same time* that it enables the victim-hero to move on and move (into the) beyond, using noble death to transform cinematic victim-heroes into legends.

CHAPTER 1

REEL PRESENCE, SACRIFICE, AND THE CINEMA

"Sacrifice is the communication of anguish." —Georges Bataille

"Experiencing trauma is an essential part of being human; history is written in blood." —Bessel A. van der Kolk

A naked man hangs from a post: blood drips down his chest; gaping wounds expose his skeletal structure; his arms have just been severed above the elbows. Two men crouch at his knees with a sharp blade embedded in his leg, which has begun to separate from his body. This gruesome image comes from a photograph taken in China around the turn of the twentieth century and depicts a frozen moment during a torture known as Leng Tch'e, or slow slicing—a form of public execution in which a victim's body is gradually dismembered. Bataille centered his philosophical writings about violence and suffering as well as his own meditative practice on this photograph, published by Georges Dumas in 1923. Taking inspiration from medieval mystics whose spiritual devotions involved contemplating images of a crucified Jesus, Bataille reportedly stared at the image in order to experience a sense of self-annihilation and the collision of "divine ecstasy and its opposite, extreme horror."[1]

This photograph offers a unique point of entry for considering the logics of trauma and sacrifice. Akin to the violent mise-en-scène of Mel Gibson's *The Passion of the Christ* (2004), the Leng Tch'e photograph embodies constructions of trauma as wounding or shattering the subject. The perforated, naked flesh, ripped from bone, literalizes Cathy Caruth's understanding of trauma as a "breach" in the self and Dominick LaCapra's figuration of trauma as "creating holes in existence."[2] The victim's severed limbs and his position in the middle of a crowd of onlookers evoke figurations of trauma as a disarticulating experience that wrenches the subject from the social. In addition to the content of the photograph, its formal qualities might also be understood as emblematic of trauma. Robert Hariman and John Louis Lucaites write that the stillness and fixity of photographs embody what is often described as the "phenomenological structure of trauma," in which "the traumatized subject remains trapped in the continually recurring scene."[3] For Bataille, meditation on this photograph furthered the work of ritualized sacrifice (given that, by his lifetime, ritual killing was largely understood as an ancient or archaic practice), offering the witness experiences of dissolution, shattering, and loss akin to what might be called "trauma."

The sacrificial films addressed in this book share striking similarities with this photograph, including a fascination with and investment in images of the male body in pain. In their onscreen depiction of violence and suffering and their reliance on overwhelming—even combative—special effects and editing techniques, these films mime, evoke, and perhaps even engender the sensations of trauma. Scenes of torture in a film such as *Braveheart* closely recall the brutal violence and public humiliation depicted in Bataille's meditative photographs, and the flashbacks in such films as *Omega Man* and *I Am Legend* enact the structure of trauma that the still photograph might be said to capture. These films, nonetheless, also differ markedly from Bataille's still photographs: they are, after all, moving pictures built on linear narratives. While the photograph appears trapped within a single moment, sacrificial films perform fantasies of moving on and recovering from trauma, quite literally leaving behind scenes of devastation and loss.

The overlaps among and distinctions between the logics of trauma, sacrifice, and the cinema elucidate how sacrificial films simultaneously indulge in the sensations of trauma *and* assert the possibility of leaving behind traumatic injury. Sacrificial films fulfill Bataillean fantasies about sacrifice and subjectivity, which are, in fact, fantasies about trauma and self-loss. These films engender the sensations of self-loss and approximate experiences of trauma as the paradoxical grounds on which subjectivity can be reconstituted and imagined as whole, intact, and masterful. Not unlike actual rituals of sacrifice, sacrificial films encourage spectators to lose themselves so that they might feel reborn. In the end, sacrificial films posit trauma and self-loss as both enabling and ennobling, offering a paradoxical vision of the male victim-hero as at once wounded and masterful, suffering and salvific, pained and privileged.

A consideration of Hollywood's Bataillean investment in the rhetoric, iconography, and phenomenology of trauma requires understanding Bataille's theoretical work on sacrifice and subjectivity as theories about trauma. Interrogating the relationship between sacrifice, subjectivity, and trauma demonstrates how Bataillean figurations of self-loss resonate with and contribute to prevailing fictions about masculinity and nationality within contemporary

U.S. culture. A Bataillean perspective also reveals how and why narrative cinema has become a unique and powerful site for enacting and reproducing the phenomena of sacrifice, trauma, and self-dissolution. This chapter aims not only to further understanding of Bataille's work but also to use Bataillean theories to explicate a variety of tropes and practices within U.S. film culture. That is, Bataille becomes both an object of critique and a useful lens for understanding the import that sacrifice and trauma maintain within the American cultural imaginary.

Although considerable scholarship attends to the pleasures and perils of film spectatorship and the experiential dimensions of the cinema, Bataille's work does not factor sufficiently into these conversations.[4] While I critique Bataille's constructs of subjectivity—which I understand to celebrate violence and to be decidedly masculinist—I do not summarily dismiss his insights. Bataille, perhaps more than any other theorist, can help us make sense of American trauma culture and its stronghold on the cinema. Bringing a Bataillean perspective to the study of U.S. film culture makes legible the attraction that so many Hollywood films demonstrate toward traumatic self-dissolution and elucidates the work that sacrifice is imagined to do on behalf of the spectator, the citizen-subject, and the nation-state.

Strange Bedfellows

Mel Gibson, a filmmaker fascinated with spectacles of suffering and pain, may have a theoretical counterpoint in Bataille, one of the most inexhaustible and controversial writers on the subject of sacrifice. Although operating at markedly different cultural registers—Gibson is a commercial actor and filmmaker and Bataille was an avant-garde writer and philosopher—both figures have inspired uproar because of their interest in sacrificial mutilation and graphic depiction of bodily torment. Both have also produced works derisively labeled "pornographic," and both have been branded as fanatical, if not unhinged. Just as *The Passion* galvanized intense debates about the film and its creator, responses to Bataille's work often fixate on his controversial persona: André Breton called Bataille an "excremental philosopher" and Jean Paul Sartre declared that he needed psychological help.[5] To focus too strictly on the apparent excesses and peculiarities of Bataille's persona, however, is to miss the consonance of his theories with U.S. film culture.

Bataille is an important scholar for understanding sacrificial economies not only because he was a theorist of sacrifice but also because he was an advocate of it, not entirely unlike Gibson. For example, Bataille founded Acéphale, a secret society that allegedly planned to stage a human sacrifice of its own—although a willing victim was found, apparently, no one would agree to commit the sacrifice.[6] Bataille is an important scholar for understanding

American cinema because so many Hollywood films bear Bataillean characteristics, reproducing similar fantasies about sacrifice and its relationship to both trauma and subjectivity. As a cultural theorist, Bataille helps explicate fascinations with the ritualized laceration of male bodies precisely because he admitted to sharing them.

The fantasy structures that underpin contemporary incarnations of sacrifice within American film culture mirror those fantasies that imbue Bataille's work. Like Bataille, these films depict trauma as a self-shattering experience with the capacity to produce new subjects. While these films characterize their protagonists as suffering from post-traumatic stress disorder in rather clinical terms, they also depict this suffering, in rather mystical terms, to be mesmeric and awe-inspiring. Also like Bataille, sacrificial films gravitate toward the violent death and consequent redemption, or rebirth, of men, positioning sacrifice as a potent form of trauma that both enables and ennobles the victim-hero. Bataille's kinship with these cinematic articulations of the sacrificial thus makes his work a useful theoretical paradigm for understanding how and why sacrifice and trauma operate as overlapping tropes within American public culture and cinema in particular.

Throughout this book, I cite clinicians and academics whose language for describing trauma and subjectivity resonates with both Bataille's work and the Bataillean images and tropes that characterize U.S. trauma culture. Such comparisons may seem unexpected, if not startling. While the aims of most mental health practitioners and trauma scholars may differ drastically from Bataille's—the therapist trained to help survivors respond to suffering would likely find little to no connection between his/her work and Bataille's erotic attraction to human suffering—analogous logics and metaphors nonetheless emerge. Without losing sight of the distinctions among these levels of trauma discourse, I expose and explicate these metaphoric connections in order to illustrate and curtail the pervasive influence of masculinist figurations of human subjectivity in sites as disparate as medical-scientific literature, literary theory, and popular film.

Sacrificial Descendents

Bataille enumerates and exclaims ritualized sacrifice as one practice, among many, through which humans seek the "communication of anguish" in order to reverse the "painful antinomy of life and death."[7] While Bataille's early writings emphasize literal sacrifice, his later work eventually addresses other practices that embody the sacrificial impulse, including meditations on violent images and the "little death" of erotic or sexual pleasure. Michael Richardson argues that "eroticism performs on the individual plane what sacrifice performs in the collective sphere." While "eroticism effects at the individual level the longing to dissolve our own separate personalities and consecrate ourselves in the body of the other," rituals of sacrifice function as "an attempt at community level to engage with what exceeds us."[8]

Bataille understands this "domain of social laceration" to be rich and varied in form, ranging "from war to the bloody cross of Christ," but unified in its efforts to engender "communication between beings" and the consequent "formation of new beings."[9] For this reason, Bataille encourages his audience not to "turn away from death" but to "stare at it, look it straight in the face."[10] Bataille also imagines that sacrifice offers the witness experiences of communion and intimacy with the victim and other witnesses, illustrating the sacrificial impulse toward "joining."[11] Bataille's vision of sacrifice as an experience that grants witnesses experiences of "a breaking loose that melts them and blends them indiscriminately with their fellow beings" also governs sacrificial films, which enact fantasies of unification at both narrative and stylistic registers.[12]

Bataille celebrates sacrifice for its capacity to create new subjects, whom he imagines as limitless and transgressive. For instance, in his essay "Sacrificial Mutilation and the Severed Ear of Vincent Van Gogh," Bataille describes sacrifice as liberating its participants. "The one who sacrifices is free—free to indulge in a similar disgorging, free, continuously identifying with the victim, to vomit his own being just as he has vomited a piece of himself or a bull, in other words free to throw himself suddenly *outside of himself*."[13] Bataille is not blind, however, to the paradox central to death's allure: once experienced, death and its pleasures can never be experienced again. As he laments, "One might say rather precisely that true joy would require a movement to the point of death, but death would put an end to [that joy]!"[14] Hence, argues Bataille, subjects seek sacrificial death at a safe remove through its representation in literature and the arts.

Calling sacrifice "a human action more significant than any other," Bataille characterizes the sacrificial impulse as instructing much, if not all, of human behavior and suggests that even cultures claiming to have abandoned sacrifice as primitive or savage nonetheless participate in sacrificial economies.[15] LaCapra concurs; if "in sacrifice an innocent or purified victim is violently torn apart in order that communicants may be regenerated or redeemed and attain a higher unity or proximity to the godhead," then this "regeneration through violence" may "itself be displaced or find a substitute in secular scenarios that disguise, or even deny, their relation to sacrifice."[16] Carolyn Marvin and David Ingle argue that war might be understood as such a culturally sanctioned (if unacknowledged) return to sacrificial practice, offering up the bodies and blood of soldiers to engender national "renewal."[17]

Likewise, Bataille positions literature and art as modernity's "heirs of religion" and "the continuation of ancient sacrificial rites."[18] Having "received sacrifice as a legacy," they aim to fulfill the human "longing to lose, to lose ourselves and to look death in the face."[19] Bataille traces throughout myriad works of art—the erotic and ritualistic violence of a Genet play, the images of sacrifice painted on the walls of the cave at Lascaux, and the writings of the Marquis de Sade or Emily Brontë—an impulse for ecstatic anguish and self-annihilation that encourages the witness to lose him/herself "as completely as the ecstatic mystic loses himself in God." Understanding the desire for self-loss as endemic to the human condition, Bataille concludes that without the attraction to anguish and a "violent instinct," humans "could dispense with the arts" entirely.[20] Echoing Bataille's assignation of a sacrificial legacy to the arts, Gil Bailie traces the roots of Greek theater to "ritual sacrifices made to the god Dionysus" and interprets sacrificial practice as crucial to modern life. Bailie asserts that just as "Greek theater emerged from . . . sacrificial rites," one can find "vestiges" of ritualized sacrifice that "survive in the arts of theater and film today."[21]

Sacrificial films simultaneously summon and expel traumatic experience and its alleged traces of the unspeakable real. These films demonstrate Bataille's claim that humans "make every effort to efface the traces, signs and symbols of death. Then, if we can, we efface the traces and signs of these efforts."[22]

> We must still revive [the shades of death] voluntarily—in a way which corresponds precisely to our needs. . . . It is to this purpose that we put the arts: they manage, on the stage, to arouse in us the highest possible degree of anxiety. The arts—or at least some of the arts—incessantly evoke these derangements, these lacerations, this decline which our entire activity endeavors to avoid.[23]

Sacrificial films recall Bataille's Leng Tch'e photograph, for like this image, they evoke the shades of death and aim to arouse anxiety in their spectators. Steeped in the iconography of trauma, these films perform and encourage the "derangements" and "lacerations" associated with terror, loss, and psychic undoing. While such performances of suffering and death demonstrate a Bataillean fascination with trauma, they also get used strategically to manage "anxiety," to prop up cultural fantasies, and to reaffirm public narratives, for "only the fictitious approach of death" can do such work safely and without too great a confrontation with risk.[24]

Sacrifice and Trauma

Bataillean fascination with sacrifice suggests displaced fascination with trauma.[25] Jonathan Boulter suggests that Bataille offers his own theory of trauma, particularly in such works as *Erotism* and *Inner Experience*. Bataille equates trauma to "expenditure, sacrifice, loss and excess."[26] Without naming "trauma" specifically, Bataille figures self-loss as a violent "disturbance" that "reopens in the mind of the man experiencing it, who also knows what death is, the abyss that death once revealed."[27] Inasmuch as Bataille envisions death as a "clarifying experience" for the subject, Boulter argues that for Bataille, "violent trauma in some ways constitutes the self" and "whether in the form of eroticism or sacrifice, works ultimately to integrate both individuals and society."[28]

Caruth includes Bataille's writing about trauma alongside the theorizing of such venerated psychiatrists as Shoshana Felman, Dori Laub, Robert Jay Lifton, and Bessel van der Kolk in her influential and oft-cited anthology *Trauma: Explorations in Memory*. Bataille's essay in the volume, "Concerning the Accounts Given by the Residents of Hiroshima," refers to the atomic bombing of Hiroshima to argue that trauma affects not only individuals but also cultures and nations, threatening to "sap the life from the social body." He argues, "The destruction of life does not just affect the moment of the individual's death: it can bring disorder and depression to the collectivity as well."[29]

Bataille also lays bare what he sees as the peculiar fact that "the death of sixty thousand [in Hiroshima] is charged with meaning" when all the while death is a "basic component of human life."[30] Bataille suggests, not unlike Van der Kolk, that trauma represents an "essential part of being human."[31] Making the claim that "horror is everywhere the same," Bataille seems principally interested in acknowledging the pervasiveness of terror and loss; but what he also admits, perhaps accidentally, is the discursive work of trauma, which marks some events, bodies, and places as worthy of its mantle while others are excluded.[32] That is, Bataille illustrates that in public discourse some experiences "count" or "matter" as trauma while others do not, and these distinctions are, as Laura S. Brown argues, largely political and ideological ones.[33] Despite this brief allusion to the politics of trauma, however, Bataille remains largely oblivious to (or at least unconcerned with) these implications in his writings about sacrifice, which he constructs as an idealized and phantasmagoric version of traumatic experience.

In fact, Bataille's interest in the dissolution of subjectivity suggests a *longing* for the experience that has been named "trauma"—a longing that Boulter describes as "traumatic nostalgia," or what Bataille himself dubs a "stirring nostalgia for death."[34] To demonstrate, Bataille figures his torture photographs and meditative practices as simultaneously horrifying and fascinating, appalling and sublime. Illustrating LaCapra's contention that responses to trauma often commingle "attraction and repulsion," Bataille writes, "On the one hand, the horror of death drives us off, for we prefer life; on the other an element at once so solemn and terrifying fascinates and disturbs us profoundly."[35] Such ambivalent fascination characterizes Bataille's description of his torture photograph.

> I would gaze at the photographic image—or sometimes the memory I have of it—of a Chinese man who must have been tortured in my lifetime. . . . In the end, the patient writhed, his chest flayed, arms and legs cut off at the elbows and at the knees. His hair standing on end, *hideous*, haggard, striped with blood, *beautiful* as a wasp.[36]

Explicating the photograph in detail that is both scientific and poetic, Bataille simultaneously marks the tortured body as "hideous" and "beautiful," excruciating and exquisite, repellent and mesmeric.[37] This oscillation exemplifies LaCapra's description of trauma as inviting "ambivalent" responses that commingle "attraction and repulsion."[38]

Having played a "decisive role" in his life, leaving him "obsessed by this image of pain, at once ecstatic (?) and intolerable," Bataille identifies this photograph and other "images of explosion and of being lacerated—ripped to pieces" as tools with which a spectator can engender, or will, his/her own experience of what some might call "trauma" or, at the very least, "vicarious trauma."[39] Understanding this meditation on the suffering of an Other as deriving from and approximating ritualized sacrifice, Bataille writes, "The method of meditation is close to the technique of sacrifice. The point of ecstasy is laid bare if I smash interiorly the particularity that encloses me within myself: in the same fashion, the sacred is substituted for the animal at the moment the priest kills it, destroys it."[40] Sacrifice and meditations on torture, argues Bataille, invite spectators to bear witness to and experience the suffering of an Other; he understands these practices as sharing a capacity to wound or open up the subjectivity of the witness.

Bataille describes his meditations as both traumatic and transcendent, allowing for communication between the self and an Other.

> The young and seductive Chinese man of whom I have spoken, left to the work of the executioner—I loved him with a love in which the sadistic instinct played no part: he communicated his pain to me or perhaps the excessive nature of his pain, and it was precisely that which I was seeking, not so as to take pleasure in it, but in order to ruin in me that which is opposed to ruin.[41]

Describing the "excessive nature" of the victim's pain, Bataille cites the unrepresentable nature of trauma (that which exceeds language and consciousness) and conflates traumatic self-loss with access to the real, or what he describes as "access to the extreme limit of what is possible."[42] Bataille figures the communication of pain as a radical freedom that unmoors the spectator/witness from the perceived limitations of his/her subjectivity.

Theorizing Bataille's interest in self-loss, Amy Hollywood understands his meditations on the Leng Tch'e photograph "as a traumatic response to the ethical call of the other," animated by the horrors of World War II and the Holocaust. She contends that Bataille's "desire for horror is not a desire to escape the demands of history but to face them."[43] Hollywood is careful to note, however, that despite whatever ethical impulses may drive Bataille's work, his "practice is problematic in that he seems to use another human being's unchosen suffering as a means toward his own ecstatic anguish." Bataille exploits the Other's "physical suffering, his literal dismemberment" in order to engender his own "psychical laceration and the explosion of his subjectivity."[44] He makes use of what he imagines to be an Other's trauma in order to produce, within himself, an experience of self-shattering, akin to that produced by sacrifice.

Although Bataille claims that witnessing the suffering of an Other allows "*Compassion*, suffering, and ecstasy" to "mingle together," his insistence that the victim is "there for" him—that it "was necessary that one die before [him]" so that he might "cease to be unprofitably closed and *communicate*"—privileges the alleged ecstasy of the encounter with trauma over compassionate consideration of suffering.[45] Hollywood wonders whether Bataille's desire to gaze at suffering—to look death in the face—can be extricated from voyeurism and the objectification of the Other.

> Can we be sure that in his encounters with photographic images of suffering flesh Bataille communicates with the suffering other rather than with the sadistic-voyeuristic eye through which the photograph is made and disseminated? Can we ever fully separate the compassionate encounter with the other from that fetishistic and/or voyeuristic-sadistic look?[46]

Bataille's emphasis on the ecstasy and joy of such encounters—on the erotics of anguish, or what Susan Sontag calls the "erotics of agony"—would suggest not.[47] In fact, Bataille's desire to experience the suffering of an Other seems to be less about answering an ethical call to communicate anguish than it is about a longing for the radical freedom that he associates with subjective undoing.

Given that Bataille never actually reenacts the experiences of the torture victim but only imagines them, his fantasies about self-loss (however shocking or extreme they might seem) relate to and resonate with contemporary U.S. cinema.[48] It is this insistence on the safe, vicarious, and fantastic experience of the suffering of an Other that links Bataille's work to the film culture I interrogate: both hinge on a privileged subject's (or spectator's) ability and desire to approximate loss without actually experiencing its ravages; both hinge on encounters with the *sensations* of violent trauma without actually risking danger to self. Like Bataille, the films I consider herein illustrate a "stirring nostalgia for death" that stops short, "approaching it closely enough to know of its terror but far enough to escape from it."[49]

The fascination with (or desire for) the traumatic loss of self that characterizes both the work of Bataille and sacrificial films illustrates what John Mowitt calls "trauma envy"—a concept echoed by both Boutler's notion of "traumatic nostalgia" and Hal Foster's conception of the "envy of abjection."[50] Such nostalgia or envy, argues Mowitt, owes to the illusion that traumatic experience gives survivors unique access to the real and endows them with "transcendental status." Mowitt writes, "Under these circumstances trauma has come to be invested with such authority and legitimacy that it elicits a concomitant desire to have suffered it, or if not the unspeakable event itself, then the testimonial agency it is understood to produce."[51] While I do not mean to suggest that clinicians and trauma scholars share the same "envy" or "nostalgia" that characterize Bataille and sacrificial cinema, by conflating trauma with the unspeakable real and by privileging survivor testimony as a particularly revered form of speech, both therapeutic and academic discourse may contribute to trauma's cultural capital and its status as an object of fascination.

Sacrificial praxis, contends LaCapra, similarly exalts suffering and authorizes the victim. LaCapra argues that "those involved in sacrifice, at times including the figure who is the (self-)sacrificial victim or the transfigured signifier, vehicle, or embodiment of the sublime, have been seen as above and beyond the moral law, perhaps transgressing it in a manner that helps give rise to a new order."[52] As much as Bataille's work claims a desire to communicate with and open up to the anguish of the Other, he positions that spectator, at a safe remove from the suffering he/she perceives, to appropriate the moral authority or truth-power assigned to the one that suffered and risks exploiting suffering as self-serving spectacle. Sacrificial films also encourage their imagined audiences to feel transformed by figuring spectatorship as a *death-defying* experience, as if the spectator is enlivened or made better by having witnessed the suffering of an Other.

In her reading of his work, Hollywood understands Bataille as eschewing the redemptive authority assigned to trauma through his refusal to narrativize self-loss, offering "guilt without redemption, anguish without salvation." She writes, "Bataille implies that the specificity of the real (this body, in pieces, radically other in its suffering yet recognizably like mine in its very bodiliness) must take precedence over any narrative contextualization" because for Bataille, "narrative and historical contextualization" become "ways of evading the real."[53] Even without soteriological narratives, Bataillean figurations of self-loss demonstrate a potentially exploitative investment in and attraction toward the imagined authority of trauma that is problematic on multiple levels.

First, by conflating trauma with the real, Bataille's understanding of the "communication of anguish," like many canonical theories of trauma, implies that pain itself can be shared between a victim and a witness, as in his claim that the photographed Leng Tch'e victim "communicated his pain . . . or perhaps the excessive nature of his pain."[54] Bataille understands his torture photograph as granting him direct access to the suffering of the victim depicted within the frame (never mind the process and formal constraints through which the image was constructed) and neglects the extent to which discourse and ideology constitute and delimit any act of communication, as if his meditative dramatizations can grant him access to "non-discursive experience."[55] If the trauma victim is imagined to gain unassailable authority based on the premise that "seeing is the origin of knowing," Bataille appropriates this privileged access to the real and implies that such knowledge can be transmitted or passed onto a witness, such that an image is said to guarantee "the communication of knowledge gained through (visual, visceral) experience."[56] This logic turns pain into a commodity or a shared social good.

Second, Bataille's theories of sacrifice construct self-loss as a productive experience through which subjects can be made stronger. This is especially true in Bataille's discussions of what may happen to the subject who chooses to "look death in the face," which depict witnessing as a specular process, reinforce fictions of masterful subjectivity, and cast trauma as an empowering act of apotheosis. Imagining that the witness might vicariously experience the self-loss of the victim, Bataille's theories position both the victim and the witness as "transcendent" and "sovereign," unhinged from the "bonds which paralyze a vertiginous movement toward the void."[57] Describing experiences of self-loss—or vicarious trauma—Bataille advises that if the witness "gives itself up to non-knowledge in this abandon, then rapture begins." Bataille assures us, however, that after such rapturous experience, the witness can gain "sense once again," rendering the experience intelligible and "giving satisfaction to [his/her] will to be everything."[58] Promising that the subject may return or "emerge" from such a fleeting experience of self-loss, Bataille anticipates what will become a commonplace timeline within American trauma culture: the notion that subjects are imagined as whole and unified, before, after, and *because of* traumatogenic injury.

For Bataille, encounters with trauma endow both the victim and the witness with the "limitless, infinite nature of sacred things" and give them access to the universality that is typically understood to belong to the gods.[59] He writes, "I become non-knowledge, I become God, unknown, unknowable ignorance."[60] What results is a fantasy in which the subject is imagined to be totalizing, untethered, and omnipotent. Bataille's construction of the sovereign man as having "no more regard for the limits of identity than he does for the limits of death" and becoming, therefore, "the transgression of all such limits" suggests, even in the absence of soteriological narratives, an interpretation of trauma as able to endow the subject with new meaning.[61]

Positing the sovereign subject as almost trickster-like, Bataille writes, "The mystic of 'joy before death' can never be seen as cornered, for he is able to laugh complacently at every human endeavor and to know every accessible enthusiasm."[62] The logic of trauma undergirds Bataille's vision of subjectivity. Trauma, it would seem, is the new knowledge—the nonknowledge—with which the subject can be rebuilt. Carolyn Dean notes that the Bataillean lexicon marks the loss of self as the "constituent moment of selfhood," illustrating Bataille's belief that the law is upheld by its transgression.[63] This notion of "paradoxical self-fulfillment through self-annihilation," like trauma discourse more generally, reaffirms prevailing fictions about subjectivity, deploying injury as evidence for the existence of the autonomous, unified self.[64]

The logic affirmed by the Bataillean assertion that one may "retrieve the self by unbinding it " mirrors the assumption of trauma discourse that a breach in self offers evidence of the self's prior wholeness or unity.[65] Dean suggests that Bataille casts sacrificial practice and its various approximations as working to reconstruct the subject. But for Bataille, this process does more than simply repair a subject that once existed; it in fact creates a new one. The fantasy of the unified, coherent, and stable (but limited) self yields to the fantasy of the universal, transcendent, and limitless subject—a subject that is better off (or more masterful) for having suffered and anguished. Bataille's emphasis on violent regeneration echoes the masculinist logic of warrior cultures, in which men earn authority and prove their worth through acts of aggression and physical force.

For this reason, Dean interprets Bataille's fantasies of self-loss and subjectivity as decidedly patriarchal. While much of Bataille's work purports to celebrate vulnerability over strength, injury over potency, and "symbolic castration" over "phallic virtue," Dean posits that his writings nonetheless perpetuate masculine privilege, abandoning traditional signifiers of virility and using tragic loss as the grounds on which to reconstitute masculine subjectivity.[66]

> Now shorn of his illusory armor—war, beginning with the Great War that so traumatized Bataille, was no occasion for glory—he refashions virility as self-loss, embraces castration in his quest for self-restoration. The pain is there, but tragic manliness still reserves the prerogatives of manhood for itself.[67]

The Bataillean fantasy of subjectivity presumes that the perfect subject of history is a masculine one. Dean argues that "the subject in question for Bataille (as well as for Lacan) is necessarily a male one," and the "moment at which the self experiences itself as loss (as mutilated, punished, castrated) is also the moment at which it is constituted as a self, or more precisely, as a man."[68] As Bataille puts it, "Man can only find himself in the condition of escaping."[69] Rather than rejecting masculinist constructions of the subject, Bataille merely refigures them, linking the imagined fullness and mastery of the subject to his ability to transgress, or violate, the boundaries that had previously defined him.[70]

While these constructions of self-loss and subjectivity might be described as distinctly Bataillean, I maintain that Bataille's traumatic understandings of sacrifice (or his sacrificial understandings of trauma) pervade American culture and lend insight into a wide range of cultural discourses and practices. Bataillean language resonates forcefully with the rhetoric of trauma in both clinical and humanistic contexts. Bataille's description of sacrifice as producing "the ecstatic loss of self" anticipates Richard B. Ulman and Doris Brothers's psychoanalytic definition of trauma as an event that "shatters the self."[71] It presages Jonathan Shay's description of trauma as obliterating a "sense of meaningfulness of the self" and the "cohesion of consciousness."[72]

His ideas also echo in Kristeva's treatment of trauma as engendering the "shattering of psychic identity" and the "falling apart of consciousness," just as his fascination with "Nothingness" mirrors Farrell's assertion that events become traumatic through their capacity to reveal the "ultimate nothingness of the self."[73] Bataille also anticipates Farrell's description of trauma as "destabiliz[ing] the ground of experience" when he exalts sacrifice as enabling the subject to give up "reason, intelligibility, the ground itself upon which he stands" and to give into "the depth of terror, the extreme limit where he succumbs."[74] Similarly, Bataille prefigures the recurrent depiction of trauma as a fall into an abyss—as in Farrell's assertion that traumatic experience "can open onto an abyss" or Eleanor Kaufman's notion of trauma as having an "abysslike structure"—when he describes self-loss as a "pure inner fall into a limitless abyss."[75] Given recurrent links between trauma and the abyss, it matters that each cycle of sacrificial films addressed here features one film about a sinking ship, in which the descent into the literal abyss of the ocean becomes a potent allegorical confrontation with trauma.

Foster also locates Bataillean tendencies within what he describes as the "cult of abjection" that he links to abject art, or, specific modes of avant-garde art that focus on the "broken boundaries of the violated body," such as Andres Serrano's controversial *Piss Christ* (1987). In such works, representations of the broken body operate as a "direct double of the violated subject, whose parts are displayed as residues of violence and/or traces of trauma." Too often, however, such works ultimately and "inadvertently support the normativity of image-screen and symbolic order alike," with depictions of subjectivity's undoing ultimately reaffirming illusions that the proper, masculine subject existed in the first place. As Foster suggests, it bears noting that most artists who deploy artistic "degradation for protection and/or profit" are male.[76]

Much American trauma discourse also recalls Bataille's description of trauma as an opportunity for a subject (or a community) to be freed and reborn. Consider, for instance, poet Gregory Orr's meditation on the enabling possibilities of trauma. He writes, "The very hopelessness of the shattered self is its hope, because this devastated self possesses a radical freedom. . . . The self is therefore free to make new connections to the world. And it has an even more primary task and opportunity: to make a new self."[77] Bataille's assertion that anguish endows the subject with "new knowledge" also mirrors the rather threadbare claim that trauma can be productive and that the survivor is better off for having suffered, anticipating what Naomi Klein calls the prominence of "shock doctrine" within late capitalism.[78] Klein notes that American culture frequently exploits disasters or "moments of collective trauma" as opportunities to produce "radical social and economic engineering," as in presidential hopeful John Kerry's 2004 assertion that the perceived traumas of 9/11 "brought out the best in all of us."[79]

Bataille's understanding of sacrifice as producing new, transgressive, and masterful subjects also accords with historical, sociological, anthropological studies of ritualized sacrifice as a masculinist institutional practice. Nancy Jay argues that sacrificial rituals—including the Catholic Eucharist, which is understood to reenact the sacrificial death of Jesus—negotiate a perceived tension "between sacrifice and childbearing women" and create "oppositions between the purifying power of sacrifice" that is associated with new life and salvation and "the pollution of childbirth and menstruation" that is associated with death and human imperfection.[80] Generating life without the need for female bodies and offering humans a "remedy for having been born of woman," Catholic rites of sacrifice thus forge "bonds of intergenerational communities between males that transcend their absolute dependence on childbearing women," exemplified by the exclusion of women from priestly roles within the ministerial priesthood of the Catholic Church.[81] Through regular sacrificial practice the priesthood maintains its hierarchical social structure, affording men positions of privilege that are denied to women and creating a lineage of subjects imagined to transgress their mortal origins and experience regeneration through loss.[82]

Marvin and Ingle's work on war as a form of ritualized sacrifice further suggests the relevance of Bataille's theories of self-loss to the study of nations and culture. Marvin and Ingle contend that war functions as a ritual of sacrifice offered up to the American totem object, the flag. The shedding of sacrificial blood functions as a kind of renewal for the in-group, helping restore group solidarity and identificatory bonds among U.S. citizens, allowing the national body to reconstitute itself again and again. As the bodies of male soldiers are defiled and dismembered, the community of onlookers and supporters is revitalized, making use of the trauma and loss of the fallen soldier—whose ultimate sacrifice marks him as the ideal citizen-subject—for the reconstitution of the body politic.[83]

Like Bataille, Marvin and Ingle understand violence as simultaneously the "greatest threat to survival and essential to existence."[84] The nation offers up cherished sons (and, of course, daughters—although U.S. public culture typically constructs the soldier and the ultimate sacrifice in masculine terms) so that those at home may live, thus constructing a civil religion modeled after the Christian tradition and its emphasis on the sacrifice of God's Son, Jesus.[85] Marvin and Ingle write, "The myth of the sacrificed Christ who dies for all men makes every sacrificial solder a remodeled Christ dying to redeem his countrymen. Every soldier becomes a redemptive sacred figure to subsequent generations of celebrants."[86] When offered up as a sacrifice, the soldier becomes a "sacred" object, a hero and sovereign subject whose death endows him/her with the transcendental status and moral authority that is, as Mowitt reminds us, associated with trauma.[87] Sacrifice creates a paradox wherein (almost exclusively) male bodies become heroic and authoritative by having been subjected to suffering and loss.

Sacrifice and the Cinema

Bataille locates the capacity to disintegrate subjectivity within all art forms generally, but film as a medium has a particular capacity to do the traumatic work of sacrifice and to engender the sensations of self-loss. If, as E. Ann Kaplan and others have argued, trauma is understood as "inherently linked to modernity" and the cinema is historically tied to the "'shock' experience of modernity," then film is an art form uniquely positioned to confront, represent, and reenact trauma.[88] Like the atom bomb, the train, or the plane, the cinema as a technology and cultural institution may signify and carry within it what has been posited as the traumatic history of modernity.

As a visual medium composed of moving images, the cinema embodies the visuality of traumatic symptoms—as in the hallucinations, flashbacks, and nightmares experienced by trauma survivors.[89] Films have a specific capacity to embody traumatic sensibilities and destabilize the purported cohesiveness of the "I" through assaults on the eye. Steven Shaviro argues that the cinema "tends toward the blinding ecstasy of Bataillean expenditure," using images and sounds to provoke physical arousal and agitation in spectators.[90] He contends that a fundamental pleasure of watching films lies in the possibility of shattering or unraveling the subjectivity of the spectator and that the cinema has the potential to overwhelm and even "endanger" the boundaries of subjectivity.

> Cinematic pleasure does not put the spectator in a position of active mastery of the gaze, and does not necessarily depend upon specular identification. Pleasure can just as well be linked to the destruction of identification and objectification, to the undermining of subjective stability, and to an affirmation of the multiple techniques that denaturalize (or de-Cartesianize) cinematic perception.[91]

This spectator thus mirrors the witness as described by Bataille: "stunned" to the "point of ecstasy."[92] Bataille's understanding of ecstasy illustrates Linda Williams's description of the ecstatic state as one in which the subject is "beside himself" with overwhelming emotion and/or physical sensation.[93] As Bataille writes in *Guilty*, "An image of torture falls under my eyes; I can, in my fright, turn away. But I am, if I look at it, *outside of myself*."[94]

Lamenting the "conservative, conformist assumption—shared by most film theorists—that our desires are primarily ones for possession, plenitude, stability, and reassurance," Shaviro argues that "what inspires the cinematic spectator is a passion for that very loss of control, that abjection, fragmentation, and subversion of self-identity."[95] He further contends that the technologies of the cinema enable this shattering of subjectivity, noting, "A wide variety of cinematic pleasures are predicated explicitly upon the decentered freeplay, the freedom from the constraints of subjectivity, that editing and special effects make possible."[96] For example, through the work of editing, films allow spectators of cinema, unlike those of live theater, to transcend the spatial and temporal limitations that typically constrain them and adopt a variety of points of view. In mere seconds, spectators can imagine themselves to be different people in different places at different times—their imagined subjectivities not unified and cohesive but flexible and mobile.

Films may also invite spectators to lose themselves in identification with a character and even to experience continuity with a range of characters variously or even simultaneously, as Constance Penley and Carol Clover argue.[97] Films can encourage such "continuity" of identifications through elements of editing and cinematography that encourage decentered looking. For instance, many films alternate between omniscient views (presented by the camera itself) that are not attached to any particular character within the story world and point-of-view shots that are anchored to specific characters; a film may offer multiple point-of-view shots from different characters, literally presenting spectators with multiple perspectives and inviting them to see the world through multiple sets of eyes. This decentered looking can encourage viewers not to create any closed or coherent identification with a single character but instead to experience multiple, shifting identifications. The subjectivity of the spectator who is offered almost limitless vision(s) may thus be torn apart or shattered.

In this sense, Shaviro suggests that film as a medium, generally speaking, should be understood as reenacting subjective annihilation, but I suggest that the impulse toward sacrificial mutilation characterizes some films more than others. While the potential for shattering subjectivity may inhere in all films, particular texts animate this potential to greater or lesser degrees; that is, some films seem more invested in sacrificial economies and Bataillean expenditure than others. For example, although she never references Bataille directly, Janet Walker's notion of trauma cinema points toward a body of films with pronounced Bataillean impulses. Films in this category, Walker argues, address a "world-shattering event or events of the past, whether personal, public or both" and share a "stylistic and narrative modality" that is nonrealist.

> Like traumatic memories that feature vivid bodily and visual sensation over 'verbal narrative and context,' these films are characterized by non-linearity,

> fragmentation, nonsynchronous sound, repetition, rapid editing and strangle angles. And they approach the past through an unusual admixture of emotional affect, metonymic symbolism, and cinematic flashbacks.[98]

It is no accident that the subject matter and stylistics of these films correspond precisely to the description of PTSD in the American Psychological Association's *Diagnostic and Statistical Manual of Mental Disorders*, argues Walker. Walker locates such war films as *Apocalypse Now* (Francis Ford Coppola, 1979), *Platoon* (Oliver Stone, 1986), *Hiroshima, Mon Amour* (Alain Resnais, 1959), and *Saving Private Ryan* (Steven Spielberg, 1998) within this body of trauma films.

These films might be said to "traumatize" film, using formal interventions to engender overwhelming and disorienting sensory experiences, in ways that mirror stylistic choices Bataille made as a writer and poet. In a meditative poem on the experience of "joy before death," for example, Bataille describes the subject as coming undone and linguistically enacts this dissolution through anaphora. Insistently repeating the phrase "I am" in a series of descriptions of being "devoured," "absorbed," and "annihilated," Bataille strives to "traumatize writing itself."[99] Hollywood argues that, through anaphora, Bataille "moves traumatic memory and its compulsive repetitions into writing" and "bring[s] trauma and catastrophe into language."[100] This literary device might be understood as an attempt not just to reference or represent the traumatic loss of self but also to embody or reenact that sensation.

Boutler also reads Bataille as "traumatizing narrative" through his "attempts to disintegrate narrative to allow the event of trauma to emerge."[101] In addition to Bataille's textual repetitions, Boutler cites his imagistic style as working "to enact, to call into being the scene of trauma or, more precisely, the moment and initial impact of trauma"; he explains of *Story of the Eye*, for example, that "repeated images of degradation, images whose power resides in their separation from narrative proper" function (or at least strive) "to reproduce the temporal effects of trauma by presenting a narrative that closes off any sense of thematic or characterological development, any sense, that is, of progression through time or space."[102] Bataille's attempts to traumatize writing and narrative through such formal strategies should be understood as analogous to cinematic efforts to traumatize film through such devices as flashback editing, visual distortions, and still images that reenact the phenomenology of trauma.

The sacrificial films addressed here share many significant characteristics with what Walker calls trauma cinema. In the case of *Saving Private Ryan*, for example, overlaps do occur between these categorizations. Like the films Walker describes, sacrificial films frequently use disorienting visual effects and flashback editing to recall the aftereffects of trauma. They also rely heavily on graphic violence and gross-out effects, which engender affective and visceral responses and are always heavily coded with metonymic implications. Many sacrificial films also feature ensemble casts whose narratives may undercut subjective stability by presenting spectators with a diverse array of anguished characters with whom viewers are encouraged to communicate.

In line with their narrative emphasis on catastrophic events or tragic loss, sacrificial films also frequently depict characters that exhibit textbook symptoms of PTSD, including nightmares, hallucinations, and repetition compulsions. In this regard, both trauma cinema and sacrificial cinema are akin to Bataille's Leng Tch'e photograph, or other traumatic still images, in their capacity to engender the sensations of trauma and encourage the dissolution and fragmentation of the spectator—an experience of self-shattering that mirrors that of the sacrificial victim-hero who is depicted first as "losing it" and then as losing himself entirely.

Sacrificial films, however, do not exactly mirror Walker's concept of trauma cinema: their efforts to traumatize film get tempered by an impulse toward order and closure. Walker's work on trauma cinema highlights films within avant-garde and/or documentary traditions, films that operate outside of mainstream and commercial conventions (an exception to this case would be *Saving Private Ryan*, a "Hollywood" film praised for its "documentary-like" style). Walker's treatment of trauma cinema also stresses the use of nonlinear narratives and discontinuous editing as markers of cinematic traumatology. In contrast, the sacrificial films addressed in this book occupy more centralized locations within mainstream U.S. cinema and adhere in most ways to Hollywood stylistics. With the exception of occasional flashbacks, the narratives of sacrificial films are largely linear, and instead of constituting the global stylistics of the film, visual disturbances (including strange angles or rapid editing) are used sparingly to manifest the protagonist's experience of trauma. Like traumatic memory, these moments become interruptions of or intrusions upon the otherwise conventional form of the sacrificial film and by the end of the film are generally resolved—as is the trauma of the sacrificial victim-hero, whose identity is stabilized and reconstituted through his ultimate sacrifice. That is, in Hollywood films, brief attempts to traumatize film get resolved alongside the recuperation of the victim-hero through noble death.

Sacrificial films should thus also be understood as distinct from still images such as Bataille's torture photographs. Unlike the still photograph, the film text can move on from or leave behind the violent scene. The traumatic memory of a lost past, which Roland Barthes understands as inherent to the photograph, does not get replicated by the moving picture, in which the "*having-been-there* vanishes, giving way to a *being-there* of the thing."[103] This sense that the film text "gets time moving again" is heightened further when narrative is present. If the "traumatic moment is stopped in time," then the forward progress of narrative suggests that the traumatic moment might "recede, dissipate, or become complicated by other elements of larger stories."[104] While Bataille understands photographs as enabling the spectator to lose him/herself temporarily before he/she regains a sense of order and new knowledge, sacrificial films take extra care to translate self-loss into regeneration and the reconstitution of the subject. By commingling the "perfect contraries, divine ecstasy and its opposite, extreme horror," sacrificial films augment Bataille's description of the horrific image as having "imprisoned [him] in "anguish" and having "at the same time delivered [him] from it."[105]

With largely linear narratives, sacrificial films reorder experience by creating a useful traumatological timeline, in which the injured or disrupted subject can be imagined as having lost a wholeness that he/she once possessed. LaCapra posits that the "beginning-middle-end plot . . . seeks to resonate closure or uplift and tends to conflate absence with loss or lack."[106] The wholeness, uniformity, and mastery that have never belonged to the subject (that have always been absent) get constructed as lost or damaged by trauma so that they may be repaired and returned. Confirming such fantasies through their negation, sacrificial films use traumatological narratives about loss to cover over the *illusory* nature of claims about proper and masterful subjectivity. Instead of acknowledging that the wholeness of the subject is a fiction, sacrificial narratives claim traumatic injury as evidence that such wholeness once existed and can be recovered. By operating at an allegorical register, these sacrificial narratives further offer the reassuring promise that one thing can become something else: loss transformed into regeneration, an end made into a beginning.

Sacrificial films thus position themselves as therapeutic responses to trauma. If trauma is understood to imprison the survivor pathologically in the continual present of a painful past, narrative is typically understood as one of the most critical steps with which the survivor can move on from his/her ordeal. Shay notes that constructing a trauma narrative "enables the survivor to rebuild the ruins of character" by offering a sense of context in which he/she can begin to know and make sense of his/her trauma.[107] Learning to tell his/her story, the posttraumatic subject can rearticulate his/her sense of self, history, and agency in an attempt to escape trauma's persistent return. Shay writes of narrative's capacity to heal, "The narrator now speaks as his or her free self, not as the captive or the perpetrator."[108] Recalling the therapeutic use of testimony, sacrificial films enact a fictive moving on or leaving behind in which trauma can be imagined as safely contained in the past—no longer intruding on and interrupting the present.

The consequences of such ostensibly therapeutic work should not be underestimated. First, as I will argue more fully below, Hollywood's sacrificial films not only perpetuate the fiction of unified subjectivity but through their exclusive reliance on male victim-heroes they also reinscribe the presumption that the perfect subject of history is a male one. In so doing, these films reinforce the privileged position of masculinity in American culture. Second, by heralding the post-traumatic (male) subject's suffering as a form of redemption, these films contribute to trauma envy or nostalgia, reinforcing cultural fascination with trauma and marking traumatic loss as a social good.

Third, the narratives of suffering and redemption that get enacted on individual levels within sacrificial films operate as instructive models for imagining how social bodies such as nations can, do, and should respond to events that are constructed as culturally traumatic. Many scholars argue that collectives or cultures use film texts to work through traumas that are said to shatter the body politic and its prevailing belief structures. Mapping fictions of the unified and coherent subject onto understandings of the national body, these arguments imply that collectives can be wounded or broken and, in response, can put themselves back together again. For instance, Thomas Laqueur contends that "nations, like individuals, sustain trauma, mourn and recover. And like individuals, they survive by making sense of what has befallen them, by constructing a narrative of loss and redemption."[109] When public discourse frames events as traumatic, popular culture often operates toward recuperative and restorative ends, reproducing the assumption that trauma is something one can (and should) avoid, leave behind, or cure. Based on such understandings of traumatogenic injury, narrative films frequently offer an avenue "through which uncomfortable histories of traumatic events can be smoothed over, retold, and ascribed new meanings," as Marita Sturken argues.[110]

Such is the work of cinematic sacrificial allegories: to construct scenes of suffering, terror, and trauma in order to redress imagined loss and offer fantasies of recovery. Speaking the language of trauma, sacrificial films represent a particular and prominent narrative strategy for transforming cultural memory so that its impacts can be imagined as uplifting rather than upending. These narratives rescript the past—if not to change its outcomes, then to change its meanings—offering tales of sacrifice and heroism that make sense of and lend meaning to terror and loss. To remember is not just to recall the past but also to attempt to piece back together what is imagined as painfully dismembered, that is, literally to re-member the past. In many cases, narrative rememberings of trauma attempt to persuade audiences to understand traumatic events and their consequences through particular lenses and in accord with specific ideological paradigms. If trauma discourse encourages survivors to piece themselves back together in order to recover and move on from trauma, Hollywood applies this same logic to America as a nation-state. Sacrificial films thus encourage the national body to restore itself to prior (imagined) states of unity and unanimity by whatever means necessary, including violence and further acts of traumatic loss.

In this regard, sacrificial films might be more precisely described as producing a *post*-trauma cinema, which ultimately privileges regeneration over loss, recovery over suffering, freedom over imprisonment. This impetus toward closure and the insistence on a "before" and "after" to injury should also be understood as consonant with the logic of sacrifice. LaCapra contends that the tendency of "conventional narrative structure" to obscure the "difference between absence and loss" also characterizes sacrifice, whose promises of unification and regeneration imply "an original full presence, identity, or intactness." In this light, LaCapra suggests that linear narrative structure and sacrificial practices might be understood as "displacements of one another."[111]

Gil Bailie also associates conventional cinematic narrative structure—in particular, Hollywood's emphasis on narrative resolution—as consonant with (and even derivative of) ritualized sacrificial practice. While sacrifice does suggest an impulse to shatter, to open up, and to create continuity and intimacy among participants, Bailie reminds us that sacrificial practice also strives toward the restoration of order and the reaffirmation of boundaries. Sacrifice serves an expiatory function that is understood to provide "a communal sense of cleansing" in which spectators can witness the expulsion of disorder and chaos from their social body through its projection onto the body of a victim.[112] This tension echoes what Jay identifies as the "joining" and "separating" impulses concurrent within sacrifice; although sacrificial practice might be understood to unite members of a particular social body, it also serves to distinguish and disconnect that collective from an imagined outside.[113]

Borrowing from René Girard's work on sacrifice, Bailie understands sacrificial practice as driven to restore order and reaffirm the bounds of the social and argues that films may work similarly to "purge the community of its conflict and violence by assigning all its sin to one figure."[114] The violent expulsion of this figure—the sacrificial victim-hero, or the scapegoat—from the world of the narrative film is framed as a restoration of the social order and a reconstitution of its boundaries, a re-drawing of the lines between what is in and what is out, what was before and what is after, what was broken and what is healed. Accordingly, Bailie argues that conventional cinematic narrative structure descends from the logic of ancient sacrifice, such that "dramatic resolution in films continues to be heavily influenced by the sacrificial recipes of antiquity."[115]

Sacrificial practice acts as a defense mechanism, not unlike displacement, in which the anxiety or perceived guilt of a community is shifted onto the body of an Other, whose willingness to die makes this transference productive, acceptable, and reassuring. The expiatory work of sacrifice and the analogous work of classical Hollywood narrative structure might therefore be understood as therapeutic in their aims to redraw boundaries and promise closure. Farrell argues that "the effort to heal psychic wounds invariably involves a need to substantiate or reconfirm the self, which often entails convictions of transcendence."[116] Trauma discourse works to construct trauma as a unifying experience that bonds survivors through shared suffering *at the same time* that the experiential authority assigned to the survivor gets used to distinguish and elevate that subject position as extraordinary and exemplary. This is not to say that either sacrificial films or trauma discourse succeed in restoring unity to the social body—or that such imagined unity ever did or could exist—but to say that their emphasis on recovery and resolution operates *as if* such possibilities did exist.

By indulging in the traumatic disorder and disorientation of death, both sacrificial practices and sacrificial films reaffirm the imagined integrity of the subject and the social. Even as much as Shaviro wishes to foreground the cinema's capacity to shatter subjectivity, he admits that the spectator "cannot escape the fatality that heightens self-consciousness whenever one seeks to abolish it, and that turns every gesture of 'sacrificial mutilation' . . . into yet another instance of self-assertion and self-validation."[117] Bataille put it this way: "At all costs we need to transcend [our limits], but we should like to transcend them and maintain them simultaneously."[118] Bataille's poetic anaphora (repeatedly declaring, "I am") may traumatize writing, but it concurrently reaffirms the presence of the subject (or the "I") that "is."

As such, sacrifice and its cinematic reenactment might be understood as both a form of trauma—a terrifying act of destruction and loss—and its alleged cure—a ritualized form of redemption and regeneration. Sacrifice is, like trauma, "a pathology that always operated as a cure"; and the pathology that acts as a cure is also self-perpetuating.[119] If the subject's (or community's) undoing guarantees its existence, then that subject (or social body), will always depend on and therefore facilitate its potential annihilation. In other words, as long as we imagine trauma and sacrifice as cultural acts of apotheosis, we will remain reliant on the sacrificial economy and its inherent violence.

I meet with caution, then, Shaviro's assertion that film "should be praised as a technology for intensifying and renewing experiences of passivity and abjection," for even the hopelessness and paralysis of trauma can be co-opted and mobilized toward the ends of mastery and transcendence.[120] Sacrificial films offer their protagonists' pain, suffering, and destruction as evidence of and justification for their valorized status as hero, I contend. Dean says of the Bataillean transformation of masculine norms that "the virile man is he who refuses our culture's definition of what it means to be whole."[121] At the same time that it reinscribes the logic of traumatic self-loss, sacrifice operates as a particularly potent remedy for traumatic undoing, conflating such categories as injury and virility, victim and hero, weakness and strength, death and life.

Reigning Men

The ritualized sacrifice of male bodies embodies what many scholars, including Sally Robinson, Tania Modleski, and David Savran, have identified as hegemonic masculinity's regeneration through victimization and self-inflicted pain. In both its assertion of male victimhood and its promise of rebirth, ritualized sacrifice demonstrates masculinity's tendency to appropriate what is culturally coded as "feminine," a strategy that Modleski and Savran cite as typical of the maintenance or expansion of hegemony. Modleski suggests that "male power" is often "consolidated through cycles of crisis and resolution," answering "the threat of female power by incorporating it" and effacing "female subjectivity by occupying the site of femininity."[122] Similarly, Savran argues that "modern white masculinities are deeply contradictory . . . offering subject positions that have been marked historically as being both masculine and feminine."[123] The cyclical emergence of sacrifice as a narrative structure within popular American film also illustrates Robinson's claim that "the post-sixties era witnesses a new white and male investment in the 'victim-function,'" which culminates in the "creation of a new category of narrative function/persona": the victim-hero.[124]

The specifically *sacrificial* variant of the victim-hero, however, does more than just "cash in on the symbolic value of victimization."[125] The trope of sacrifice does not simply position men as victims, nor does it offer just another tale of male pain and suffering. Assuredly, "there is much symbolic power to be reaped from occupying the social and discursive position of subject-in-crisis," but sacrifice engenders a much more complex discursive position: the subject-without-limitations, the subject-above-reproach, the subject-beyond-subjectivity.[126] The sacrificial object is not just a victim, nor is he just "any" hero. The sacrificial object is constructed as nothing short of holy.

As the literal definition of sacrifice ("to make holy" or "to make sacred") suggests, noble death endows the sacrificial object with sacrality and power; although the object's authority is predicated on its destruction, the sacrificial offering becomes hallowed, revered—consecrated to a state in which its sacrosanct authority is, like that of the trauma survivor, not to be challenged or disrespected. In other words, the sacrificial object becomes almost divine, or is, at least, touched by the authority of divinity; and when this object is almost exclusively male, the ideological and material implications of sacrifice cannot be underestimated. Not only does sacrificial practice allow masculinity to appropriate and efface Otherness, but it also aligns the masculine with the allegedly immutable power of the godhead. The sacrificial subject is thus not one merely in crisis but one that uses crisis to engender new life for itself (and for others). Farrell notes that "by sacrificing himself in a climactic rescue, the Son saves humankind—the other children of the Lord—and dies reconciled with the Father, identifying with him and sharing his power."[127]

Calling male sacrificial death the preeminent model of traumatic heroism, Farrell describes Christian narratives of Christ's Second Coming as a revenge narrative, in which the wounded Son of God may find himself vindicated for his traumatic undoing. He writes, "Once victimized by the bloodthirsty mob, the scapegoat comes to rule the world. Triumphal mastery preempts sacrificial love, celebrating a righteous cosmic slaughter akin to traumatic berserking."[128] In sacrificial cinema, such a second coming rarely occurs within the diegesis of a particular film, as most sacrificial films end with the deaths of their victim-heroes and do not depict their resurrections. Rather, this return gets enacted intertextually, as sacrificial deaths structure the narrative of a multitude of films. The second coming of the cinematic sacrificial victim-hero is guaranteed by the cyclical and repetitive nature of this body of films. As each cinematic death reenacts the logic of its predecessors, a new victim-hero emerges to enact his own traumatic heroism and to bask in the glory of noble death. It matters, then, that many of the sacrificial films considered in this book are part of larger cinematic lineages as sequels to or remakes of prior sacrificial films: the transgenerational bonds that Jay identifies within institutional religious practice also get enacted within film culture, in which some characters are resurrected so that they may live, suffer injury, and die again.

CHAPTER 2

UNHINGED HEROES AND ALPHA TRAUMAS

"In the twentieth century only Vietnam seriously punctured our idealized self-image. (It was no accident that Vietnam elicited a new name for what Freud called 'the war neuroses': posttraumatic stress disorder remained widespread in part as a correlative of our collective disillusion and its effects on returning veterans.)" —Claire Kahane

Biological warfare, a capsizing cruise liner, demonic possession, the Antichrist, serial killers, and an evil empire may seem to be disparate and unrelated (if not unbelievable) social harms, but according to 1970s Hollywood, these problems shared a common solution: redemptive male death. During the final years of the Vietnam War, a cycle of sacrificial films emerged as part of the industry's turn toward violent cinema laden with special effects, inaugurating what would become a recurrent cinematic strategy for constructing and making use of trauma discourse.[1] The sacrificial films of the Vietnam and post-Vietnam era include *Omega Man* (Boris Sagal, 1971), *The Poseidon Adventure* (Ronald Neame, 1972), *The Exorcist* (William Friedkin, 1973), *The Omen* (Richard Donner, 1976), *Alice, Sweet Alice* (Alfred Sole, 1976), and *Star Wars* (George Lucas, 1977). These films deploy the perceived traumas of Vietnam as imagined threats to and reconfigurations of the U.S. national masculine, using sacrifice as a symbolic suture to refigure prevailing public narratives about the nation and its leading men.

A number of scholars, including Marita Sturken, Susan Jeffords, and James William Gibson, have noted that public culture framed the Vietnam War as disrupting the nation's imagined identity and prevailing gender norms. Sturken suggests that Vietnam "refigured the image not only of American technology and global power but also of American manhood and its relation to the feminine," unsettling the overlapping master narratives of "American imperialism, technology, science, and masculinity."[2] Further compounded by the discourses of feminism, civil rights, and gay rights, the Vietnam War has been constructed as marking a "definitive exit point in American history" and interrupting the nation's ability to narrativize itself, resulting in what Tom Engelhardt calls "a collapse of story."[3]

Cultural memory also framed Vietnam in the language of trauma and injury. Philip Windsor notes that "in US political discourse . . . the horrors of the Vietnam War have been treated not in the obvious terms of tragedy—hubris, retribution, and expiation—but as a 'syndrome' that had to be 'got over.'"[4] This syndrome is imagined as affecting not just those directly touched by violence, terror, or loss but also the nation as an imagined community. Sacrificial films, such as *Omega Man* and *The Poseidon Adventure*, rescript this traumatic history, allegorizing national trauma and recovery through narratives in which humanity's so-called achievements become instruments of despair and destruction. These films transform the bodies of male sacrificial victim-heroes into vehicles for national redemption and regeneration.

Trauma Returns

The concept of trauma, argues Judith Herman, has a cyclical history, experiencing great publicity at some moments and virtual neglect at others. The clinical consideration of psychological trauma, which originated with Freud, flourished in the immediate aftermath World War I but then largely disappeared. The concept reemerged and "reached a peak" in the 1970s in the context of the crumbling "cult of war and the growth of an antiwar movement."[5] For example, in 1970 psychiatrists Robert Jay Lifton and Chaim Shatan joined forces with the organization Vietnam Veterans Against the War to orchestrate rap sessions as therapeutic contexts in which returning soldiers could offer testimony about combat trauma. This group worked as advocates for veterans' right to psychiatric care and strove to create public understandings of war as a traumatic experience.

The psychiatric community expressed concern about the "remarkable number of delayed psychiatric problems that emerge only after the veteran returns to civilian life."[6] Evidence of psychological distress among veterans prompted a session at the 1972 American Psychiatric Association's annual meeting devoted solely to the topic of postwar trauma; a year later the National Council of Churches sponsored an entire conference on the subject of "The Emotional Needs of Vietnam-Era Veterans."[7] Shortly thereafter, psychiatrists developed the phrase "post-Vietnam syndrome" (PVS) to describe a host of symptoms ranging from "rage reactions, anxiety, depression" to "psychophysiological symptoms," including flashbacks and recurrent nightmares.[8] Shatan explains the plight of veterans suffering from post-Vietnam syndrome: "Unable to forget, unable to endow their Vietnam experience with meaning, they live through some things forever," stuck in a "never-ending past [that] deprives the present of meaning."[9] By the middle of the decade, hundreds of rap groups had formed, and at the end of the decade this activism led to the creation of Operation Outreach, a psychological treatment program run by the Veterans' Administration.[10]

Not limited to psychiatric communities or to those directly linked to veterans, trauma discourse circulated widely in public rhetoric. In fact, PVS received substantial coverage in such national newspapers as the *New York Times* and the *Washington Post* and in *Life* magazine, now famous for publishing graphic wartime photographs. For example, a 1970 article in the *Washington Post* profiled three anonymous Vietnam veterans, allowing them to describe their experiences before, during, and after war. Although the article notes that these men were not like the many "basket cases" that "lapsed into that special world of the maimed who never return," it implies that these survivors were lucky to have been spared such a fate, citing others that had been betrayed by the false promises of "grandeur" central to the rhetoric of sacrifice.[11]

In 1972, the *New York Times* published a front-page story describing postwar shock as a "shattering experience" in which journalist Jon Nordheimer critiqued the government's "blindness and intransigence" to the issue of trauma. Nordheimer argued that the nation's mistreatment of veterans upon their return as much as the war itself could be blamed for the suffering of soldiers. He explained: "The PVS proponents have charged that the Government's refusal to accept Vietnam as a trauma . . . has resulted in a policy of official neglect to the young men it had asked to serve the country" and argued that this infrastructural injury compounded the public's hostility toward returning soldiers.[12]

This article supports Jeffords's contention that the trope of victimization predominated in public rhetoric in the Vietnam and post-Vietnam era, positioning male veterans as "emblems of an unjustly discriminated masculinity" or, as Engelhardt puts it, "emblematic figures of loss."[13] This construction of Vietnam veterans mirrors what Kirby Farrell calls the Christological model of "traumatic heroism," and supports his assertion that "Western culture is grounded in traumatic stories."[14] To illustrate such fascination with woundedness, Jeffords refers to A. D. Horne's collection of essays, *The Wounded Generation* (1981), in which the trope of injury figures largely. Consider, for example, John Wheeler's essay in this collection, which describes the Vietnam veteran as the "nigger of the 1970s." Wheeler explains, "You create a nigger by depriving a person of part of his or her personhood. Ignoring that person or inflicting traumatic hurts is the traditional way to treat a nigger."[15] Wheeler uses not only the rhetoric of race to position the American veteran as disenfranchised, he also makes recourse to what was the newly emergent language of trauma in order to construct the veteran as psychically scarred.

Lifton links Vietnam veterans' traumas to the lack of a clear narrative about the "purpose or significance" of the war.[16] He links veterans' individual experiences of "storylessness" to the perceived storylessness of this particular war, implying that greater potential for trauma inhered in this war than in others. Lifton frames the Vietnam veteran as experiencing an unusual degree of wartime and postwar suffering, which he interprets as endowing the returning soldier with a particular kind of wisdom, because of their divided reception at home and the unsuccessful nature of the war itself. He writes, "There is something special about Vietnam veterans."[17] Contrasting Vietnam veterans to those of earlier wars, he suggests that "these men give the impression of something more" and says this "something more" derives directly from the trauma they are said to have endured.[18] Lifton implies that the trauma survivor possesses a unique moral authority and an experiential knowledge that is beyond reproach—an attitude that John Mowitt understands as characterizing most trauma discourse and as fostering "trauma envy."[19] Lifton's suggestion of the trauma survivor's elusive access to "something more" recalls Bataille's fascination with those that have suffered and the fantasy that pain offers access to the real.

The frame of psychic injury applied to combat veterans also became a wider heuristic for thinking about the nation, substituting prevailing psychic models of the subject for understandings of the larger collective. This logic mirrors that of sacrificial films, in which the victim-hero operates as an "individuated aggregate" whose personal story is meant to stand in for that of the national collective.[20] This allegorical and synecdochic substitution of "the one" for the whole hinges on and forwards the belief that both individual subjects and national bodies can be broken and therefore were once whole (and can be again). For instance, in 1972, the *Washington Post* relayed a belief that in addition to describing the mental condition of traumatized veterans, the concept of "Post-Vietnam Syndrome also includes a feeling that the society that sent them to Vietnam was ill." This sentiment was also illustrated by a letter to the editor of the *New York Times* that described America as a "nation wounded."[21]

The language of psychic trauma and mental illness also instructed presidential rhetoric during the Vietnam era. Engelhardt argues that the public presentations of President Richard Nixon consciously deployed "the mantle of madness" as a political tool. Adopting what Nixon reportedly called "the madman theory," his administration offered "a carefully crafted vision of a mad president," making use of international perceptions that Nixon was "unhinged" in order to explain his unrelenting (if not irrational or insane) pursuit of victory in Vietnam.[22] This depiction of the mentally unhinged leader mirrors cinematic constructions of the sacrificial victim-hero, who is frequently depicted as on the edge and losing it, and illustrates Farrell's discussion of "berserking," or the enactment of "berserk frenzy" brought on by trauma. Farrell describes berserking as a style that is "readily manipulated" and put toward a "bewildering range of uses."[23]

Trauma also became a frame for thinking about the cinema. In a film review for *Newsweek* in 1975, for instance, Paul Zimmerman describes many Hollywood films as responding to a "new age of ambiguity" that left America "adrift in the uncharted waters of the 1970s, bobbing in the wake of a decade of trauma."[24] During the late 1960s and 1970s, a number of psychiatrists and psychologists posited a special relationship between cinematic images and traumatic injury. In 1969, psychiatrist Mardi J. Horowitz argued that films might offer a unique tool for understanding how traumatic memory works. Using what he dubbed "stress films" to prove that disturbing memories "would more likely follow a traumatic film than a neutral film," Horowitz's research helped validate the commonly held belief that traumatic memories return as "vivid and potentially intrusive images and, more generally, that psychic trauma tends to be re-enacted."[25] In 1975, James C. Bozzuto posited a *causal* relationship between cinematic images and trauma, coining the diagnosis of "cinematic neurosis." Drawing from a case study published about a woman who claimed to have been traumatized by seeing *The Exorcist*, Bozzuto suggests that films could produce traumatic shock within spectators.[26]

Despite being identified as potential sources of trauma, films were also marshaled during the Vietnam era to end the nation's perceived "storylessness" and to produce new narratives that could account for and manage history's imagined traumas.[27] Farrell argues that far from disavowing the perception of national injury, many of these stories "actually heightened the atmosphere of crisis and reinforced the sense of injury" in order to make use of trauma as an interpretive trope, or what might be called a defense mechanism.[28] Sacrificial films make use of tropes of crisis and victimization but move beyond the rhetoric of victimhood, asserting a rhetoric of national rebirth based on masculine sacrality and constituting trauma as an experience that can be transcendent and transformative.

It's a Jungle Out There

Omega Man (which is based on Richard Matheson's 1954 novel *I Am Legend* and which remakes the film *Last Man on Earth* [Ubaldo Ragona, 1964]) depicts a near-apocalypse caused by biological warfare over the spread of communism. It displaces consideration of the Vietnam War but not beyond visibility, marking its protagonist, an army colonel named Robert Neville (Charlton Heston), as traumatized and on the verge of psychological collapse. In its depiction of "the last man on earth," whose body eventually becomes the post-apocalyptic source for new life, *Omega Man* dramatizes traumas of human existence and posits cultural anxieties about the dangers of science, technology, and war.

The film contributes to what Sturken describes as two central narratives within cultural memory about the Vietnam era: "the divisive effect of the war on American society and the marginalization of Vietnam veterans."[29] With faith in technology and modern science shaken by global disaster, *Omega Man* posits that humanity's salvation and rebirth hinge on the body of its unhinged male hero and in particular his blood. At the same time that the film marks Neville as wounded, vulnerable, and deserving of empathy—he bears characteristic symptoms of psychological trauma—it also casts him as a source of Bataillean fascination—a figure who is exotic in and ennobled by his lonely suffering.

At the film's outset, Neville believes he is the only human unaffected by the plague. An army officer and a scientist, Neville bears partial responsibility for the catastrophe and survives by inoculating himself with the only available vaccine, which he created. Both complicit in and condemned by destruction created in the name of science, Neville wanders the desecrated streets of Los Angeles during the day and seeks comfort in such mundane activities as driving his car, watching movies, and playing chess against himself. At night, Neville defends himself against The Family, a group of nocturnal plague victims led by Matthias. A television journalist prior to the plague, Matthias celebrates the apocalypse as a kind of revolution that cleansed the planet. He and The Family strive to destroy everything and everyone associated with modern civilization, ranging from technology to literature. Neville eventually discovers other survivors—Lisa, Dutch, Richie, and a group of children—who are susceptible to the plague. Realizing that his own blood can be used to inoculate others, Neville asserts that the most effective remedy for the shortcomings of the modernist project is one of life's most elemental substances: human blood, at least blood that is "genuine 160-proof old Anglo-Saxon," as Neville puts it.

The mise-en-scène invites an understanding of the film in relation to the perceived traumas of Vietnam. *Omega Man* uses a "sustained jungle metaphor" to construct Los Angeles as an "urban jungle" and anticipates what would become the "conventions of the Vietnam/jungle/patrol movie," casting Neville as hunting and being hunted by his enemies.[30] The opening shots of the film depict Neville driving his sports car around the streets of Los Angeles, wearing safari gear with his gun in tow. Like the heroes of the Vietnam War films that would follow in the coming decades, he patrols and searches.

Omega Man also constructs a war zone in which *visibility* is a central problem. Blinded by light, The Family emerges largely at night, forcing Neville to fight them under the cover of darkness; this scenario recalls cultural figurations of U.S. troops as hunting and being hunted in the dense and dark jungles of Vietnam and as constantly forced to confront the "invisibility of a barbarous enemy."[31] Consider, for instance, a veteran's description of the Vietnam experience as recounted in Lifton's *Home from the War*.

> No matter how much effort you put into it, you can't find him. You can't lay your hands on him. And the fact that he might also be anywhere, you know . . . as though you were hunting a specific deer and you don't know which one it is and there's a deer herd all over you.[32]

In this scenario, Lifton contends, "the invisible enemy, being able to track down the GI, becomes the hunter, the GI the hunted."[33] *Omega Man*'s images of The Family resemble what would become canonical representations of the enemy in Vietnam as "elusive, invisible, disguised."[34] As Family members, cloaked in dark robes, dart in and out of hiding places waiting to ambush Neville, he often mistakes debris—including store mannequins and corpses—for living bodies. And, like the passage Lifton quoted, *Omega Man* casts The Family as an animalistic herd, which Neville calls "vermin."

Images of rotting corpses and blood-strewn bodies blasted by machine-gun fire evoke the wartime iconography with which Vietnam-era American audiences were becoming familiar. For instance, during the war, *Life* magazine published numerous cover photos that exposed the wounded and scarred bodies of American soldiers, including a cover from 1965 that depicts the maimed body of a dying helicopter pilot; a cover from 1966 that portrays bandaged soldiers huddled in jungle trenches; and a cover from 1970—only a year before the release of *Omega Man*—that features the injured bodies of American veterans as part of a photo essay entitled "Our Forgotten Wounded." Traces of these bodies mutilated in combat haunt the landscape of *Omega Man* and encourage interpretation of the film in relation to its historical context.

One Is the Loneliest Number

Omega Man emphasizes the psychological tolls of war. The film's opening shot, a high-angle, extreme long shot on Neville's convertible driving through the ruined city, renders Neville small, unreachable, and isolated. Neville comes continually in and out of view, his face often hidden by the position of the camera (the camera shooting Neville from behind and over his shoulder) or mise-en-scène (shadows obscuring his face). This lack of access to Neville underscores his isolation and alienation and reaffirms understandings of trauma as producing social detachment that cuts off the survivor "from all human community."[35]

Neville speaks to himself but never provides any explanation for the scenes of destruction in which he is immersed. His self-directed dialogue hints at the possibility that he is psychologically unhinged, and the lack of explanation denies audiences any narrative context or empathetic ground on which they might build a relationship with his character. Casting Neville as the loneliest man on the planet, *Omega Man* also strategically hinders the audience's initial ability to forge identifications with him. As distanced from the film's imagined spectators as he is alone in the world, Neville appears as the ultimate embodiment of the traumatized subject, cut off from any chance for connection to or communication with others.

This figuration of the abandoned male hero in the film recalls prevailing constructions of the Vietnam veteran as especially mistreated and victimized not only by the war but also by the divided reception at home, as if foreshadowing Lifton's 1973 assertion that the Vietnam vet was "different from veterans of other wars. A favorite word to describe them is 'alienated.'"[36] The absence of exposition and relative lack of dialogue in *Omega Man*'s opening scenes also means that no narrative frame exists that would enable spectators to make sense of the scenes of destruction, thus introducing Neville's condition as one of "storylessness." Beyond contributing to the film's figuration of trauma, the lack of an expository frame also effectively positions Neville as a synecdoche for the nation. Neville's initial anonymity introduces him as a stand-in or substitute for the national audience, an aggregation of the imagined suffering of the collective.[37]

Omega Man further depicts Neville as suffering from many of the symptoms associated with psychological trauma, including hallucinations, flashbacks, and repetition compulsions. The phrase post-traumatic stress disorder was not coined until 1980, so in the film Neville suffers from what at the time would have been called "shell shock," "combat fatigue," or PVS. His symptoms mirror canonical descriptions of trauma as an "unwitting reenactment of an event that one simply cannot leave behind."[38] Framing trauma as "the literal return of the event against the will of the one it inhabits," *Omega Man* constructs Neville's traumatic memories as being triggered by a seemingly unrelated and inconsequential experience that revives his experiences of terror and loss.[39]

After a minor car accident, for instance, Neville experiences auditory hallucinations, imagining the sounds of ringing pay phones—one of many technologies that plagues him throughout the narrative. The sounds torment Neville, reminding him that he has no one to call. These hallucinations also trigger a traumatic memory of a ringing phone that two years earlier had brought Neville the news that the effects of biological warfare were devastating the United States. Significantly, *Omega Man* introduces this information in the form of a flashback that intrudes upon Neville's consciousness and interrupts the narrative. This disruptive device not only offers evidence of Neville's trauma, but it also embodies the "phenomenological structure of trauma" in which the subject "simultaneously feels stopped in time while constantly repeating the actions within that isolated moment."[40]

Through flashback editing, the film's otherwise linear narrative bears signs of traumatic disruption, in which the "flow of time has been fragmented into shards of isolated events."[41] Traumatizing the film text itself, *Omega Man*'s flashbacks contribute to a "poesis of trauma."[42] Inasmuch as these flashbacks get marked as both psychological and narrative *aberrations* in an otherwise linear narrative, their disruptive presence also works (as the proverbial exceptions that prove the rule) to confirm the normativity and hegemony of linearity within Hollywood storytelling—the logic of which, as LaCapra might suggest, reinscribes fictions about the proper, unified, and whole subject that is said to exist before and (presumably) after trauma.

The content of Neville's flashbacks also matter. They reenact images of warfare, Neville's failed attempts to engineer defenses against the spreading plague, and news stories about the escalation of war and the spread of disease. The first flashback, which takes place shortly after Neville's car crash, is triggered when he presses a button on an elevator. This simple act unearths a host of traumatic memories that disrupt the present time of the diegesis, including images of bombs exploding and a rocket launch. Another flashback depicts news stories about plague victims and images of dead bodies throughout the city.

A subsequent flashback reveals that a helicopter crash prevented Neville from disseminating the vaccine that would have saved the population. This flashback embodies the film's ambivalence about modern technologies and might also be understood as specifically invoking the iconography of the Vietnam War—as in the 1965 *Life* cover that features a wounded and "vulnerable" helicopter pilot. Taken together, these flashbacks expose Neville's psychological instability and his complicity in the catastrophe he suffers. This construction of Neville mirrors public presentations of the Vietnam veteran as both party to and damaged by the horrors of war.

Insinuations that Neville is disturbed (and disturbing) are reinforced when he debates whether or not to use his curative blood to save The Family. Richie, Lisa's younger brother and the first survivor to have been cured of the plague, challenges Neville about his enmity toward The Family. Insisting on the humanity of The Family, the young Richie asks why Neville's enemies cannot be saved, as Richie had been. Neville refuses Richie's empathetic gesture, calling The Family "homicidal maniacs" and "vermin." Richie responds, "You're hostile. You just don't belong. Sometimes you scare me more than Matthias does."

This construction of Neville is similar to Vietnam-era concerns about whether veterans would be able to abandon their warrior culture and reintegrate, suggesting that Neville suffers from the Vietnam veteran's "adjustment problems."[43] Richie's concern that Neville is violent, dangerous, and "hostile" prefigures what would become canonical representations of the Vietnam veteran in American cinema. For example, one year after *Omega Man*'s release *Welcome Home, Soldier Boys* (Richard Compton, 1972) depicts scenes of soldiers "berserking," and *Skyjacked* (John Guillermin, 1972) pits an airline pilot (played by Heston as well) against a berserk Vietnam veteran hijacking a commercial airplane.[44]

The debate between the older and younger generation that seeks "to find out who's right," as the character Ritchie says in the film, also mirrors what Adam Lowenstein offers as another perceived trauma of the Vietnam era: dissent at home. Lowenstein argues that cultural memory frames Vietnam-era America as experiencing an "extraordinary national crisis," in which the "definition of 'America' is subjected to such fiercely opposed forces that the nation often verges on tearing itself in half." Chief among these divisions are such polarizations as "right/left, old/young, prowar/antiwar, bourgeois culture/counterculture, white/black"—all of which get staged, rather acutely, in this debate between Neville, an older, white establishment figure, and Richie, a young African American outlier.[45]

The fight between Richie and Neville contributes to the cinematic depiction of Vietnam as a war waged between U.S. citizens, "fighting themselves" over competing definitions of heroism, morality, and justice. It configures the nation as traumatized and disabled by the "indecisive psyche" of a culture "that could not agree on a narrative under which to fight."[46] This sense of domestic struggle is heightened by the fact that Neville's primary enemies, The Family, are other U.S. citizens that have become symptomatic of the plague and that Neville himself contributed to the development of biological warfare in the first place. The battle being waged in this film is imagined as one internal to the nation and its leadership structures, making clear that at stake in *Omega Man* are definitions of the body politic and contemporary rhetoric about the nation itself as being ill and in need of healing.

Modern Warfare

Omega Man expresses historically specific ambivalence about the master narratives of modernism and the ensuing emphasis on scientific and technological progress. Its depiction of a global plague caused by biological warfare and engineered by human hands contrasts with both Matheson's source novel and its first filmic adaptation, *Last Man on Earth*, which attribute the plague to naturally occurring bacteria. As a result of the human actions in *Omega Man*, Matthias argues, Neville has "nothing to live with but his memories, nothing to live with but his gadgets, his cars, his guns, gimmicks." Matthias's invective associates Neville's traumas with the signifiers of modernity and the technologies on which he has grown dependent.

Technological malfunctions and breakdowns torment Neville. Within minutes of the film's opening, for example, his Ford Mustang fails him. Surprised by an abandoned armored car piled high with corpses, Neville drives his car off the road. Although minor, the wreck mirrors a series of much greater technological failures that give shape to the traumatized landscape in which Neville is trapped, or paralyzed—including the earlier helicopter crash and a later scene in which a jammed machine gun precipitates Neville's death.

For Farrell, the failures of humanity's tools, embodied by such incidents as plane crashes and car wrecks, hasten trauma in popular culture. As the "prosthetic extensions of us," planes, trains, ships, and cars can signal human progress and strength, but their breakdowns can also expose "how radically vulnerable and ephemeral we are." The image of a crash, Farrell contends, can singularly "evoke the traumatic potential of modernism," and in the case of *Omega Man*, the destruction of Neville's *muscle* car also suggests that the vulnerability of this technology might signal a potential threat to Neville's masculinity, which is intimately tied to the phallic tools and weapons he wields.[47] On multiple occasions, *Omega Man* underscores the possibility that Neville's traumas directly implicate his troubled masculinity, as in the scenes in which Neville gets trapped and must be rescued by a woman (Lisa, his lover) or in the final scene in which a moment of technological impotence—he can't fire his machine gun—leaves him vulnerable to The Family.

Omega Man's ambivalence about modern technology also includes its anxious treatment of mediation, especially television. In Neville's first flashback, for instance, much of the memory centers on a news report detailing the outbreak of biological warfare, and the reporter featured in this flashback is Neville's post-apocalypse enemy Matthias. In casting Matthias as a journalist, *Omega Man* invites understanding of television as a technology with a destructive potential not unlike the actual weapons of warfare. The film's portrayal of the medium of television as a dangerous weapon of modern warfare also informs Neville's second flashback. In addition to more news footage of plague victims and images of dead bodies scattered throughout the city, this flashback depicts two corpses sitting upright in their living room, squarely in front of their television set—killed while watching television. The entombment of the bodies in front of their television set implicates the act of watching television in their deaths, as if the images onscreen may have somehow precipitated their demise. With their eyes opened and their mouths gaping, the corpses appear almost as if they died of shock at what they saw on their television.

The insinuation that television was complicit in the deaths of these characters bears particular historical significance given the public perception that much of the trauma of the Vietnam War owed to its mediation as the first "television war." Also called the "living room war," a phrase coined just two years before *Omega Man*'s release by television critic Michael Arlen, Vietnam has been cast as a war fought and lost in its mediated representations at home.[48] Such cultural memory has also marked news coverage of the war as injurious to American citizens as war's helpless spectators. Marshall McLuhan opined in

Figure 3. Two corpses sitting in a living room in front of a television as the nighttime news recounts devastation wrought by biological warfare. *Omega Man* (Warner Bros.)

1968 that television coverage of the Vietnam War meant that "the public [was] now participant in every phase of the war, and the main actions of the war [were] being fought in the American home itself."[49]

Marking American spectators as not only participants in but also victims of the war—their living rooms turned into battlefields and tombs—*Omega Man* contributes to anxious discourse about the effects of war's mediation, which lingers even today within American cultural memory about Vietnam. Whether television coverage of Vietnam "really" did (or did not) affect public opinion about the war, *Omega Man* operates as part of a larger discursive formation in which television is taken to task for its perceived contribution to the war and in which the American public is imagined as wounded and damaged by representations of atrocity. Like Bataille, this film asserts the power of images not only to capture suffering but also to *produce* trauma, as in Buzutto's construction of "cinematic neurosis." Although the narrative overtly indicates that biological warfare killed these characters, their positioning as spectator-corpses decaying in front of their television sets also evokes understandings of the image as able, in Bataillean terms, to communicate pain and anguish directly—to transmit trauma to its witnesses.

Neville's second flashback also features him watching Matthias on television as the reporter editorializes about the implications of war. Matthias asks, "Is this the end of technological man? Is this the conclusion of all our yesterdays, the boasts of our fabled science, the superhuman conquest of space and time, the age of the wheel?" In what will become one of many speeches Matthias gives about the dangers of modernity, this soliloquy airs the widespread anxiety about American master narratives during and after the Vietnam era. Matthias frequently voices concerns about the destructive forces of modernity, as in his speech in which he deems Neville the "refuse of the past" and his later declaration that art and science are an "illusion" and a "nightmare." *Omega Man* thus performs and contributes to anxiety about the nation's technological failures, or impotence.

Because these critiques come from the film's chief villain, however, *Omega Man* remains ambivalent about modernity and technology. While the film chronicles technological failures and dangers, technology also operates as both a source of Bataillean pleasure for Neville and as a useful weapon against The Family. *Omega Man* also manages the cultural anxiety that mediated technology contributed to the world's devastation by using televisions and screens as defenses against The Family and by enabling Neville to use this equipment productively and toward salvific ends. Matthias exploits television as a platform to spread his social dis-ease, but Neville uses technology to seek out a cure. *Omega Man* also manages its uncertainties about Neville's masculinity, prosthetic dependence, and hero status by reconstituting his troubled subjectivity through tropes of traumatic heroism and returning to the body as humankind's most potent resource.

Near-Death Experiences

Omega Man's constructions of Neville resonate in many ways with Bataillean fantasies of the subject, as demonstrated, for instance, by recurrent depictions of him as a spectator of film and television. In these scenes, movie and/or television screens function as Neville's prosthetic extensions, for example, helping him to unwind while watching a movie or enabling him to monitor his enemies via surveillance cameras. Neville's repeated positioning as a spectator of film and television screens and his fascination with images of others suggest an impulse toward dissolution and self-loss, or what Steven Shaviro calls a "Bataillean ecstasy" of "self-abandonment."[50] To demonstrate, after his car accident in the opening sequence of the film, Neville enters an abandoned movie theater and screens the film *Woodstock* (Michael Wadleigh, 1970).[51]

His familiarity with both the projection equipment and the film's dialogue suggest that Neville reenacts this event frequently, illustrating what might be considered a repetition compulsion that concurrently reveals the etiological role of the screen in Neville's trauma and illustrates his attempts at mastery over his isolation. The film's ritualized and euphoric images of people dancing, embracing, and communing with one another underscore Neville's attempts to find continuity with others and to experience something *outside of* himself. As he speaks and sings along with the figures onscreen, Neville reveals his longing to be a part of their world, which is, significantly, a counterculture.

This desire for communication with others also motivates, even if unconsciously, Neville's compulsive confrontations of and interactions with another counterculture, The Family. Neville yearns to know, understand, and (at times)

Figure 4. Illustrating the tensions between his countercultural tendencies and his traditional masculinity, Robert Neville drives to see *Woodstock* in his muscle car. *Omega Man* (Warner Bros.)

become a part of The Family. He insists on maintaining close contact with them, hunts down their nests, captures a Family member for research purposes, and constantly surveils them on television monitors in his living room. Although these acts subject Neville to the risk of "becoming contaminated" by the objects of his gaze, he cannot stop himself, as if possessed by his fascination with them.[52]

Despite the dangers posed by The Family, Neville often leaves his windows open, stepping onto his balcony, provoking the angry mob and rendering himself the object of their gaze. He is drawn to the trauma and abjection of The Family, reproducing a Bataillean construction of the abject as that which "fascinates and disturbs us profoundly."[53] Mark Sample argues that "like Freud's Rat Man, like Hitler himself, Neville is both fascinated and horrified by what he perceives as vermin."[54] To Neville, The Family becomes like the torture victim to Bataille: hideous *and* beautiful.[55]

The camera also directs its gaze toward trauma; a significant portion of *Omega Man*'s screen time is devoted to the abject bodies of the plague victims, frequently offering extreme close-ups of their lacerated, colorless skin and white eyes. *Omega Man* encourages fascination with the ecstatic anguish of the Other and invites its spectators to experience the Bataillean self-abandonment that Shaviro identifies as so central to the cinematic experience. Sample notes that the "grotesque" bodies of The Family become carnivalesque spectacles, the camera placing their abjection on conspicuous display. Not simply invested in depictions of Neville as a spectator or witness to the grotesque spectacles of suffering, however, *Omega Man* does not construct what Sample describes as a clear or tidy "opposition between the classical [Neville] and the grotesque body [The Family]."[56] Instead, *Omega Man* hints at the *likeness*, or continuity, of these bodies, as evidenced by the film's frequent fixation on Neville's spectacular and public experiences of pain.

Neville endures many near-death experiences, including an incident when The Family attempts to murder him publicly in the devastated remains of a stadium. In a position reminiscent of Christ on the cross or the Leng Tch'e torture victim, Neville is tied to a fence, his arms outstretched, while hordes of plague victims taunt him and threaten to set him on fire. This scene exemplifies *Omega Man*'s fascination with trauma and the trope of wounded masculinity. Exposed, paralyzed, and passive, Neville suffers conspicuously, and his pain becomes a source of pleasure for onlookers, whose gazes fixate on his body. Like the trauma survivor, Neville is trapped—held hostage—until he is unexpectedly rescued by Lisa and Dutch, the other survivors with whom Neville eventually joins forces. This near-death experience also catalyzes Neville's rather sudden romance with Lisa, which echoes the characters' Bataillean impulse toward self-dissolution; interrupting their fight against The Family, Neville and Lisa seek erotic self-loss in the middle of a battle for self-preservation.

Omega Man's treatment of self-dissolution, abjection, and Otherness might invite understandings of the film as offering ethical imperatives and political critiques specific to its historical context. For instance, it is not incidental that the film Neville watches is *Woodstock*, a documentary about the music festival that took place in 1969. As Lifton notes, *Woodstock* signified Vietnam-era youth culture, counterculture, and, by extension, the antiwar movement. "Woodstock imagery" and the film itself had "special meaning for young Americans who fought in Vietnam."[57] Lifton's description of one Vietnam veteran who saw the film multiple times upon his return home from the war mirrors the scene in *Omega Man* where Neville recites dialogue that he seems to know by heart.[58]

Neville's pleasure in watching *Woodstock* might imply that this film and its protagonist embrace what Lifton describes as the countercultural rejection of the hegemonic masculine attitudes that celebrate violence and war-making, trading in the John Wayne model of masculinity for the "alternative modes of maleness put forth by the counter culture: being gentle, open, noncompetitive, 'soft' (to the point of being able to cry)"—as Neville almost seems to do when he watches scenes from *Woodstock*.[59] In addition, Neville's fascination with the abject counterculture of The Family and his relationship with a woman marked with multiple indices of difference—not only is Lisa (Rosalind Cash) black but she is also a former follower of Matthias and lacks Neville's immunity to the plague—might also be read as evidence that *Omega Man* espouses a critical or oppositional stance toward violence and Othering. It bears noting that at the time of *Omega Man*'s release, Heston was known as being in opposition to the Vietnam War and as being a civil rights activist; thus, his extratextual persona may have invited understandings of the film as critiquing the war and advocating acceptance of the Other.[60]

Despite such potential signs of productive critique, however, *Omega Man* ultimately and violently reinscribes boundaries between self and Other, bolstering what Lifton describes as the "masculine attitudes" that perpetuate violence, Othering, or war-making.[61] The film's reassertions of masculinist mastery and reliance on a sacrificial economy overwhelm its potential for hospitality, rejection of phallic values, and engagement with the suffering of an Other. As much as *Omega Man* allows its protagonist to indulge fantasies of self-shattering, dissolution, and Otherness, it also insists that Neville shore up the boundaries of his subjectivity; confirm the distinctions between healthy and sick, healed and broken, right and wrong; and redraw the lines between inside and out, before and after.

Seeing Is Being

Omega Man maintains assertions of the "super-masculinity promoted within the military" by preserving the oppositional frame that differentiates Neville from his enemies.[62] If Neville appears on the verge of psychological breakdown and is marked by trauma, his enemies are coded as even farther gone than he, having been diagnosed by Dutch as having "psychotic delusions" and "occasional stages of torpor"; and if Neville becomes an abject object of the gaze, he also maintains his authority as an all-seeing voyeur. Neville deploys surveillance cameras and monitors as weapons in his fight against The Family, using his ability to see as a strategy for gaining mastery and validating his sense of agentive selfhood.

Neville's apartment features surveillance cameras and a wall of televisions, a "modern-day panopticon" from which the elevated Neville may look down upon and constantly watch The Family.[63] These television screens allow him to experience visual mastery—a totalizing gaze over the dark urban jungle—in contrast to the self-loss he experienced while watching *Woodstock*. These cameras and television monitors, consequently, mirror what Sturken has described as the two roles of the camera during war: on one hand, they claimed to provide photographic evidence of or access to the past (what really happened) and, on the other hand, they worked as a device for waging warfare that tracks and monitors the enemy.[64] While *Omega Man* constructs television news as a source of trauma (visceral, visual evidence of the horrors of war), the film also deploys cameras and screens as trauma's remedy (the tools with which horror is contained). This paradoxical figuration of the screen also mirrors the figuration of sacrifice as a ritual praxis that both produces traumatic self-loss and reconstitutes subjectivity.

Neville uses technology to overcome the partial blindness produced by the nocturnal strikes of his enemies. Sequestered in his townhouse, high above the streets, Neville becomes Michel de Certeau's "voyeur-god," using his power of sight to fulfill his "scopic drive" for mastery. The "all-seeing power" of his "totalizing eye" gives him an advantage over and makes him superior to his blind enemies.[65] If Vietnam-era public rhetoric blamed television news for its chaotic, disordered, and uncertain participation in the war and if the screen might also signify Neville's radical passivity, Neville recasts visual technology as purposeful in his able hands. This narrative device reasserts the productive potential of technology and recuperates Neville's masculinity as agentive and masterful, armed with a controlling gaze.

At the center of this wall of televisions, one screen—the biggest of all—displays Neville inside his own apartment. Looking at his super-sized image onscreen, Neville comments to himself, "I'm a narcissist." This television screen thus embodies the transformation from self-loss to subjective reconstitution. Constantly visible to himself, Neville—outside of (or beside) himself—mimes Lacan's figuration of the child in the mirror stage, confirming his own existence and (mis)recognizing himself as whole, stable, and unified, a proper subject. Neville also uses this screen to find himself, as if confirming Shaviro's concern that cinematic experiences of self-dissolution get turned, all too often, into opportunities for "self-assertion and self-validation," as opposed to the experiences of abjection and self-abandonment that Shaviro advocates.[66] This screen operates as a specular technology that allows Neville to become a witness to his own fictions of subjecthood, and this act of subjective reconstitution helps undo the damages already wrought by the television—the self-declared narcissist as the antithesis of and antidote to the spectator-corpse.

Neville also asserts himself as a masterful subject through his romance with Lisa, which recuperates his white masculinity by restoring him to a position of relative authority within the film and reaffirming his heteronormativity. Having lost his place in the social order, Neville's sexual relationship with Lisa confirms his status as a man inasmuch as hegemonic masculinity is tied to presumptions and performances of heterosexuality. Neville's adherence to such heteronormative and masculinist norms becomes especially prominent when Lisa becomes infected and joins The Family, requiring Neville to rescue her. Saving Lisa confirms Neville's heroic authority and atones for earlier moments of weakness in which Neville had to be rescued by Lisa.[67]

Neville's relationship with Lisa also anticipates what Sturken identifies as a common tactic of post-Vietnam films: using narratives of racial reconciliation as stand-ins for narratives about the reunification of the war-torn nation. While Hollywood's Vietnam War films typically eclipse the subjectivities of Vietnamese soldiers and citizens and ignore their traumas, they focus almost exclusively on the experiences of U.S. soldiers—as if the war only happened to (and for) Americans. Sturken argues that many Vietnam War films "provide absolution and a sense of redemption" through depictions of the war "as a site where race relations were transcended—where at a time of racial turmoil

Figure 5. Neville and other survivors admiring his expansive and narcissistic surveillance equipment. *Omega Man* (Warner Bros.)

at home, men of all colors saw each other as equals and treated each other as brothers." In a war that was otherwise considered not to have a clear purpose or outcome, Hollywood films depicting racial reconciliation between American soldiers retroactively claim that racial harmony was "something good produced by the experience of Americans in the war."[68]

Omega Man's depiction of Neville and Lisa's interracial relationship offers similar promises of racial harmony and equality. Such promises cannot overcome, however, the violent politics of Othering that undergird sacrificial violence: despite Neville's love for Lisa, a former member of The Family, the film scapegoats Matthias and his followers as vile, abject Others, worthy of destruction. Unlike Matheson's novel, *Omega Man* ends with Neville both mourned as victim and vindicated as hero; the film denies The Family any empathy. What's more, although Neville shares his blood with Lisa and her brother, Richie, the film links Neville's salvific authority with his whiteness, describing his blood as "genuine 160-proof old Anglo-Saxon" in contrast to the infected and allegedly impure blood flowing through Lisa's and Richie's black bodies.

The suffering of The Family does not compel Neville to seek a cure; only the pain of other survivors that he imagines as more similar to himself—as healthy, normal, human—motivates his messianic mission. After Neville reveals that he could use his own immunized blood as a serum against the plague, Dutch responds, "Christ. You could save the world." In addition to the rather obvious pun in this remark (as in "Christ, you could save the world"), this comment introduces both the central paradox of this film—redemption and salvation lie in the draining of Neville's life source—and one of its chief symbols, Neville's blood.

Offering up his blood allows Neville to undo the damage to which he has contributed, winding back time, fictively rewriting history, and creating a future on his terms. This process allows Neville to become a hero without relinquishing the moral authority imagined to accompany his position as victim, for in order to heal others, Neville must first be wounded. Multiple scenes depict Neville in the process of painfully drawing and transfusing his own blood, quite literally opening up his body for the sake of others. Like blood itself, which is necessary for life but also signifies the possibility of death, Neville's cure embodies the sacrificial paradox wherein "life is mingled with death, but simultaneously death is a sign of life, a way into the infinite."[69]

Neville hopes that by inoculating his fellow survivors with his blood he can create a utopian community, which he likens to "the beginning of the world." Consequently, Neville no longer fashions himself as the "omega" but as the "alpha" man: the first, the origin. The world will be reborn not by a return to its maternal origins but by a rebirth through the father, who was "the last" and is now "the first." Neville's cure attempts to create transgenerational bonds that transcend reliance on maternal bodies and endow his body with sacral, even god-like, authority, just as most ritualized sacrificial practice does, as Nancy Jay reminds us.[70]

Omega Man thus reproduces the Bataillean fantasy in which self-loss is imagined to give the subject access to the "limitless, infinite nature of sacred things" and the "universality" that is the province of the gods.[71] Bataille says of the sovereign subject, "He is not a man in the individual sense of the word, but rather a *god*."[72] *Omega Man* bears out its divine aspirations for its victim-hero through its titular reference to the biblical *Book of Revelation,* in which the phrase "I am the alpha and the omega" is God's own appellative declaration.[73] As if this allusion might not suffice, *Omega Man* confirms Neville's deification when one of the surviving children asks him, "Are you God?"

Although Neville and Lisa's coupling does position them as father and mother, or Adam and Eve, of the world's newest family, *Omega Man* quickly displaces Lisa from the position of mother, leaving (white, male) Neville to grant new life to the survivors. Having succumbed to the plague, Lisa abandons Neville's family and returns to Matthias. Neville must save his symbolic offspring *and* his love interest, requiring him to play father and mother to the fledging clan; but before he can collect his blood in a scientific and orderly fashion, Neville resigns himself to the urgent, violent, and fatal spilling of his blood.

Moving On and Falling Down

In his final fight with The Family, Neville's gun jams—another failure of modern technology and a signifier of his potential emasculation. Matthias throws a dagger at Neville, piercing the protagonist in the chest. Neville falls into a water fountain, where his blood spills profusely and mixes with the water. Rather than seeking help, Neville bottles his blood to cure Lisa and to give to Dutch so that he may regenerate the world's population. Both Neville's blood and Lisa's infected body get translated into property to be inherited by Neville's successor, Dutch, who heads to the hills to create a new generation of survivors and leaves Neville to die in the fountain. Yet another white man inherits the task of giving new life to the world.

Instead of a military man or a government official, the leader of this new world is a member of a counterculture (who is also a medical student) charged with the responsibility of healing the sick and dying world. Neville's death functions, at least in part, as an expiatory gesture; if he has been responsible for the destruction around him, his death atones for such complicity and makes room for a new version of masculine heroism—one built on giving life, not making war, on curing, not conquering. With Neville also exalted in and by death, however, *Omega Man* does not entirely relinquish its investment in the violent logics of war and sacrifice. Dutch may lead a new generation of survivors but only *because* Neville was first willing to fall in the line of duty.

As they pack up and move on, Dutch and the other survivors perform what might, in therapeutic discourse, be called a "healthy" response to trauma. Dutch says, "Well, let's move, kids. We've got a long way to go." Able to leave the devastated Los Angeles behind them, these survivors enact fictions of closure and recovery. Rather than compulsively repeating their encounters with suffering—what LaCapra might call melancholic "acting out"—the survivors mourn their losses and move on. The trauma of near-annihilation does not possess them or hold them hostage but is abandoned as the past. In contrast to constructions of the veteran as trapped in the past, the narrative directs the survivor to let go of his/her past injuries, positing a clear trajectory of the experience of trauma—one in which there is a *before* and an *after* to trauma—and a subject that, once undone, can be made whole (and healthy) again. Built into this promise of restoration is the fantasy that this repaired subject was ever (or could ever be) whole in the first place.

The iconography and rhetoric of rebirth of this scene corroborate such a redemptive understanding of the film's resolution. As Neville falls into the fountain, he assumes a position reminiscent of Christ's crucifixion: arms outstretched, head drooping, and blood pouring from his side. Returning to this root paradigm for interpreting sacrifice, *Omega Man* positions Neville, and by extension the body politic for which he stands, within a Christological lineage of salvific male subjects.[74] Referring to Neville's final position as "a pose self-consciously reminiscent of Christ on the Cross," Sample argues that "Neville's blood, like Christ's, is the blood that heals, the blood that renews, the blood that gives life." Because "Neville's blood is the only blood on earth immune to the deadly contagion," *Omega Man* assigns its victim-hero a hallowed and inimitable position; although Dutch can carry on his legacy, only Neville is marked as the source of life.[75]

Continued emphasis on suffering and trauma, however, complicates this film's rhetoric of restoration and rebirth. As much as the diegesis encourages recovery from trauma, the final images of the film remain suffused with trauma envy, demonstrating the allure and symbolic import that traumatic self-loss and the white male body in pain sustain in this film. A high-angle shot depicting Neville's corpse floating in the cruciform fountain constructs the male subject not as virile or agentive but as lacerated and defeated; his body is limp, unmoving, and left to decay under the rising sun. Recalling Bataille's torture photographs, this victimized version of masculinity remains on public display—an object of a collective gaze. This scene completes the film's deconstruction of the perceived oppositions between the "classical and grotesque body": Neville's body may be "raised on a pedestal" but it is not, as Sample argues, self-contained. Neither is this body a "finished product" with its "orifices sealed or hidden entirely."[76] This body is—like those of The Family—open, gaping, seeping, and exposed; but being undone in this final scene does not render Neville monstrous or reviled. Instead, it endows his abject remains with a regenerative force.

The film's investment in the restorative capacity of the disarticulated, injured, and even grotesque male body further drives the formal construction of the film's final frames: a relatively inert, long take of Neville's corpse in the fountain. The use of the long take embodies the phenomenology of trauma and its "mythic sense of eternal recurrence," producing an unresolved tension at the end of the film.[77] While the resolution of Dutch and Lisa's narrative emphasizes the process of moving past trauma, the form of the film's final image remains relatively trapped in the violent scene of Neville's sacrificial death, refusing to let go of suffering and loss. Although not actually a still frame, the long take resembles a photograph; there are only faint traces of movement along the edges of the frame. Accordingly, this final shot recalls what Lowenstein calls the "photo finish ending," a common device in the cinema of the late 1960s and 1970s that had both political and phenomenological implications.[78]

First, the shot's likeness to the photo finish offers an "evocation of news photography" associated with the Vietnam War.[79] This allusion anchors the film, linking Neville's subject position to prevailing constructions of the traumatized Vietnam veteran. Second, this use of the almost-but-not-quite photo finish recalls the photograph's capacity for signifying absence and "connoting death": what Barthes describes as the cinema's capacity to suggest "being there" is met with the photograph's ability to evoke "having been there." Hanging limply in the fountain, Neville resembles the victim of Bataille's Leng Tch'e photograph. Both men are trapped, lifeless, and immobile. There is no dialogue, no narration—only a fixed and (relatively) immutable representation of trauma. *Omega Man* maintains a traumatic frame, laying bare the important and alluring role that trauma plays in American culture.

This scene also lays bare what Marvin and Ingle describe as the nation's unspoken (and rather unspeakable) dependence on ritualized sacrifice for cultural renewal. The new world does not begin without a sacrifice of the old, but *Omega Man* never articulates such impulses overtly. In fact, once Neville dies, no further lines of dialogue are spoken. This literal silence recalls figurations of trauma as unspeakable and the survivor as beyond censure. At the same time, the ending becomes party to the nation-state's unwillingness to confront its reliance on a sacrificial economy. As one of the final acts of this film—as is the case with all sacrificial films—this redemptive act of self-loss is both definitive and unquestioned. No one within the diegesis dares to speak about or question this ultimate act, which is understood both to demand reverent silence and to speak for itself.

Although the content of the image remains unchanged, the image is *not* a still photograph or even a photo finish; traces of movement at the edges of the frame—as in the water rippling slightly around Neville's body—suggest that this final scene should not be understood as trapped in a perpetually recurring past. In contrast to the still photograph, the movement detectable within the frame—however slight—insists on getting time moving again. This long take simultaneously evokes the specter of trauma *and* the promise of recovery, recalling Bataille's description of the Leng Tch'e photograph as having concurrently imprisoned him within and delivered him from anguish.[80] As the image undergoes one final transformation—gradually dissolving into its negative, with hues of blue and red filling the screen—this final shot recalls but is not exactly like Bataille's torture photographs.

On the one hand, these onscreen colors suggest that trauma has, quite literally, enveloped the film's victim-hero. While his followers are encouraged and enabled to move on by his suffering, the sacrificial victim-hero maintains a unique claim on the markers of suffering and, consequently, the moral authority that suffering is imagined to impart. On the other hand, the movement and transformation in the frame refuses to abandon itself entirely to hopelessness, for the traumatic "*having-been-there*" of the photographic image gives way to the recuperative "*being-there*" of the moving image, right before the spectator's eyes. Demonstrating trauma's capacity to become "profoundly equivocal in its interpretive possibilities," this final shot positions self-loss as both an end and a beginning, trauma as both a loss and a victory.[81]

Neville has been annihilated, and, yet his sacrifice also renders him eternally present. Having become the serum that will preserve life on earth, Neville's blood, once liberated from his body, will be dispersed and made continuous. Having been negated, like the final shot itself, Neville becomes like Bataille's sovereign: nothing and everything, nowhere and everywhere, no one and everyone at the same time. Neville earns his sovereignty by letting go, giving in, falling apart, but, as is cued by the sanguine and buoyant nondiegetic music

Figure 6. Neville lying dead in the fountain in a shot that recalls a photo-finish ending. *Omega Man* (Warner Bros.)

that plays over the final shots of Neville, *Omega Man* codes this act of self-loss not as tragic or meaningless but redemptive and productive. Shortly before we see Neville for the final time, floating lifelessly in the fountain, a close-up of his colonel's cap, which sits on the edge of the fountain, underscores the authority that he maintains, even (or especially) in death.

A Grand Lady

The Poseidon Adventure tells the story of a group of survivors on board a cruise ship capsized by a tidal wave. As the ship overturns and begins to sink, most passengers get trapped in the ballroom. Despite orders to stay put and await rescue, one group, led by a reluctant and renegade hero, Reverend Scott (Gene Hackman), climbs to what was once the bottom of the ship in order to attempt escape. Expressing anxiety about "modernity's gamble," *Poseidon Adventure* questions whether the "long-term dangers of a technology-intensive society will be avoided by continued progress."[82] *Poseidon Adventure* also illustrates Bataillean fascination with trauma and self-loss while using sacrificial violence to validate and confirm fantasies of agentive, masterful subjectivity. Unlike *Omega Man*, however, *Poseidon Adventure* addresses the politics of war implicitly, dramatizing Scott's spiritual and physical struggles onboard a sinking ship to rewrite allegorically cultural memory about national trauma.

Poseidon Adventure viscerally manifests its Bataillean fascination with self-dissolution and trauma through graphic depictions of destruction and loss onboard a technological marvel, the SS *Poseidon*. After the ship overturns, a gruesome scene of tangled bodies and debris remains. During the first disaster sequence, the film features over three minutes of uninterrupted carnage. The sounds of roaring waves, shattering glass, groaning steel, and—above all—panicked screams fill the soundtrack. Bodies crushed by large objects, pinned against walls, lacerated by broken glass, and piled on top of one another populate the mise-en-scène.

The repeated assaults on individual passengers' bodies get reenacted on a grander scale: the destruction of the *Poseidon*, which shatters as explosions and flooding waters ravish its structures. If the destruction of passengers' bodies can be understood to offer allegorical figuration of the nation as under attack and falling apart, the ship's devastation offers an additional register of allegorical synecdoche. Consider, for instance, how the wave's assault on the ship mirrors Kai Erikson's metaphorical description of psychic trauma. Based on interviews with survivors of the 1972 Buffalo Creek flood, Erikson describes trauma as "an assault on the person so sudden and so explosive that it smashes through one's defenses and does damage to the sensitive tissues underneath." In traumatic encounters, Erikson contends, in which "the outside threat is too abrupt or too strong," the mind's protective "barrier is breached and the mental processes within are disturbed."[83] Similarly, *Poseidon Adventure*'s images of the bombarded ship—attacked from the outside, breached, flooded, and sinking fast under the pressure—offer a visceral and visual figuration of the traumatized subject or collective.

Just as Erikson uses a bodily metaphor to describe psychic or subjective undoing, *Poseidon Adventure* figures its damaged ship in corporeal terms, as a wounded body. Once imagined as an impenetrable vessel, the *Poseidon* becomes a mass of detritus and gaping wounds; as the ship becomes increasingly traumatized, the mise-en-scène codes it as feminine. While maritime tradition personifies the ship as female—the captain calls the *Poseidon* a "great lady"—visual depictions of the ship initially construct it as a masculinized structure, as exemplified by repeated exterior shots of the ship that emphasize its magnitude and force. For instance, the film opens with a series of extreme long shots of the exterior of the ship that depict it as a phallic apparatus dominating the sea; in many of these shots, the ship exceeds the borders of the frame, as if it is too large and mighty to be contained. Other shots on the outer decks of the ship emphasize its hardness and the presumed impenetrability of its steel husk, while low-angle shots of passengers make them seem small in comparison to the massive vessel.

After the tidal wave, however, the *Poseidon* transforms from a masculinized technological marvel to a decidedly feminine corporeal structure. For example, as Scott and his followers search for an exit from the sinking ship, the body of the ocean liner appears to be nothing more than a collection of tunnels, canals, tubes, ducts, and pipes. With incessant depictions of channels through which the passengers must crawl and holes into which they must squeeze, the mise-en-scène constructs the journey out of the ship as a traumatic birth process through a monstrous vaginal canal. As passengers travel through the bowels of the ship, laboring to get out, they struggle against the dying, maternal body of the *Poseidon*, translating the process of dying itself into a form of rebirth. This physical transformation of the ship mirrors and contributes to anxious constructions of "the nation as feminized and susceptible to violation in the Vietnam era."[84] It further embodies what Lowenstein describes as historically specific assertions "that America, divided against itself over the Vietnam War, might be in danger of losing its disembodied, masculine integrity and succumbing to an overly embodied, feminine vulnerability."[85]

The mise-en-scène and catastrophic special effects matrix of *Poseidon Adventure* recall Bataille's torture photographs, fixating on corporeal fragility and turning violence into a spectacle. Just as the Leng Tch'e photograph depicts the brutal disarticulation of the torture victim's body, *Poseidon Adventure*'s disaster scenes reproduce the chaotic sensibility of panic; and given assertions that "trauma *destabilizes the ground* of experience" and threatens to "open onto an *abyss*," it matters that this film dramatizes a ship that, following an underground earthquake, is turned over on its head—ground having become ceiling and bottom having become top—and is sinking toward the ocean floor into the abyss.[86] These frenzied scenes reproduce understandings of trauma as what Jackie Orr describes as a "vertiginously relational scene" that "undoes the psychic architecture of inside and out."[87]

It also matters that so many of the film's death scenes feature falling; although you see dozens of dead bodies—many of which were destroyed by drowning and fire—the majority of *dying* depicted onscreen involves bodies falling. In a rapid succession of shots, dozens of bodies fall as the ship capsizes, and three of the four primary characters who die, including the film's sacrificial victim-hero, do so by falling. This recurring plot device illustrates the recurrence of falling as a signifier of trauma. Like the tortured body in Bataille's photographs, which hangs flaccidly from a post, the body that falls from the sky is helpless, forced "from one station in life to another." Falling, Eleanor Kaufman contends, embodies the "abysslike structure of trauma"—the disorientation, the loss of control, the unrelenting nature of suffering that overwhelms the subject.[88] In *Poseidon Adventure*, falling operates at both phenomenological and allegorical registers, performing both the sensations of trauma and constructing fictions of the subject as once whole and then "falling apart."

These disaster sequences produce an overwhelming display of violence that may leave the spectator's gaze "at once fascinated and distracted."[89] This experience of self-shattering thus might be understood as enacting the phenomenology of trauma, inundating the spectator with a barrage of sights and sounds so powerful and quick that none of it can be fully assimilated or processed. Presenting an unrelenting torrent of sights and sounds—falling bodies, rushing waters, fiery explosions, collapsing structures—*Poseidon Adventure* invites the viewer "into a realm of Heraclitean flux, a time and space from which all fixed points of reference and self-reference, all lines of perspective, and all possibilities of stabilizing identification and objectification are banished," at least temporarily.[90] With the ship itself turned on its head and sinking fast, fixity and stability are quite literally undone; and the film's camerawork manifests this instability with multiple canted frames and kinetic shots.

The sights and sounds of destruction paralyze the narrative, leaving only the spectacle of catastrophe. Not only do the ship's hostage passengers represent established figurations of tramautized subjects—they are, as Scott says, "cut off from the rest of the world"—but the film also formally and viscerally invites viewers to adopt a besieged position of spectatorial captivity. This film might therefore be understood as producing an experience of spectatorship akin to what McLuhan described during Vietnam, compelling spectators to participate in violence through its relentless and visceral mediation.[91]

Communicable Dis-ease

Poseidon Adventure also dissolves subjectivity by encouraging multiple and shifting identifications. With an ensemble cast, *Poseidon Adventure* asks viewers to share in and identify with the traumatic experiences of a diverse group of passengers. This narrative structure induces what Bataille calls continuity, or the fusing of the self, with others. Like Neville's fascination with the community in *Woodstock*, *Poseidon Adventure* offers a range of figures that invites the spectator to step outside of him/herself. Shaviro contends that this structure of potential identifications encourages the spectator to be "captivated and 'distracted,' made more fluid and indeterminate, in the process of sympathetic participation," not with just one character but with a diverse array of them.[92]

This focus on a group of survivors at war with themselves relates to the film's historical and political context, evoking cultural memories of the divided American populace. With a variety of characters clashing over survival plans and responses to loss, the pervasive mood of dissent offers allegorical figuration of the conflicted nation. In fact, the majority of the film's dialogue centers on conflicts between the characters, which range from philosophical debates to familial spats to full-throttled fistfights. For instance, the opening sequence of the film features multiple disagreements: the captain of the *Poseidon* argues with the ship's owners about the safety of the cruise liner; a husband and wife, Mr. and Mrs. Rogo, fight with each other over her past as a prostitute; a brother and sister, Robin and Susan, bicker about their absent parents; and Scott, the film's sacrificial victim-hero, and the ship's chaplain debate about the merits of prayer and the efficacy of institutional religion. Almost all of the dialogue in the film's opening scenes conveys conflict, suggesting that no harmonious or untroubled relationships exist on this ship, and some characters—especially Mr. and Mrs. Rogo—communicate only by yelling.

One of the most significant acts of dissent occurs when Reverend Scott and his followers decide to disobey the purser's orders and leave the ballroom—a decision that certainly invites reference to what would have been contemporary debates about whether or not America should pull out of (or escape from) Vietnam. Amid panicked cries for help and violent disagreements, Scott finds his authority immediately challenged; suspicious and fearful passengers shout "You don't know what you're talking about!" This discordant tone continues throughout the entire narrative, as his followers frequently doubt or question his escape plans. The most intense and ongoing example of these conflicts conflict takes place between Scott and Mr. Rogo, who assumes the position of second in command.

For instance, when Scott's escape route leads to the death of Rogo's wife, he accuses Scott of being a "lying, murdering son of a bitch" and laments, "I started to believe in your promises that we had a chance." The narrative frames this constant conflict between these leading men as painful and disruptive, as illustrated by the words of one conciliatory passenger who reminds the bellicose men, "The rest of us would feel much more secure if you two would stop shouting at one another," thus suggesting that the lack of clear leadership and the constancy of dissent are themselves traumatic injuries. *Poseidon Adventure* constructs these battling leaders as embodying ideologically opposed subject positions: while Scott describes himself as a revolutionary, Rogo is a police lieutenant described as playing "everything by the books."

Pitting a visionary outcast against a member of the "establishment" in a struggle for authority, this conflict helps constitute cultural memory about political dissent between the cultural center and the counterculture. Like *Omega Man*, divisions also play out along lines of age, mirroring the generational and cultural divides that became visible during the Vietnam War.

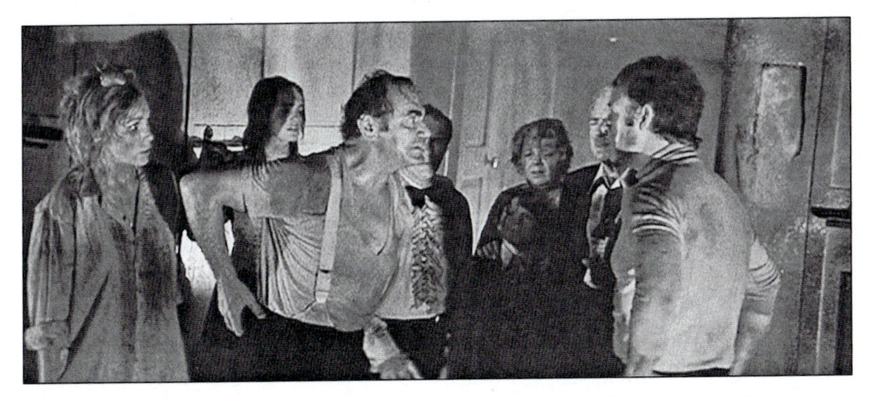

Figure 7. Mr. Rogo and Reverend Scott vying for positions of authority and arguing about an escape route. *The Poseidon Adventure* (Twentieth Century Fox)

Robin, the youngest survivor of the cruise ship disaster, proves himself to be an expert on the *Poseidon*'s construction and inner workings, but even though he offers helpful advice and information throughout the escape process, Robin is consistently dismissed as "just a kid." The film's infantilized women don't fare much better, as the young women are constantly advised to gain composure or "pull [it] together." *Poseidon Adventure* thus frames the battle for authority in the midst of crisis as one to be fought by men. In this way, the film not only reenacts the drama of national dissent but also positions masculine authority and privilege as primarily at stake in such conflicts.

Cast Out

Conflict plagues Reverend Scott, whom the film marks as troubled and disarticulated from his place in the social order. *Poseidon Adventure* depicts Scott as a man struggling against his profession, his peers, his followers, and himself. At the outset of the film, Reverend Scott calls himself an outsider, a revolutionary within the traditional ranks of the church, fed up with the passivity, hypocrisy, and bureaucracy of institutional religion. In his first lines of dialogue, Scott aggressively confronts the ship's chaplain, rejecting prayer as ineffectual "garbage" and describing himself as "angry, rebellious, critical, a renegade stripped of my so-called clerical powers."

Like canonical constructions of the trauma survivor, Scott figures himself as isolated, alienated, on the margins of his own life, and such displacement throws masculine authority and privilege into question. Because he has been stripped of his powers and institutional authority and exiled to a remote place in Africa, Scott lacks the signifiers of hegemonic masculinity. He is a man without a home, without a title; Scott's displacement reenacts the Vietnam-era destabilization of prevailing cultural fictions about masculine hegemony and patriarchal authority.

Positioning himself as an outsider rejected by his institutional home, Scott also suggests particular evocations of the figure of the Vietnam veteran. Like the veteran, whom Lifton describes as having "rage close to the surface," Scott is angry, resentful, and unhinged.[93] If, as Lifton argues, one of the central and most traumatic narratives about the veteran's experience was the lack of a clear purpose for the war, Scott attaches an analogous sense of futility and frustration to the institutional church, whose purpose seems dubious to him. Adopting what might be understood as an anti-establishment or countercultural position of oppositionality, Scott echoes descriptions of Vietnam veterans as having "degrees of bitterness, distrust, and suspicion of those in positions of authority and responsibility."[94] He articulates such suspicions as he laments God's inability or unwillingness to respond to the suffering of the individual, warning, "You can wear off your knees praying to God in a coldwater flat in

February, and icicles would grow from your upraised palms." He similarly advises listeners during a sermon, "God is pretty busy. It's not reasonable to expect him to concern himself with the individual."[95]

Poseidon Adventure constructs Scott's position of marginalization and crisis as endowing him with a kind of wisdom. As an outsider, he *alone* has the insight and experiential authority to bring about salvation on the *Poseidon*. In response to the frequent challenges to his authority—he's often told "You're going the wrong way!"—Scott forges ahead by himself and convinces others to follow because only he has seen the way out. For example, when the passengers doubt that the exit lies in the direction Scott has chosen, he compels them to follow with the simple and frank response, "I saw it." Scott's unique ability to lay claim to what only he has seen recalls the kind of incontestable authority that is often assigned to trauma survivors, whose experiences cannot be questioned by those that have not shared them and can only imagine what survivors saw. Joan Scott argues that "when evidence offered is the evidence of 'experience,' the claim for referentiality is further buttressed—what could be truer, after all, than a subject's own account of what he or she lived through?"[96]

Scott's ability to see things that others cannot extends to both his metaphorical vision—his ability to fabricate an escape plan—and his willingness to go first and bear witness to the horrors unfolding on the *Poseidon*. It is Scott that prepares his followers for things to come; he warns, for example, "There's a lot of dead bodies in there. It's not a pretty sight." Scott's willingness to face, and even experience, trauma privileges "the communication of knowledge gained through (visual, visceral) experience," as in the popular notion that true understanding comes only from having been "in the trenches," and helps to confirm—if only obliquely—assumptions about the special wisdom of the (male) veteran.[97]

Although his professional banishment might suggest anxiety about the wartime emasculation of the nation and its imagined heroes, Scott constructs his marginalization from his ministerial community as offering him the radical freedom that Bataille idealizes as a consequence of self-loss. Having been banished to work in Africa, Scott describes his punishment as precisely what he wanted: "elbow room . . . freedom . . . real freedom to dump all the rules and all the trappings . . . freedom to discover God in my own way." His description of himself as an uncompromising rebel—even defector—with unique access to God mirrors Bataille's fantasy of "the ecstatic mystic [that] loses himself in God."[98] Scott begins to reconstitute his loss of status as catalyzing the acquisition of something else: the wisdom, vision, transcendence, or "something special" he might be imagined to share with the Vietnam veteran.

Marked as an outcast and rejected by those that refuse to believe in his plan for salvation, Scott also bears a likeness to Christ, whom leftist Christian discourse posits as a radical hero misunderstood by many as a dangerous insurgent. *Poseidon Adventure* confirms this lineage visually. For instance, as he is engineering escape efforts from the ballroom, Scott commandeers (of all things) a giant Christmas tree as a makeshift ladder. Carrying the tree on his back, its trunk resting on his shoulder, Scott reenacts Christian iconography in which Jesus carries the cross on which he would be crucified. Paradoxically, it is also this early scene that demonstrates that Scott has not yet come to understand the full measure of his traumatic heroism, despite his earlier glorifications of his professional victimization.

Before ascending the tree, Scott begs the ship's chaplain to join him and the others who have decided to leave the ballroom, but the chaplain insists on remaining in order to care for those who cannot escape. Scott critiques the chaplain for being weak, asking, "What good's your life been? What's it all been for?" Scott worries that death will negate his companion's life work; giving in, Scott warns, will undo the good of his life. He utters a similar warning to another passenger who wants to abandon the escape efforts after suffering the death of his beloved wife. Urging the widower to move on, Scott says, "If you don't come with us, her death is meaningless." In his final moments, Scott wrestles with such doubt again, asking God, "What more do you want from us?" This anxiety about meaninglessness—which Shay depicts as a prominent aspect of traumatic experience—reveals Scott's lingering fear of self-shattering trauma; although he recognizes the enabling possibilities of his professional ostracism and social marginalization, Scott still doubts what *Poseidon Adventure* imagines to be the enabling potential of *radical* self-loss.[99] Not until the film's final scenes does Scott fully accept that he must participate in the nation's sacrificial economy by offering up his own life.

Figure 8. Reverend Scott carrying a Christmas tree on his back as a makeshift escape ladder. *The Poseidon Adventure* (Twentieth Century Fox)

This initial refusal to accept the logic of sacrifice is underscored by Scott's proclamation to the chaplain, "I will not give up," which articulates a traditionally masculinist perspective that values action and aggression over compassion and passivity. This emphasis on virility echoes an earlier sermon in which Scott advised his listeners, "God wants brave souls. He wants winners, not quitters." So on the eve of a new year, Scott directs his audience, "Resolve to let God know that you have the guts and the will to do it alone. Resolve to fight for yourselves and for others and for those you love." With these directives, Scott reaffirms phallic discourses of mastery and triumphalism. His highly individualist rhetoric suggests fantasies of the subject as volitional and agentive; but, as the chaplain warns Scott, his perspective only speaks and accounts for the strong and must be adapted to respond more effectively to the vicissitudes of life and, in particular, to trauma.

The chaplain's warning anticipates Scott's struggle to accept a model of traumatic heroism. The film requires Scott to reconcile traditional expectations of masculine agency with the necessity (and inevitability) of vulnerability—a realization with particular historical significance given what, by 1972, were becoming prevailing constructions of the Vietnam War as the end of American "victory culture."[100] Scott's difficulty accepting this paradigm of trauma—finding mastery in self-loss, agency in passivity—might be understood allegorically to dramatize the nation's own reckoning with and reconstitution of its identity at the end of a losing war. Before he can reach (or resign himself to) this conclusion, however, *Poseidon Adventure* first establishes Scott as wounded and vulnerable by subjecting him to unmeasured suffering.

As the group's leader, Scott authorizes every choice the collective makes, always facing each new obstacle first himself. This positioning clearly establishes Scott as an authority figure and given his willingness to brave death, Scott's role as leader might be understood as reaffirming his traditionally masculinist rhetoric. His super-masculinity operates as a prophylaxis, protecting his followers from encounters with pain, terror, or loss. Yet this scenario also places Scott in positions of extreme vulnerability, revealing the film's investment in the injured white male body. For example, when Scott discovers he must lead the other passengers through a flooded portion of the ship, he insists that he go first in order to ensure that the path is passable and to leave a guide rope for other passengers to follow. As he swims toward the exit, Scott becomes trapped under debris and nearly dies. Mrs. Rosen—an older, obese woman hitherto characterized largely as a nuisance, if not an obstacle—dives into the water and brings Scott's nearly lifeless body to the surface.

Like Neville, Scott requires rescue at the hands of a woman—and a grandmother, no less—suggesting a level of fragility that contrasts with Scott's masculinist discourse. This moment of weakness depicts the submission of the disembodied, masculine leader to an "overly embodied" femininity.[101] Redressing Scott's apparent vulnerability with Mrs. Rosen's resourcefulness and expertise, *Poseidon Adventure* dramatizes the potential failure of Scott's masculinist rhetoric and subject position. The film codes Scott's frailty and need for rescue as feminizing.

Far from renouncing the hegemonic privilege of masculine subjectivity, however, *Poseidon Adventure* both atones for and makes use of Scott's vulnerability. Such compensation can be seen, for example, in Mrs. Rosen's death, which immediately follows Scott's rescue. After exerting herself to carry Scott's body back to the surface, Mrs. Rosen suffers a heart attack and dies suddenly. It is significant that Mrs. Rosen's death occurs *after* her salvific gesture toward Scott. First, her death highlights the anomaly of her heroic role; it is out of character for this female figure to act in such an agentive and physically demanding way, and this burden is too much for her body to bear. Mrs. Rosen's moment of strength becomes an exception that confirms her thoroughgoing and characteristic weakness and, by contrast, confirms the presumed naturalness of the male body as heroic authority. As she dies in Scott's arms, Mrs. Rosen resumes a more traditional iteration of feminine passivity.

Second, because Mrs. Rosen dies *after* she has rescued Scott, her death itself is not productive; her dying is not what saves Scott. Her death might be considered traumatic and her actions heroic, but it is not *sacrificial*. Death is, at best, a tragic consequence of her actions or, at worst, an expiatory gesture that punitively expels her for having transgressed gendered norms and stepped out of bounds. Having threatened Scott's emasculation, Mrs. Rosen gets quickly disposed of in order to return Scott to his position as hero. In the logic of this film, as in the sacrificial economy more generally, the capacity to give life through death belongs largely to the male body.

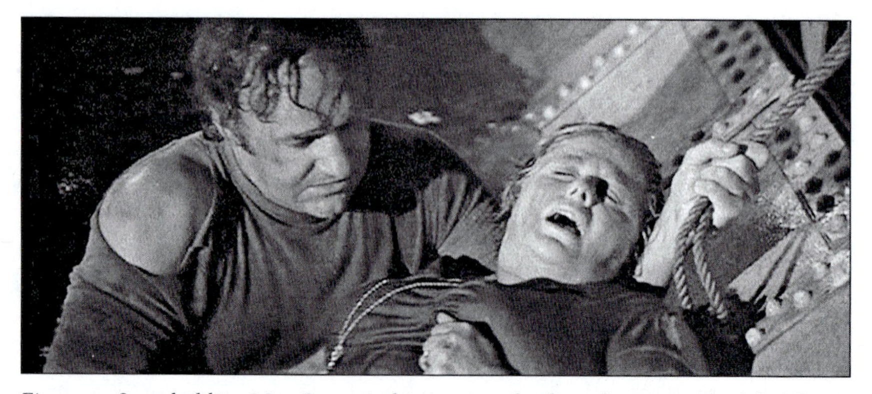

Figure 9. Scott holding Mrs. Rosen in his arms as she dies after saving his life. *The Poseidon Adventure* (Twentieth Century Fox)

Death Becomes Him

Scott's ultimate sacrifice completes *Poseidon Adventure*'s paradoxical conflation of authority and vulnerability as a unique marker of masculine subjectivity. In the bottom of the ship, the survivors discover a propeller shaft through which they can escape. Elated, they cross a platform that hovers above a pit of flaming water, only to be blocked by a sudden explosion of piping hot steam in front of the would-be exit. This startling accident flings Rogo's wife, Linda, to her death in the water below them, prompting both further dissent among the group about Scott's efficacy as a leader and immediately compelling Scott to atone for the loss with his own self-destruction.

Looking up, Scott asks God angrily, "What more do you want from us?" Like the Christ story, which depicts its hero as expressing momentary doubt toward God moments before accepting his fate, *Poseidon Adventure* demonstrates Scott's final and futile attempts to resist self-loss before he resigns to his fate. Having asked God, "How many more sacrifices? How much more blood? How many more lives?" Scott realizes that it is his own life that must be offered up, declaring, "You want another life? Then take me!"[102] This language constitutes Scott as a sacrificial object to be offered up, and this ritualized act effects Scott's destruction at the same time that it endows him with the authority of the sacred.

Accepting the terms of the sacrificial economy, Scott jumps from the platform to shut off the steam. Dangling above the sea of fire, Scott hangs onto a wheel that he must turn in order to stop the flow of steam; his back is turned to his followers. A series of close-ups on his face and hands shows Scott's struggle to hang onto his life. Like Bataille's torture photographs, these close-ups fetishize Scott's corporeal fragility and suffering; he hangs, quite literally, in the balance between life and death, another spectacle of white male pain. In contrast to the hyperbolic soundtrack to much of what preceded them, these shots are distinguished by their relative silence. Nothing distracts viewers from the conspicuous sight of Scott's suffering, which is also on display for his followers, whom we frequently see in reaction shots. Similar to *Omega Man*'s "photo finish" ending, the silent and relatively still shots of Scott in the moments before his death fixate on his helplessness and his inability to escape, and this brief moment of silence seems to enact understandings of trauma as an experience that is unspeakable.

As much as this moment embodies Jonathan Boulter's description of trauma as a "moment of anguished *though necessary* suspension in full exposure to the moment of radical loss," it also constitutes a transformation; as Scott dangles above the water, the film depicts him as translating hopelessness into courage, meaninglessness into purpose.[103] Once he has shut off the steam valve, Scott slowly rotates himself to face his followers, his directional change literalizing

Figure 10. Scott hanging tenuously seconds before resigning himself to noble death. *The Poseidon Adventure* (Twentieth Century Fox)

his changed perspective. Delivering his final sermon, Scott's words of encouragement break the silence, "You can make it. Keep going!"

Quite overtly, Scott (like Dutch in *Omega Man*) encourages the other passengers to move on, not to linger or remain fixated on his death but to push forward and seek rescue. Scott passes on his mantle of leadership to Rogo, who after losing his wife has become another wounded man. Ordering him to "get them through," Scott asks Rogo to take up his position of authority and help the survivors heal—further mirroring the transgenerational bond established between Neville and Dutch at the end of *Omega Man* and reproducing the all-male lineage that Jay posits as one of the primary institutional aims of sacrifice as a ritualized praxis.

Then, without asking or reaching for help, Scott drops into the fiery water, his arms outstretched—returning, once again, to Christological iconography. As he lets go of the wheel, Scott also lets go of his conventional assumptions about life, death, and heroism. He recognizes that he cannot always be strong or in control and relinquishes traditional understandings of mastery as he relinquishes his grip on life. Scott's death, not unlike Mrs. Rosen's, implies an act of expiation that atones for his failures as a leader, including the many deaths in which he was directly involved along the way. *Poseidon Adventure*, not unlike *Omega Man*, disposes of an outmoded version of masculine heroism, one that speaks only for the strong and that could not sustain itself effectively in the midst of the traumas of the Vietnam era.

However punitive and compensatory, Scott's death is also ennobling, for it guarantees his followers' salvation: Rogo does effectively "get them through." Scott's death also changes Rogo; the once hard and angry cop softens at the end of the film and becomes a compassionate leader. As one passenger says, Rogo stops being "always negative, always destructive" and seizes his opportunity "to do something positive for a change." For the first time, the group overcomes its conflicts and stops fighting. Resignation to radical passivity has allowed Scott to reconstitute himself as an authoritative and purposeful subject, an effectual and life-giving leader. As Dean argues of Bataillean constructions of sovereign subjectivity, Scott refashions his understanding of mastery: "the loss of the self is lived as the constituent moment of selfhood."[104] That his death effectively reconstitutes Scott's subjectivity can be seen in Rogo's transformed attitude toward the minister. Having only moments earlier renounced Scott as a "lying, murdering son of a bitch," Rogo reassesses Scott's value as a leader, admitting, "The preacher was right. That beautiful son of a bitch was right."

Scott reaffirms the value of the sacrificial economy through his willingness to offer up his own life; the minister that once identified himself as a renegade who was alienated from the institutional church reenacts Christianity's most cherished narrative: noble death. Positioning Scott within this Christological lineage, his death also gives him exclusive ownership over his trauma. This loss belongs to him and not to his followers, whom he directs to push through and move on; Scott's unique access to trauma is underscored when seconds after his death, Susan—a young survivor who has come to see Scott as a surrogate father—longs to jump in after him and is forcefully pulled back to safety. Susan cannot follow where Scott has gone, nor can she reproduce his regenerative act of self-loss.

It also matters that Scott falls to his death.[105] A prominent signifier of traumatic self-loss, falling signifies ambivalence. Kaufman writes, "the disorienting vertigo of falling is a sign both of trauma and of hope and at times . . . operates on both registers at once." She continues, "falling is at once a marker of the abysslike structure of trauma and, more importantly, a kind of apparatus that lands at the end of the text to save the day."[106] Scott's death sustains a marked tension between an understanding of death as a traumatic loss and as a hopeful new beginning, between a melancholic attraction toward trauma and a normative expectation of moving on. The fiery pit of water into which Scott falls signifies both the destructive, punitive fires of hell and the cleansing, healing power of water.[107] The tension surrounding the film's construction of trauma—as both a frightening end and a hopeful beginning—is also suggested by Susan's desire to follow Scott. Her response, which might be considered an example of melancholic acting out, signals the envy of trauma that characterizes trauma culture; but the efforts of the others to save her demonstrate the necessity of moving on, leaving trauma (like Scott's corpse) behind.

Both *Omega Man* and *Poseidon Adventure* cite the discourse of recovery, or moving on, *at the same time* that they insist on the inexorable impact of trauma, and both films use sacrifice to negotiate what might otherwise be considered an impasse between the possibility of healing and the intransience of trauma. By becoming both the emblematic signifier of trauma and its only resolution, these sacrificial deaths imply that the experience of the (male) sacrificial victim-hero matters most, for his loss is the gravest and the greatest. These films assert that the province of trauma and the transcendental status it bears belong solely to the redemptive male subject. In relinquishing his ability to move on from or leave behind suffering, the victim-hero makes room for his followers to escape.

While Sample reads the protagonist's death at the end of a film such as *Omega Man* to be a dystopic sign of his "downfall," asking "What good is a dead hero?," I contend that both Neville's and Scott's deaths guarantee their heroic subject positions, hinging not on Neville's reproduction of the "trademark Hestonian bearing" or on Scott's adherence to his own action-oriented teachings but on their traumatization and dissolution.[108] So what good is a dead hero? Within the logic of the sacrificial economy, the dead hero is the most useful hero of all because he can be lifted above the limited and limiting constraints of everyday life and made legend. Having been shattered by trauma, this hero can be emptied out and endowed with mythic signification. Sacrificial films mythicize history and engender a paradigm of trauma that instructs American cultural memory again and again. Consonant with allegorical form, this "eternal return" to the paradigm of traumatic heroism embodies the repetitive nature of trauma and commemorates the ruins of the past as the font of new beginnings.

CHAPTER 3

FREE FALLS IN THE 1990S

"This is a culture centered on trauma (Greek for wound): a culture of atrocity exhibition, in which people wear their damage like badges of identity, or fashion accessories." —Mark Seltzer

In January 1994, a jury acquitted Lorena Bobbitt for the crime of severing more than half of her husband's penis from his body. Her defense of temporary insanity persuaded the jury that chronic abuse by her husband, John Wayne Bobbitt, led her to snap on the night of the attack. Mrs. Bobbitt reportedly suffered from symptoms akin to those of PTSD, including being inundated with flashbacks, or what she called "pictures."[1] One of the most notorious scandals of the decade and tabloid fodder for months, the Bobbitt case exemplifies the American "fascination with torn and open bodies and torn and opened persons, a collective gathering around shock, trauma, and the wound."[2]

As much as the case of penile amputation might be described as shocking, anomalous, or bizarre, the spectacle of the body in pain—and the white male body, in particular—actually became quite routinized in the 1990s. Illustrating trauma's currency in 1990s-era public discourse, the Bobbitt case also demonstrates the imagined effects of trauma (as in causing Lorena to "snap") and the ways trauma is used (as in the defense's claim that trauma justified her "irresistible impulse" of revenge).[3] The logic with which Lorena Bobbitt is understood to disintegrate psychologically and then snap resembles cinematic depictions of sacrificial victim-heroes driven to breaking points by terror and loss.

The discourses of trauma that flourished in the 1990s in the United States constructed trauma as both a problem to be solved (as in popular constructions of masculinity as being in "crisis") and as a redemptive, purifying, and unifying experience (as in the rhetorical canonization of World War II veterans as the "Greatest Generation"). In Hollywood, this discourse shaped and was shaped by a number of sacrificial films, including some of the most successful films of the decade (if not the century). This cycle of sacrificial films includes *Braveheart* (Mel Gibson, 1995), *Independence Day* (Roland Emmerich,

1996), *Executive Decision* (Stuart Baird, 1996), *Titanic* (James Cameron, 1997), *Armageddon* (Michael Bay, 1998), *Saving Private Ryan* (Stephen Spielberg, 1998), *Deep Impact* (Mimi Leder, 1998), *Fight Club* (David Fincher, 1999), the re-release of *The Exorcist* (1999), and *Gladiator* (Ridley Scott, 2000).[4] The subjects of this chapter, *Titanic* and *Armageddon*, valorize wounded, traumatized working-class victim-heroes as uniquely able to balance sentimentality with phallic masculinity. Using trauma to galvanize the unification of an otherwise fractured and troubled community, these films mark sacrificial death as a man's most noble and productive act.

Trauma Drama

Mark Seltzer describes American culture as dominated by a "pathological public sphere" in which scenes of death and dying operate as "theater for the living."[5] Emblematic of this culture is the image of a "crowd gathered around the fallen body, the wrecked machine, and the wound," which Seltzer understands as characteristic of public culture in the 1990s.[6] Seltzer finds examples of this attraction toward the wound in popular television series such as *ER*, in news coverage of mass murder, and in fictional depictions of serial killers, including *Silence of the Lambs* (Jonathan Demme, 1991) and *Copy Cat* (John Amiel, 1995).

Seltzer also locates this wound culture in what he refers to as the "current a-la-modality of trauma—the cliché du jour of the therapeutic society of the nineties." He argues that the discourse of trauma was so prevalent and compelling that it largely governed the rhetoric of the 1996 presidential contest between Bob Dole and Bill Clinton: "The election was a contest about trauma and wounds: the shattered and already posthumous war veteran—dead man talking—and the make-love-not-warrior whose tag-line is, 'I feel your pain.'"[7] Seltzer also tracks the resurgence of trauma in a wide array of sites in the contemporary public sphere, ranging "from the art and culture scenes to tabloid and talk TV."[8]

E. Ann Kaplan corroborates Seltzer's claim that trauma reemerged as an organizing discourse in the 1990s, noting that Vietnam-era progress in the study of trauma "was not widely disseminated until the mid-1990s." Kaplan attributes this transformation to such works as Judith Herman's successful 1992 book *Trauma and Recovery*, which was reprinted in 1997, and Denise Grady's 1997 *New York Times* article, "War Memories May Harm Health."[9] As a result, argues Kaplan, a "veritable flood of media attention and printed books [on the subject of trauma] followed in the 1990s."[10] Throughout the decade, for instance, the topic of PTSD was a frequent subject in such national newspapers as the *New York Times* and the *Washington Post*; in fact, the number of articles in the *New York Times* whose subject was PTSD tripled during the 1990s from the number of the previous decade.[11] A number of 1990s-era books have become canonical in the psychological study of trauma, including Shoshana Felman and Dori Laub's *Testimony* (1992); Jonathan Shay's *Achilles in Vietnam* (1994), which was one of many books written in the 1990s about veterans of the Vietnam war; and Bessel van der Kolk's *Traumatic Stress: The Effects of Overwhelming Stress on Mind, Body, and Society* (1996).[12]

In the humanities, both Holocaust studies and trauma theory gained prominence. A number of literary scholars began working on trauma in the mid-1990s, including Cathy Caruth, Dominick LaCapra, Geoffrey Hartman, and Michael Rothberg, as did a number of film scholars, such as Janet Walker, Susannah Radstone, and Thomas Elsaesser.[13] In fact, so pervasive were discussions of trauma in the mid- to late 1990s that the journals *Screen* and *Cultural Critique* dedicated special issues to the study of trauma within the humanities. As John Mowitt puts it, the 1990s witnessed an "academic (but not merely academic) 'trauma industry' that had risen up around [Caruth's] work" that he calls nothing short of an "academic obsession."[14]

The fact that the topic of trauma had taken hold of the academy did not go unnoticed. In 1999, the *New York Times* announced that the study of trauma had graduated "at last," citing a number of universities that had established trauma studies programs and degrees, such as New York University's International Trauma Studies Program, which was founded in 1998, and a new degree in disaster psychology from the University of South Dakota.[15] Patricia Cohen describes "frequent episodes of historical amnesia" as characterizing the study of trauma and credits political alliances (among feminists, veterans, and antiwar activists) that formed during the Vietnam era with the gradual rise of trauma to clinical and academic prominence.[16] Cohen's *Times* article traces the history of thought about trauma in scholarly communities and lists a number of assumptions central to the logic of trauma discourse. It is thus a useful source for considering how trauma was imagined to work in the 1990s.

First, Cohen identifies trauma as a rather ubiquitous, if not inevitable, experience in human life, echoing Bataillean understandings of suffering as a "basic component of human life."[17] "From the cycle of violence in the Balkans to the string of teen-age killing sprees at high schools, trauma has become nearly as commonplace as the weather on the evening news. It has rippled through boardrooms and bedrooms, emergency rooms and courtrooms across the United States," Cohen wrote.[18] The notion that trauma is everywhere and that "everything is potentially traumatic" was replicated widely in the popular press in the 1990s.[19] Discussions of trauma centered on such varied experiences as "being raped or criminally assaulted, witnessing a murder or severe beating, being a victim of or witness to a vehicular or industrial accident, being a victim of child or spouse abuse, being a hostage or a prisoner of war, having a child struck by an automobile or found to have cancer or being involved in a natural disaster like a flood or a hurricane or one inflicted by humans, like the Oklahoma City bombing."[20] A peculiar paradox results: at the same time that public culture associates trauma with relatively extraordinary events such as war, terrorism, and natural disasters, it also defines trauma as a common (if not ubiquitous) problem that affects both victims, witnesses, and rescuers.[21]

Second, Cohen discusses the phenomenology of trauma as an event that is imagined to paralyze the subject. Cohen cites Van der Kolk's neurobiological research, which understands trauma as having the capacity to short-circuit the human brain and to hijack the subject's ability to process extremely painful memories. Cohen's language in the article reproduces the logic of trauma. For example, Cohen quotes Charles Figley, director of the Traumatology Institute at Florida State University, as describing the academy as "being overtaken by what is happening in the real world."[22] Imagining the academy, like the trauma survivor, as being taken hostage by the threats of the traumatic real, Cohen metaphorically depicts academe itself as a body that has been shocked by trauma's power and unable to fully digest its impacts: "Trauma's sprawling character has made it difficult for universities to swallow." After such initial shock and awe, Cohen suggests, the academic community was finally responding; Cohen quotes Judith Herman as saying, "The field is exploding."[23]

Third, like most discussions of trauma in public discourse, Cohen equates the recovery process with the survivor's ability to reintegrate his/her subjectivity. The notion that a once-coherent but now-damaged subject might piece him/herself back together is affirmed by a 1993 *New York Times* article offering readers a "how to" guide for healing psychological wounds. Journalist Isabel Wilkerson asserts, "Just as a broken leg must be bandaged and allowed to heal, psychological wounds from catastrophic events need care and attention."[24] Similar assumptions underlie Robert Jay Lifton's understanding of trauma. As he explains in a 1990 interview with Cathy Caruth, "extreme trauma creates a second self," and this new self must be managed (if not eliminated) if the subject is to recover. "In extreme trauma, one's sense of self is radically altered. And there is a traumatized self that is created. . . . And recovery from posttraumatic effects, or from survivor conflicts, cannot really occur until that traumatized self is reintegrated."[25] For Lifton, trauma therapy should "reconstitute the self into the single self, reintegrate itself," assuming, of course, that such a "single" or unified self did or could exist.[26] What is at stake in such trauma discourses are masculinist and individualist fantasies of a subject whose presumed initial wholeness is confirmed by claims of injury.

The rhetoric of recovery was also applied to the nation itself. Just as the hypermasculine spectacles of the Gulf War have been read as trying to cover over the wounds of Vietnam, much 1990s-era trauma discourse offered implicit absolution for the perceived failures of the Vietnam era.[27] For example, a 1991 article the *Washington Post* congratulates the military's improved treatment of veterans returning from the Gulf War, asserting, "The lessons of Vietnam reach even into the hospital wards, where they have changed they way Americans are greeting, treating and caring for veterans who suffered and returned from the gulf."[28] Celebrating the nation's redemption, the article continues, "Over the last 20 years, the military medical system has tried to remedy the flaws that left it unprepared to deal with the psychological scars of an unpopular war and the traumatic wounds that helicopter-borne soldiers could survive. By all accounts, it is getting high marks all around."[29] This article endows the nation itself with insight and experiential authority earned by suffering and loss. In this construction, trauma is conceptualized as the foundation for a new beginning even for military hospitals—a rebirth from which the agonized subject (or system) can emerge stronger, better, wiser.[30]

Man Overboard

Given the assertions of trauma's ubiquity and its association with a wide range of experiences, PTSD was often constructed as a disorder affecting men, women, and children. For instance, Daniel Goleman indicated in 1996 that the "chance that a person will suffer from post-traumatic stress disorder at some point in life is 5 percent for men and about 10 percent for women."[31] Feminists and other activists strove in the 1990s to frame women's experiences of rape and gendered violence in the language of trauma.[32] Despite such assertions of trauma's omnipresence, however, 1990s trauma discourse remained tethered most forcefully to white male bodies, as illustrated by commonplace descriptions of a "masculinity crisis."

Numerous scholars have demonstrated the prevalence of crisis rhetoric in constructions of masculinity in the 1990s, including Sally Robinson, Tania Modleski, David Savran, and Susan Jeffords. Robinson wrote that "images of wounded white men, manufactured traumas, and metaphorical pains abound in post-sixties American culture," arguing that in the mid- to late 1990s, "images of physically wounded and emotionally traumatized white masculinity" became routine. She locates key examples of this "white and male investment in the 'victim-function'" in such popular films as *Misery* (Rob Reiner, 1990), *The Prince of Tides* (Barbra Streisand, 1991), *Falling Down* (Joel Schumacher, 1993), and *Disclosure* (Barry Levison, 1994), all of which feature white men experiencing trauma.[33]

The popular press in the 1990s also framed white U.S. men as in crisis, under attack, and falling apart.[34] For instance, in a 1993 cover article for *Newsweek* prompted by the release of *Falling Down*, David Gates posits the image of the "beleaguered white male in multicultural America." He depicts white men as "surrounded by feminists, multiculturalists, P.C. policepersons, affirmative-action employers, rap artists, Native Americans, Japanese tycoons, Islamic fundamentalists and Third World dictators, all of them saying the same thing:

You've been a bad boy."[35] Gates offers as an example a white male firefighter who illustrated white men's anxiety about the sense that they do not belong in their own country. Attributing the loss of a promotion to affirmative action, the man describes himself as wounded and coming unhinged. He confesses, "A few years ago I was a walking keg of dynamite; I was the Rolaids king. If I talk too much about this I start getting wound up and I can't sleep."[36]

This testament to men's feelings of oppression and alienation illustrates a typical strategy in trauma culture, in which members of a group "suffering or fearing social death defen[d] themselves by embracing a rhetoric of traumatic victimization."[37] The challenges to and critiques of male privilege were not ignored by those who shape public culture, including journalists and filmmakers; in fact, popular culture in the 1990s emphasized white men's alleged injuries as evidence of masculinity's state of crisis. Like most trauma discourse, such claims of wounded or weakened masculinity imply that at one time a strong and certain masculinity existed that should be restored.

A cover article from *Time* the following year echoes this rhetoric of trauma. Lance Morrow laments, "Masculinity is in disrepute. Men have become the Germans of gender." Using combat metaphors, Morrow characterizes white men as under assault, asserting, "The war has now escalated to a new stage of attack and counterattack at higher and higher frequencies. Men feel frustrated."[38] He names academics and feminists as the primary enemies but also identifies Hollywood as part of the problem, saying that one genre of films "routinely assumes the awfulness of men, and portrays them in a way that would be judged bigoted and stereotyped if applied to blacks, Jews, Orientals or, for that matter, women" and that another genre was populated by "fantasies of disassembled masculinity."[39] Robinson notes in her analysis of Morrow that the article features a host of "images of mutilated and wounded white men (most notably John Bobbitt)," all of whom make a claim to "victimization by appealing to representations of bodily trauma."[40]

In order to demonstrate this "sustained assault" on masculinity, Morrow deploys the overlapping discourses of trauma and sacrifice, answering claims of patriarchal oppression with assertions of men's heroic victimization, asking, "If women are victims, why is it the men who wind up dead?" Morrow singles out combat as a fundamental site of traumatic heroism, heralding sacrificial death as a means through which men—not women—prove their worth to the nation-state.

> Not so long after [Virginia] Woolf wrote [about male power], for example, World War I destroyed an entire generation of European men on the battlefield—8.5 million of them. Woolf and her sisters did not fight in that war. Similarly, the names of more than 58,000 men are on the wall of the Vietnam Memorial in Washington—and those of eight women.

> Feminism's stated goal of real equality between the sexes will begin to be credible when females are required to register for the draft at 18, as males are, when 50% of combat units must be women—in short, when women are paying 50% of the *real* price, not only in war but also in society's other *sacrificial* exercises.[41]

According to Morrow, the value of men's lives is greater (more "real") than that of women because more men have died in combat—a discrepancy that is attributable, in large part, to the fact that historically men have denied women access to combat experience. Morrow distinguishes the rite/right of sacrificial death as an incomparable trauma *and* the most cherished performance of civic duty, privileging the experiential authority of the (male) veteran as unassailable.

After asserting that women should accept "real responsibility and risk" through participation in the sacrificial economy, Morrow diagnoses America as overrun with "rape-crisis hysterics" whose real victims are men.[42] Dismissively naming rape "the ur-crime that unites women," Morrow attributes a "borderless outrage at rape, wife battering, child abuse by men" with making men feel ashamed, frightened, angry, "diminished," "bashed," "unappreciated"—in a word, traumatized.[43] Rejecting the assertion that every man is a "potential rapist," Morrow also censures women who designate themselves as "potential survivors" for ratcheting "American victim-wailing" on behalf of actual and potential survivors of rape "up to a higher octave."[44]

Morrow labels certain uses of trauma as inappropriate or less significant than others, exemplifying what Mowitt refers to as a "strategy of comparative trauma calculation."[45] Like debates about whether Lorena Bobbitt's experience of abuse and rape was more or less traumatic than John Bobbitt's experience of having his penis severed, Morrow stages a gendered battle among those who make different rhetorical claims to trauma. Laura S. Brown suggests that such a tactic is not uncommon; in fact, she notes, what "counts" as trauma in our culture is typically that which is imagined to affect men.

> The range of human experience becomes the range of what is normal and usual in the lives of men of the dominant class; white, young, able-bodied, educated, middle-class, Christian men. Trauma is thus what disrupts these particular human lives, but no other. War and genocide, which are the work of men and male-dominated culture, are agreed-upon traumas; so are natural disasters, vehicle crashes, boats sinking in the freezing ocean.[46]

What appears to matter about these events is their publicity and visibility. Although the events themselves might get constructed as aberrations, they threaten our perception of what is "normal." Brown describes events that take place in the public eye, such as natural disasters, and "things that can and do happen to men," such as wartime violence, as defining "trauma in the official lexicon."[47] The prominence of these accepted understandings of trauma contrasts with what Brown describes as more "secret" or "insidious" forms of oppression, such as racism, rape, and incest, which happen every day.[48] Gendered and sexual violence against women might receive attention in public discourse but is almost never (if ever) labeled as a national or a cultural trauma. So, while Morrow writes off trauma discourse in anti-rape activism as "victim-wailing," he associates "real" trauma with men and their experiences in combat, asserting that it is sacrifice that makes men the "real" victims and "real" heroes of American culture. In this construction, male trauma is both a problem to be solved and an exemplary and noble expression of citizenship.

Mowitt understands such calculated comparisons of injury as "trauma envy."[49] Taking "possession of the wound," this rhetoric simultaneously discredits accusations of masculine privilege and lays claim to the moral authority that has been assigned to injury.[50] Robinson notes, however, that such crisis rhetoric "is not merely a cynical exploitation of the power of victimization; nor is it simply an opportunistic or appropriative gesture on the part of the privileged."[51] It is these things *and more*; specifically, for Robinson, recourse to victim discourse also constitutes an effort to negotiate the neoliberal conflict between individualism and collectivism in a context in which belonging and "grouping" are almost always "linked to perceived experiences of victimization." For example, the white firefighter envies black spaces of belonging, noting, "If you're black and belong to a black group, you're an activist. If you're white and you belong to a white group, you're an asshole."[52]

Trauma culture, in contrast, constructs traumatic experience as unifying, creating unshakable bonds between individuals imagined to have endured the unimaginable and said to have survived the unspeakable. Psychiatrist Kai Erikson argues that although "trauma is normally understood as a somewhat lonely and isolated business," collective suffering is capable of drawing one back to the social world. Erikson understands extreme suffering as creating a spiritual kinship among survivors: "Trauma shared can serve as a source of communality in the same way that common languages and common backgrounds can." He offers as an example "veterans haunted by dark memories of Vietnam" and advocates a "gathering of the wounded" as a step toward healing.[53]

This emphasis on trauma's centripetal force mirrors Bataille's understanding of sacrifice as uniting communities. The "domain of social laceration," which Bataille understands as including a "multiplicity of forms extend[ing] from war to the bloody cross of Christ," is marked by its capacity for "the creation or maintenance of a new unity of being." Bataille claims, "The individual who participates in loss is obscurely aware that this loss engenders the community that supports him."[54] The perceived unifying effects of trauma also mirror what Nancy Jay calls the "joining" impulse of ritualized sacrifice, which believers and practitioners imagine to unite a community of participants. But,

Jay contends, joining coexists with separating: if sacrifice is understood to join one community, it also separates this community from an imagined outside.[55] Sacrifice is thus both inclusive and exclusive, as is trauma.

Perhaps no better example of such logic exists in recent discourse than the 1990s-era canonization of the "Greatest Generation": while contemporary white men were declared to be in crisis and victimized by women and non-whites, these mythic figures of the past were heralded as having suffered nobly and been strengthened by trauma.[56] Like Morrow's celebration of male participation in "sacrificial exercises," hagiographic rhetoric about the veterans of World War II exalted these men for their suffering. In addition, this nostalgic rhetoric also used these men's shared experiences of the "good war" to discredit contemporary identity politics.

Barbara Biesecker contends that "popular rehabilitations of WWII" operated as "civic lessons for a generation beset by fractious disagreements about the viability of U.S. culture and identity."[57] Biesecker reads the film *Saving Private Ryan* and Tom Brokaw's book *The Greatest Generation* (1999) as positing the veteran of the "good war" as a solution to "the urgent need for national reunification."

> By manufacturing and embracing a particular kind of American, a certain idea of what it means to be a "good citizen," these popular cultural texts, best understood as technologies of national cultural transformation, promote social cohesion by rhetorically inducing differently positioned audiences—by class, race, ethnicity, sexuality, and gender—to disregard rather than actively seek to dismantle the inequitable power relations that continue to structure collective life in the United States.[58]

The rhetorical celebration of WWII and its veterans becomes a soporific, aiming to dull national attention to identity politics and such issues as race, class, gender, and sexuality.

At the same time, however, that the trauma of war is said to have joined together this band of brothers, trauma rhetoric also functions to set this population of veterans apart from others—lifting them above other citizen-subjects as a civic ideal. In a graphic film such as *Saving Private Ryan*, for instance, "the white pained male body of war begins to function as a ground for the production of knowledge and judgment," endowing the World War II veteran with the experiential and moral authority imagined to belong uniquely to the trauma survivor.[59] Positioning spectators as if they are "bearing witness to material, corporeal, sensual pain," it claims an illusory hold on "the preideological, apolitical, universal and, thus, universalizing experience out of which truth ('what really counts') and prudential wisdom ('what should be done') may emerge."[60] Like Morrow's adulation of the male soldier or Lifton's celebration of the "special wisdom" of the Vietnam veteran, the discourse Biesecker describes constructs the World War II veteran as the ideal citizen-subject whose authority is born out of suffering, enjoining the nation's factions to give up their differences and to find in the "Greatest Generation" evidence of "what really counts." The films addressed in this chapter similarly imagine trauma as an abyss from which real heroes emerge and presume that the act of witnessing transmits the strength and nobility of the trauma victim directly to (some of) those that survive.

Troubled Waters

The sinking of the White Star Line's *Titanic* is one of the most famous and widely discussed large-scale catastrophes in recorded history. Patricia Leavy observes, "It has been claimed that Titanic is the third most written about event in human history, following the life of Jesus Christ and the assassination of President John F. Kennedy." Leavy further notes that "Titanic" has been cited as "the third most recognizable word worldwide, following 'God' and 'Coca-Cola.'"[61] The same notoriety characterizes James Cameron's 1997 docudrama about the ship's only voyage, for *Titanic* is one of the most expensive, most acclaimed, and most profitable films ever made: with a production budget of $200,000,000, *Titanic* reportedly grossed over $1.8 billion dollars worldwide and won eleven Academy Awards.[62]

Combining the conventions of the melodrama and the disaster film, *Titanic* tells a love story about penniless Jack Dawson (Leonardo DiCaprio) and wealthy Rose Dewitt Bukater (Kate Winslet), in the process constructing a sentimental celebration of working-class masculinity that encourages men to be simultaneously emotive and agentive, sensitive and strong, wounded and steadfast. Like many sacrificial films of this era—including *Braveheart*, *Gladiator*, *Saving Private Ryan*, and *Armageddon*—*Titanic* resurrects mythic figures from the past as exemplars of citizens who prove their worth through hardship, suffering, and trauma. *Titanic* lays claim to the discourse of trauma and attempts to diminish the perceived injuries of history.

The logic and iconography of trauma predominate in *Titanic*, as is made clear from the film's outset. Following a short, grainy, and sepia-toned sequence resembling "real" historical footage from the *Titanic*'s departure, the film shows members of a treasure-hunting crew probe the wreckage of the cruise ship to find a missing treasure, the Heart of the Ocean Diamond. Televised news coverage of this controversial expedition reaches Rose, a survivor of the *Titanic* disaster, who joins the salvage crew in order to give them her version of what "really" happened on the ship's fatal maiden voyage. After being shown a computer-generated re-creation of the ship's sinking, Rose rejects this "fine forensic analysis" because it misses the truth of what she experienced. She then embarks on a detailed description of her time on the ship, which is presented to the film's audience as flashbacks that constitute the majority of the narrative. *Titanic*'s use of this frame story and flashback structure, akin to that in *Saving Private Ryan,* is important for a number of reasons.

First, as noted earlier, flashbacks reenact the structure of trauma as something that intrudes, invades, and takes hostage. For example, as Rose sees the ruins of the *Titanic* through the treasure-hunters' array of cameras and television monitors, a flashback suddenly overtakes her and interrupts the film's narrative. Rose's memories, triggered by the sight of the ship's skeletal remains, are abrupt and fragmentary, constituting a decisive interruption to Rose's experience and that of the film's audience. This flashback clearly marks Rose as a traumatized subject who is wounded, even haunted, by a shocking and overwhelming past. When Rose arrives on treasure-hunter Brock Lovett's (Bill Paxton) salvage ship in a wheelchair, for instance, carrying mounds of suitcases and multiple pets, *Titanic* implies that she has baggage that is both literal and figurative. The film also asserts the magnitude of her personal history by emphasizing her age through frequent close-ups of her eyes, putting on display her wrinkled flesh, which contrasts distinctly with the skin in similar shots of the younger Rose featured in the flashbacks.

Second, by presenting Rose's memories directly to the audience via flashbacks, *Titanic* offers what Maureen Turim refers to as the "image-as-truth" and frames history as "an essentially individual and emotional experience."[63] Although the first flashbacks suddenly disrupt the present-day of the narrative, Rose's voiceover narration contextualizes her traumatic memories. *Titanic* privileges the wisdom of Rose's experience and the authority of her testimony over that of Brock's cameras, computers, sonar equipment, and other scavenging machinery. As Rose reminds the scavenger crew and the film's imagined audience, the digital re-creation of the ship may be fine, forensically speaking, but it can't compare to her own personal account of what happened.

Rose's position as authoritative narrator reinforces what Joan Scott describes as the privileging of visual and visceral experience as unassailable. The frequent close-ups of Rose's eyes emphasize that the events she recounts are ones she experienced with her own eyes (despite the fact that much of what is depicted in the flashback clearly exceeds what Rose could have seen for herself).[64] *Titanic* lauds survivor testimony as a special mode of speech that is above reproach and beyond question in ways that mirror and reinforce some scholars' emphasis on the special wisdom of the Vietnam veteran and the public's veneration of the "Greatest Generation" as exemplary citizens. Although a female speaker offers this testimony, her narration tells the story of a great and special man, and *Titanic* makes it clear that Rose inherited her wisdom (and storytelling ability) from Jack.

This reliance on testimony shown through flashbacks constructs Rose's near-death experiences as giving her unique access to the real and romantically equates trauma with transcendence. This brings to mind Bataille's opinion that "no less a loss than death is needed for the brilliance of life to traverse and transfigure dull existence."[65] Similar assumptions can be seen at work in Lifton's 1990 discussion of the "transformative" power of death. Lifton contends that "death potentially changes anything and everything. . . . To take in death, that is, to be open to a death encounter, always means reassessing what is ultimate, significant, or . . . 'what counts.'"[66] He claims that the survivor might be understood as somewhat like the mythological hero who earns "a knowledge of death and therefore a knowledge of life," which he describes as "a profound new knowledge."[67]

According to *Titanic*, a confrontation with death not only transforms the survivor of an event but may also be passed along to those who witness the survivor's testimony. The film depicts Rose's testimony as changing those around her—just as Jack first changed her—and thus reinscribes both Bataille's assumption that anguish can be communicated directly and former president Bill Clinton's more recent assertion that he could "feel your pain."[68] Brock's question to Old Rose, "Will you share it with us?" suggests that he wants to know not simply Rose's story but the "reality" of her experience and pain. Brock does not just want to hear Rose's accounts of her past—he wants to be a part of them, to have a share in them.

In the few instances when the film interrupts Rose's flashback narration and returns the present day, a captivated and emotional audience always surrounds her. Once callous and irreverent, the treasure-hunters have been stunned into silence, many of them with mouths agape and eyes full of tears. While at the outset of the film, the crew was greedily exhuming the rubble from the *Titanic*—putting their agentive, investigative gazes to work—Rose's testimony paralyzes them into states of passivity. *Titanic* most clearly signals the impact of this collective transformation through the character Brock.

Famous primarily for finding "Spanish gold," the mercenary Brock approaches the wreckage as another lucrative landscape to mine and wants the diamond for its monetary value. Early in the film, Brock videotapes the wreckage from inside a submarine. Providing voiceover narration for his video, Brock gives a maudlin description of the ship as captivating: "Seeing her coming out of the darkness like a ghost ship still gets me every time." In response, one of his crewmembers snickers, calling Brock "full of shit." Brock laughs in agreement, cuts off his camera, and declares, "Enough of that bullshit." *Titanic* reveals Brock's reverence toward the ship to be disingenuous play-acting that he abandons when he gets signals about how his companions expect him to respond to the spectacle of such catastrophe. The ruins of the *Titanic* don't really "get" Brock; he simply wants to get *at* what is hidden within them.

Rose's testimony, however, reforms Brock, who admits that he now "truly" understands the power and impact of the disaster. He woefully discloses,

"Three years, I've thought of nothing except *Titanic*, but I never got it. I never let it in." But, now it seems, he does "get" it—the catastrophe has gotten him, gotten in. In the language of trauma, *Titanic* has invaded Brock, taken hold of him, but instead of lamenting this change as detrimental, Brock imagines himself to have been redeemed, as if he has now discovered a treasure more "real" than a diamond. *Titanic*'s use of narration enables Brock and his fellow witnesses to appropriate Rose's experiential authority, creating a transgenerational lineage through which trauma is passed on and inherited as a special, immutable currency.

The apparent longing that characterizes Rose's audience (and, by extension, the film itself) enacts a complex nostalgia for this historical catastrophe that is akin to Mowitt's trauma envy. However, the frame story and flashback structure mitigate trauma's perceived disruptions and at the same time make use of its allegedly ennobling and enabling potential. Vivian Sobchack contends that because *Titanic*'s "absolutely crucial frame story" is set in the present day, it "narratively encircles the irreversibility of the historical past—reconstituting it in the 'roundness' of the film as a whole as a felicitous and comforting 'eternal return' that undoes catastrophe and death."[69] *Titanic* moves fluidly between past and present, simultaneously remaining tethered to the violent scene of a traumatic past and offering reassuring promises that one can indeed move on.

Sobchack argues that *Titanic* offers up "a nostalgic utopia, its narrative structure not only enabling a descent into and submersion in the 'past' as an 'impossibly pure context of lived experience,' but also enabling a very present and contemporary search for this 'place of origin.'" In its "utopian dream of a 'future-past," *Titanic* also creates "a 'past-perfect' and a longing for its perfect repetition in the future, a future-perfect."[70] Envisioning a present day and a future that are better off for having returned to the injuries of the past, *Titanic* re-creates the phantasmagoric before and after of trauma. For Sobchack, this frame story works as a protective device, engendering "a mediated but seemingly 'authentic' experience, one that keeps real trauma, but not real emotion, at bay."[71]

Titanic also imagines trauma to be valuable for its capacity to unite communities. While Rose's flashbacks emphasize the divisions and inequalities onboard the *Titanic*—as in the treatment of passengers in steerage as expendable animals and Rose's description of herself as a "slave" to her wealthy fiancé—Rose's testimony reveres the poor and working-class passengers for having worked together and put others' needs before their own, as if attention to inequalities can (and should) vanish in moments of strife. The dramatization of the selfless coming-together of these downtrodden passengers not only reaffirms the fantasy that trauma may have centripetal effects on its survivors but also illustrates what Biesecker describes as prevailing 1990s-era claims that citizens should "turn a blind eye to the social differences that still make a difference."[72]

The process of unification is also reenacted among Old Rose's witnesses. As Brock speaks privately to Rose's granddaughter, the film alludes to an unspoken connection between the pair, forged by their shared experience of Rose's testimony and visualized through mise-en-scène. Brock and Lizzy (Suzy Amis) physically resemble the young Jack and Rose, as if offering a picture of what the two might have looked like as a mature couple. Standing close to one another and leaning against the ship's rails, the two virtual strangers appear to share an ineffable connection that mimes scenes of Jack and Rose's developing romance on the *Titanic*. Trauma seems to have produced an "eternal return" and a new beginning. Recalling both Erikson's appraisal of large-scale disasters as potential sites for rebuilding community and what Biesecker describes as the call for unification in the rhetorical canonization of the "Greatest Generation," the film encourages others to bear witness to suffering as a foundation for creating communality.

Individual agendas or self-serving desires no longer beset the imagined community envisioned by Rose's story because, according to the logic of the film, what "really matters" in life transcends politics, history, time, and place. Like President Clinton's appeal to citizens on Veterans Day in 1995 to "summon the spirit that joined that generation, that stood together and cared for one another," *Titanic* echoes Clinton's contention that the nation should "grow strong together, not be divided and weakened."[73] *Titanic* translates Clinton's assertion that Americans should "find that common ground for which so many have fought and died" in an effort to persuade audiences to find unity in the waters in which so many died by emphasizing—again and again—*how many* died.

Tears for Fears

Although *Titanic* begins as a melodrama, it becomes a disaster film fixated on death and dying. During the primary disaster sequence, *Titanic* offers an unrelenting series of death scenes: body after body falls, slides, jumps, and is hurled from the ship. As the ocean liner sinks, snaps in two, rises, and falls again, it propels hundreds of bodies through space, dropping them into the dark waters of the Atlantic Ocean. In one moment, for instance, Jack and Rose dangle on the outer edge of the ship, after the aft section has become totally vertical. This precarious position recalls and replays the couple's first meeting, when Jack tenderly persuaded Rose to come down from the ship's railing and abandon a suicide attempt. In both scenes, the literal fear of falling commingles with the metaphorical "falling in love," illustrating the ambivalence that Eleanor Kaufman assigns to the concepts of trauma and the fall: the "disorienting vertigo of falling" operates concurrently as a sign "of trauma and of hope."[74]

The film depicts the destruction of the *Titanic* twice—in the digital re-creation produced by Brock's team of treasure-hunters and in Rose's vivid flashbacks—and visualizes the loss of over one thousand lives.[75] Although Brock's re-creation is scientific, carefully calculated, and contextualized by the technician's narration of the events being digitally reproduced, director James Cameron's version of the event is explosive, overwhelming, and full of carnage—producing a sensation of "excessive, undischargeable excitation," which Shaviro depicts as characterizing many Hollywood films.[76] Like the disaster sequences in *The Poseidon Adventure*, *Titanic*'s scenes of catastrophe are loud (full of sounds of glass breaking, wood snapping, steel groaning, water roaring, people screaming, bones cracking) and visually chaotic (torrents of water furiously sweep objects and bodies through the ship's corridors, often flooding the frame and occasionally jarring the cameras). As the disaster unfolds, the film's hitherto steady camera becomes mobile, kinetic, and even frantic. Canted framing enacts the ship's own tumbling, and frequent edits visualize the sinking ship from every possible angle and distance.

Echoing what Shaviro describes as a tendency of many films to leave the spectator "depositioned and dispossessed by the film's incessant modulations of visibility," Cameron encourages the viewer to imagine him/herself being overtaken, as if undone by the viewing experience.[77] Shaviro suggests that such a spectatorial experience "disrupts the traditional, historically sedimented habits and expectations of vision; it undoes the transcendental and phenomenological structures that claimed to regulate perception and to ground and unify the ego."[78] *Titanic* invites the spectator to lose sight of which way is up, down, in, and out. For Shaviro, "the rush of film images is simply too quick, too immediate, to allow the spectator the breathing room necessary for traditional, detached aesthetic contemplation." As the world of the camera "violently impinges" on the spectator, he/she "can no longer regard [the scene], unaffected, from a safe distance."[79] This Bataillean cinematic experience mimes the phenomenology of trauma, wherein the subject is imagined to be vertiginously undone through unexpected shock.

Reviews of *Titanic* confirm Shaviro's understanding of the cinema's capacity to produce visual fascination with an image that "becomes an obsession" and "*haunts*" the viewer.[80] Todd McCarthy's review for *Variety* states that *Titanic* "is utterly stunning and effectively places the viewer in the jaws of death." Stephen Hunter's review for the *Washington Post* similarly celebrates *Titanic* for putting viewers "aboard the sinking ship, palpably and as never before." Janet Maslin's *New York Times* review describes the film as "a huge, thrilling three-and-a-quarter-hour experience that unerringly lures viewers into the beauty and heartbreak of its lost world." She continues, "Astonishing technological advances are at work here, but only in the service of one spectacular illusion: that the ship is afloat again, and that the audience is intimately involved in the voyage."[81]

Each review positions the spectator as being at the mercy of the film, palpably experiencing the diegetic terror and loss, lured into the violent scene. The rhetoric of trauma depicts the film as possessing viewers, taking them hostage. Recalling Bataille's description of the torture victim as both haggard and beautiful, these reviews also describe *Titanic*'s scenes of suffering and sorrow as stunning, wondrous, and thrilling; to paraphrase Maslin, they are beautiful and heartbreaking all at once. The "trauma" of *Titanic* does more than simply horrify or repel; it also entices and mesmerizes. In response to such celebratory reviews of the film's power to involve its viewers in such scenes of destruction, one may question *why* filmgoers might seek such a return to the depths of terror and loss. What is the appeal of such intimate involvement in what is constructed as a harrowing and devastating experience?

For Shaviro, this appeal should be understood in Bataillean terms as a demonstration of the subject's desire for self-shattering annihilation. He writes, "What inspires the cinematic spectator is a passion for that very loss of control, that abjection, fragmentation, and subversion of self-identity that psychoanalytic theory so dubiously classifies under the rubrics of lack and castration."[82] Shaviro concludes, therefore, that cinematic experiences of "a forced, ecstatic abjection before the image" have "radical potential to subvert social hierarchies and decompose relations of power" and to undermine Cartesian constructions of the subject through their "extreme capacity for seduction and violence."[83] In contrast, Mowitt's description of trauma envy suggests that fascination with suffering also indicates an impulse toward self-validation and confirmation, fashioned through a vicarious (or imagined) experience of trauma. Just as Brock allegedly finds new meaning and purpose in his life after he hears Rose's testimony, *Titanic* invites its spectators to experience its devastating scenes of loss as a way to reconstitute themselves. As much as *Titanic* seems to remove the distance between film text and spectator, the safe distance between spectatorship and trauma remains.

Consider, for instance, another remark from Hunter's review: "Cameron captures the majesty, the tragedy, the fury and the futility of the event in a way that supersedes his trivial attempts to melodramatize it. . . . I left with an ache for those lost 1,500, rich and poor alike, for the big ship in ruins, and for the inescapable meaning in it all."[84] Hunter's earlier description of feeling as if he were aboard the sinking ship gives way to a description of his own departure from the theater, intact and unharmed, and his own sense-making process. Ennobled by an "ache" for those that died on the *Titanic*, Hunter—not unlike Brock—now "gets" the experience; the tragedy now has "inescapable meaning." The focus remains the surviving subject who has been transformed and endowed with new knowledge. Reenacting (and perhaps producing) the shocking, paralyzing vertigo of trauma, *Titanic* uses its cinematic spectacles of self-loss to reconfirm the existence of whole and proper subjectivity and to assert that trauma produces new and better subjects. These qualities are most clearly illustrated in the character of Jack.

Jack of All Trades

Jack begins the film poor and homeless. He reveals to Rose that he was orphaned at the age of fifteen, a "tumbleweed blowing in the wind." Aboard the *Titanic*, Jack continues to find himself marginalized and disenfranchised. Quite literally pushed aside and kept below decks with the other passengers in steerage—he is told on the first-class deck to "get back to where he belongs and stay there"—Jack is treated as refuse. When Rose grants him access to the world of first class, Jack experiences frequent abuse by the wealthy elite and is, at one point, falsely accused of burglary and imprisoned.

Even though *Titanic* depicts Jack as an historical figure from the early twentieth century, the film allegorically casts him as an idealized version of the "nineties man." Like the men Gates and Morrow constructed, Jack is put-upon and downtrodden, constantly assaulted and under scrutiny, and automatically marked because of his class status as a potential thief.[85] Unlike the protagonist of a film like *Falling Down*, however, Jack does not snap under the pressure of such attacks. Instead, he maintains a remarkable degree of flexibility and mobility, moving between the worlds of third and first class with relative ease. Once in a borrowed tuxedo and later in a stolen gray overcoat, Jack disguises himself effectively as one of the elite.

Rather than bemoaning or avenging the offenses against him, Jack remains tirelessly optimistic and at ease. The snapping, or going berserk, is left to upper-class Caledon Hockley (Cal), whom the film casts as domineering and abusive, and Rose. The unflappable Jack embodies what Brent Malin describes as a historically specific paradox: he is "broken yet strong, sensitive but tough."[86] U.S. public culture in the 1990s constructed President Clinton as the embodiment of this paradoxical version of masculinity. Like Clinton, Jack embodies a "new, sensitive, nontraditional masculinity" at the same time that he performs a "powerful, thoroughly established sense of 'real American manhood.'" *Titanic* credits Jack's ability to perform this new version of masculinity to his working-class background and experiences of personal hardship, which, argues Malin, echoes public constructions linking President Clinton's masculinity to his working-class background.[87]

Although *Titanic* lampoons Jack as "hilariously uncivilized and uncouth," it marks him as a hero for such violations of middle-class norms.[88] Jack's contravention of bourgeois norms allegedly gives him greater access to the real. Malin sees the film as a "romanticized look at a working-class free spirit," suggesting that Jack is an "instinctive creature" who is uniquely in touch with "everyday folk," himself, and his emotions.[89] *Titanic* asserts that unlike the overly pedigreed passengers in first class, Jack knows what really matters. As Rose says, Jack "really sees people." He demonstrates his wisdom and insight, for instance, at dinner in the first-class dining room as Rose's guest, where he regales his upper-class audience with tales of independence and adventure. While Rose's mother repeatedly tries to embarrass or unnerve him, he embraces his rootlessness not as a humiliating signifier of his poverty or lack of agency but as a condition of possibility akin to what *Poseidon Adventure*'s Reverend Scott calls "elbow room" or "real freedom." Jack tells his listeners to "make each day count."

There is no question that Jack suffers: for example, he nearly dies (and must be rescued by Rose) after being handcuffed to a pipe in a flooding portion of the ship as punishment for a crime he did not commit. Nonetheless, he uses his injuries as evidence of and resources for his own redemptive narrative of self. He is a good card player, conversationalist, dancer, artist, and lover, and his life story and experiences of hardship seem to have endowed him with a special kind of wisdom and agency. While Jack remains composed, however, Rose appears to be on the brink of disaster. *Titanic* features a female protagonist on the verge of coming unhinged, while the working-class everyman seems affected but not undone by injury. In *Titanic*, trauma and victimization happen to men, but it is women who become traumatized victims.

For instance, in voice-over narration, Rose describes herself as being on the verge of collapse before she met Jack. Reiterating the link between trauma and falling, Rose says, "I felt like I was standing at a great precipice with no one to pull me back, no one who cared or even noticed." The flashback reveals Rose running to the bow of the ship, distraught and tearful and ready to jump. Spotting Rose in her moment of crisis, Jack gently coaxes her down from the railing, not by coercion or with reprimands but by relying on his own experiential authority and recounting a childhood story about a near-drowning in ice-cold water. In contrast to her fiancé—who will later call Rose "melancholy" and attempt to cure her with the extravagant but unwanted Heart of the Ocean Diamond—Jack enables Rose to make her own decision by offering her a new perspective on life, death, and what really matters. His vow that he will share her suffering—Jack promises her, "You jump, I jump"—convinces Rose to step down.

Jack further demonstrates his unique access to "what really counts" when he sneaks Rose into a party in steerage, which the film marks as a "real" party with "real" people. In contrast to the stifling rules and expectations of the elite dinner party (what Reverend Scott might dismiss as "all the rules and all the trappings"), this party is loud, raucous, seemingly unconcerned with social norms governing decorum. The film constructs a literal descent into steerage

Figure 11. Rose Dewitt Bukater considering suicide as Jack Dawson steps in to save her. *Titanic* (Paramount)

as liberating and as giving Jack and Rose closer access to the real, using the same logic at work in the film's frequent construction of trauma as an actual fall or plunge "through which one gains access to the Real."[90]

Titanic argues that below decks people understand what counts, while those in first class concern themselves only with questions of status and upbringing. In steerage, men, women, and children from different cultures who speak different languages mingle and celebrate together, unconcerned with the social differences or inequalities among them. While Jack's presence in first class provokes extreme discomfort and scrutiny there, no one registers Rose's presence in steerage as shocking or bothersome; they welcome her warmly and without reservation. Although the film claims to critique class discrimination—Cameron describes it as stopping "just short of Marxist dogma"—*Titanic* ultimately encourages spectators to turn a blind eye to difference, whether economic, social, or cultural.[91]

In contrast to the way *Titanic* constructs Jack's mobility as either innate or hard earned through life experience, the film marks Rose's agency as something she inherits from Jack, not unlike her storytelling ability. Hospitality and acceptance may come naturally to the diverse and disenfranchised populations below decks, but Rose must learn how to transgress her own social category and be "real." It is Jack who teaches Rose to spit and how to "fly," and it is Jack who unlocks Rose's courage and sexuality.

Jack enables Rose not by guiding her with a strong hand but by stepping aside and making room so that his female counterpart may emerge stronger, more independent, and liberated. Jack understands Rose's desire for freedom (in contrast to the regulation and control that her abusive fiancé imparts); he "gets" Rose, he sees who she "really is." His metaphorical insight and vision are overtly confirmed by his good eye for fine art and his talents as an artist. Jack's

Figure 12. Rose and Jack enjoying a "real" party below decks in steerage. *Titanic* (Paramount)

treatment of Rose attends allegorically to public discourse about masculinity in the 1990s. As a synecdochic stand-in for all men, Jack's actions refute accusations of patriarchal oppression, misogyny, and privilege and recast the idealized hero as sensitive and responsive to the plight of others.

The exaltation of the sensitive man notwithstanding, *Titanic* does not entirely renounce masculinity's claims to phallic authority. As Peter Lehman and Susan Hunt suggest, *Titanic* upholds the value of a "powerfully phallic masculinity" at the same time that "it implies that such masculinity is not what it is cracked up to be."[92] As evidence of this unresolved contradiction, Lehman and Hunt point to the scene in which Jack and Rose have sex. Although Jack is generally compassionate and gentle, the sex scene depicts a more aggressive version of masculinity, and the "hyperphysical sex that Jack performs would be in keeping with that of the lower-class, earthy body man or of the phallically powerful male action hero."[93] Hence, "while Jack is presented as an attractive 'soft' alternative to dominant masculinity throughout much of the film, in the sex scene, he is suddenly empowered with the very qualities he seems to lack."[94]

Lehman and Hunt also note that however much *Titanic* contributes to 1990s-era rhetoric about the "sensitive man," discourse about the film reinforces phallocentric affirmations of mastery. They suggest that masculinist logic characterizes studio promotions for the film as the "most expensive movie ever made" and Cameron's public discourse about the film. When he accepted his Oscar for best picture, Cameron "waved the statue above his head and declared, in a repetition of Jack's line from the film, 'I'm the King of the World.'"[95]

Likewise, the *New York Times* describes Cameron as a "supremely focused taskmaster." Depicting Cameron in terms more similar to Cal Hockley than Jack Dawson, the article quotes a description of Cameron as "the ultimate scuba-diving Navy seal filmmaker." Describing "Cameron's tendency to browbeat cast and crew when things didn't go his way," the article notes that the name of Cameron's production company, Lightstorm, "seems oddly appropriate, reflecting his inclination toward brief, intimidating outbursts."[96] In addition to constructions of Cameron as something of a berserk on-set tyrant, discussions of *Titanic* also stress his filmmaking heroics and sacrifices. Justine Elias writes, "Mr. Cameron also has a reputation for getting things done under adverse circumstances, and that reputation will be enhanced now that 'Titanic,' despite its troubled history, is arriving in theaters, to much early acclaim." Elias compares the "troubled history" of Cameron's *Titanic*—which was released almost six months late and went grossly over budget—to the troubled history of the RMS *Titanic*, noting, "The history of the movie is almost as familiar as that of the Titanic."[97]

In its casting of Cameron as a self-sacrificial and radical hero, this discourse parallels that surrounding Mel Gibson as the director of *The Passion of the Christ* (2004). Lehman and Hunt argue that promotional focus on "the 'heroics' of a filmmaker who forfeited much of his salary to complete the film" constructs Cameron as "throwing himself into the *Titanic* project with near maniacal commitment and against all odds, even saving the production itself."[98] At the same time that Cameron is imagined to embody the aggressive machismo that characterizes Cal Hockley, attention to his alleged sacrifices and difficulties also places him in a position of vulnerability similar to Jack's.

Discussions of Cameron's persona as a director also focus on his technical mastery as a filmmaker and *Titanic*'s unprecedented use of special effects technology. Lehman and Hunt suggest that the "concern with (and desire for) masculine size and power that was displaced from the film's love story" gets projected onto "promotional discourses about the film." If Jack himself typically eschews masculine grandstanding and displays of mastery, "Cameron, the studios, and the press all combined to impress the public with the very kind of masculine spectacle of size that Rose refuses to be impressed with."[99] Discourse about the film and its filmmaker reinscribes the conventional logics of masculinity that the diegesis claims to challenge.

Letting Go

Titanic's reliance on ritualized sacrifice further illustrates the film's conflicted treatment of masculinity: as Jack dies rather passively in the freezing waters of the Atlantic, *Titanic* endows him with a totalizing gaze and prescience akin to Bataille's figuration of the sovereign subject. When the RMS *Titanic* completely submerges, Jack puts Rose on a floating plank; hanging from its side in the water, he gives up his own life. As he weakens, Jack bolsters Rose's spirit with his vision of her future, "You're gonna die an old lady, warm in her bed."

This prediction comes true: at the end of the film, having told her story, Rose retreats to her bed on Brock's ship, surrounded by personal photos, and dies peacefully. Jack's final moments thus seem to grant him prophetic knowledge. Like Bataille's sovereign subject, *Titanic* imagines Jack as limitless, and like the saccharine Celine Dion song that plays throughout the film's soundtrack ("My Heart Will Go On"), Jack's ability to see into Rose's future marks him as nothing short of transcendent. As Jack and Rose await lifeboats, he persuades Rose to fight for her life, insisting that she "never let go" of her promise to survive. When Jack dies, Rose repeats this refrain, "I'll never let go."[100] The particular language of this mantra bears noting. As Rose repeats the phrase, its meanings proliferate, pointing toward the film's overlapping and contradictory attitudes toward trauma as both a problem to solve and an experience to revere.

On one hand, Rose's promise not to "let go" recalls times when she sought to avoid actual falls, as in her aborted suicide attempt and her efforts to survive the *Titanic*'s final submersion. Rose's determination to hang on implies an aversion toward traumatic descent, a promise to Jack that she will not give into the "abysslike structure of trauma."[101] And yet Rose's refusal to "let go" also implies the possibility that she will never move on from or leave behind the trauma of the *Titanic*, corroborating Cal's diagnosis of Rose as "melancholy."[102] Rose may survive, but she will never truly "let go" of the experience, which she will carry with her, quite literally, as baggage.

When the lifeboats arrive, Rose forcibly detaches Jack's stiff hand from her own, dropping his lifeless body into the ocean. As she literally "lets go" of Jack, an overhead shot depicts Jack's fall into the ocean's impenetrable abyss. Rose hides her true identity from her rescuers and introduces herself as Rose Dawson (not Rose Dewitt Bukater), as if reborn through trauma. While Rose *Dewitt Bukater* verged on psychological implosion, Jack's traumatic heroism has enabled Rose *Dawson* to find freedom and independence, a new beginning, just as Rose's testimony is also imagined to revitalize her listeners. Rose is not reborn completely anew, however; she has appropriated Jack's identity as part of her own and now bears his name. Disguising herself in a gray blanket, Rose reenacts Jack's earlier costuming trick and makes herself more like her lost love object, having become melancholic indeed.

Titanic visualizes melancholia during Rose's death scene. Cameron's camera cranes over the collection of still photographs that Rose carried aboard Brock's ship. Each photo depicts Rose on adventures around the world, fulfilling her promise to go on and lead a full life. The photographic image, however, also evokes absence and loss, and its fixity recalls the stasis associated with the phenomenology of trauma. It reminds Rose and the cinematic viewer of what Roland Barthes calls the "that-has-been," what was but is no longer. In the end, the evidence of Rose's freedom and mobility becomes a reminder of the trauma that reconstituted her identity. Although Rose does "go on," this photographic

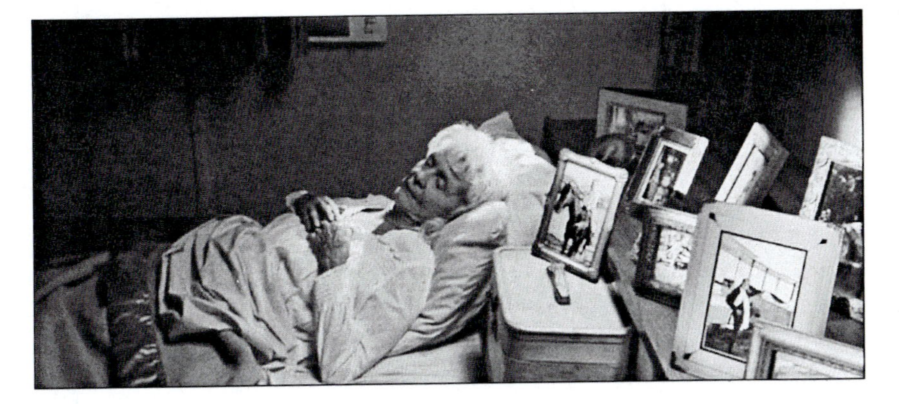

Figure 13. Old Rose dying peacefully in her bed, surrounded by still photographs of her life's adventures. *Titanic* (Paramount)

archive seems to reveal that she also remains tethered to past loss, never fully able to let go—her accomplishments bearing traces of Jack's memory and, therefore, of Rose's trauma. The film's coda, a vision of Rose and Jack in the afterlife aboard the *Titanic*, makes clear that Rose is stuck in the past. Not only does Old Rose return to the etiological site of her trauma—an ocean liner—to die, but in death her spirit returns to the ship, now returned to its full glory. There, she and Jack, both restored to youth and health, begin their narrative again through this mythic and eternal return.

In the end, *Titanic* replicates Lance Morrow's assessment of trauma, sacrifice, and American "victim-wailing." While Jack suffers a number of injuries, he is never fully undone by them—until his death, of course. But this death gives Rose new life and is therefore endowed with meaning. Jack's fall into the ocean signifies both trauma and hope, an end and a beginning. *Titanic*, therefore, echoes Morrow's praise of "sacrificial exercises" as noble deeds. In its depiction of Rose as coming undone (often actually wailing), *Titanic* also reproduces Morrow's assertion that while it is men who die, it is women who (hysterically) claim injuries.[103] *Titanic* lays claim to the discourse of trauma—Jack's death is, after all, the greatest loss of the film—at the same time that it pathologizes and feminizes those who openly mark themselves as victims.

All Over Again

Armageddon opens with Charlton Heston speaking in voice-of-God narration, describing the near-destruction of Earth millions of years earlier as digital images re-create the events Heston describes. *Armageddon* uses past catastrophe to evince the inevitability of future disaster: "It happened before.

It will happen again. It's just a question of when." Not unlike Jack's predictive vision, this prophecy immediately gives way to its own fulfillment, as debris from an asteroid fatally bombards an astronaut repairing a satellite in space.[104] *Armageddon*'s audience witnesses this tragedy alongside spectators in the diegesis, including room full of (mostly) men who watch the disaster on dozens of television monitors in mission control and one fanatical "space watcher" (a navy veteran) who accidentally glimpses the explosions with his high-powered telescope.

With this emphasis on spectatorship repeated throughout the narrative—multiple scenes depict citizens from around the world huddled around television sets, watching news of the space shuttle explosion and the impending apocalyptic event—*Armageddon* conflates catastrophe with spectacle. Dramatizing global panic caused by an asteroid (which is described in the film as an "anomaly" that is "the size of Texas") heading for Earth, the film deploys elaborate special effects to depict the destruction of such major world cities as New York, Shanghai, and Paris. Unrelenting scenes of disaster—raging tidal waves, uncontrolled fires, blankets of smoke, crumbling skyscrapers, overturned cars, dismembered bodies, mounds of rubble—rupture the narrative again and again; similar to *Titanic*, the spectatorial experience engendered by the film is excessive, affective, and visceral, inviting audience members, as Shaviro puts it, "to stay in the orbit of the senses."[105]

Armageddon also launches emotional attacks, coupling sensations of panic with sentimental catharsis. As asteroid debris rains down, NASA and the U.S. government seek unconventional solutions. The physically impaired but brilliant NASA engineer Dan Truman (Billy Bob Thornton) summons an unruly bunch of "roughnecks" led by heartbroken and alienated oilman Harry Stamper (Bruce Willis). These unlikely and largely unstable men aim to land on the asteroid, dig an 800-foot hole, and bury a nuclear warhead that can explode the orbiting rock from the inside out. As these roughnecks prepare for their journey into space on two space shuttles named *Freedom* and *Independence*, *Armageddon* oscillates between fixation on literal and spectacular scenes of destruction and the psychic dissolution of its male characters.

Armageddon traffics in what Walter Benjamin calls the "physical shock effect," inviting spectators to feel as if they are being undone.[106] Consider, for instance, Dennis Lim's review of the film for the *Village Voice*: "*Armageddon* decisively crosses the line from mindless, relatively painful garbage into a whole new dimension of summer-movie hell. Like being yelled at by idiots for 144 minutes, the *Armageddon* experience is pointlessly *traumatizing*."[107] Michael O'Sullivan's review in the *Washington Post* echoes this emphasis on trauma, describing the film as "emotionally and physically exhausting." O'Sullivan writes, "It's an intensely visceral pleasure, not unmixed with pain, like the multiple g-force acceleration experienced by an astronaut during lift-off. 'Armageddon' peels your eyelids back and blows your eardrums out until rational analysis is moot."[108]

This assault is enacted, quite viscerally, in the form of the film; few individual shots last longer than four seconds and many are only as long as one or two seconds.[109] The breakneck pace and constant barrage of images produce a violence of form that discourages the audience from erecting stable spectatorial ground. Bay's rapid-fire editing and aggressive special effects in *Armageddon* embody the logic of the U.S. military's doctrine of rapid dominance of the 1990s. This doctrine, which was formulated in 1996 by Harlan K. Ullman and James P. Wade and later popularized during the second Bush administration as "shock and awe," advocates a military praxis that overloads the sensorial and perceptual faculties of the enemy.

> The key objective of Rapid Dominance is to impose this overwhelming level of Shock and Awe against an adversary on an immediate or sufficiently timely basis to paralyze its will to carry on. In crude terms, Rapid Dominance would seize control of the environment and paralyze or so overload an adversary's perceptions and understanding of events so that the enemy would be incapable of resistance at tactical and strategic levels. An adversary would be rendered totally impotent and vulnerable to our actions.[110]

In addition to describing Michael Bay's cinematic stylistics, Ullman and Wade's definition of "Shock and Awe" closely recalls the language of trauma.

Naomi Klein notes that the "shock doctrine" reproduces the traumatic logic of torture, which according to a CIA interrogation manual, aims to exploit moments of "psychological shock or paralysis" that are caused by "a traumatic or sub-traumatic experience which explodes, as it were, the world that is familiar to the subject as well as his image of himself within that world."[111] Like the prevailing approach to war in the late 1990s—which would instruct U.S. military action for at least the next decade—*Armageddon* seems driven by the logic of trauma and an impulse to undo the spectator. It comes as little surprise, then, that reviews of the film also spoke the language of trauma.

The first depiction of disaster on Earth shows asteroid debris as it wreaks havoc on New York City. As the scene opens, citizens are busying themselves primarily in the pursuit of information and spectacle; they are reading newspapers and watching television coverage of a recent space shuttle disaster. With little warning, debris falls from space, disrupting this typical urban scene and violently grinding the city to a halt and a relative pulp. The streets become the site of carnage, piled high with devastated signifiers of modernity (cars and skyscrapers) and injured or dead bodies. The sequence ends with a long shot of a gaping hole in a city street, followed by an extreme long shot of the downtown skyline, in which both World Trade Center towers have been punctured by asteroid debris. Although both towers remain standing, one has had its top floors completely destroyed and appears injured, with smoke billowing out like blood from the cavity.[112]

This disaster sequence insists that such catastrophe is neither entirely new nor surprising. Like Heston's warning, "It happened before; it will happen again," the sequence alludes to its own longstanding cinematic history by referencing Godzilla. Seconds before the asteroid debris hits Earth, two minor characters quarrel over an inflatable Godzilla doll. An icon from one of the earliest and most enduring disaster film franchises, Godzilla has become associated with the historical trauma of war, images of urban destruction, and ambivalence about "modernity's gamble."[113] For example, in the eponymous 1954 film, directed by Ishirô Honda, Godzilla originates as the unforeseen outcome of atomic weapons testing; in turn, this by-product of human efforts comes to destroy Tokyo, one of Japan's biggest and most modern cities. Consequently, scholars often read the Godzilla films as addressing cultural memory about the traumas of World War II.[114]

Acknowledging *Armageddon*'s participation in a long-standing cinematic tradition of graphically dramatizing the destruction of civilization, this self-reflexive scene lays bare trauma culture and the peculiar pleasures of the disaster film—as further evidenced by the choice to cast Heston, a staple figure in the Vietnam-era disaster subgenre. (Heston starred in such films as *Omega Man* [Boris Sagal, 1971], *Skyjacked* [John Guillerman, 1972], *Airport 1975* [Jack Smight, 1974], and *Earthquake* [Mark Robson, 1974].) Hinting at its generic predecessors, *Armageddon* admits to disaster's capacity to fascinate or enthrall, asking its audience, whether wittingly or not, to recognize its own rather Bataillean participation in the spectacle of catastrophe.

In addition to signaling its generic past, this scene also acknowledges the currency of catastrophe in the American 1990s, during which a number of disaster films circulated, including, most significantly, another installation in the Godzilla franchise, *Godzilla* (Roland Emmerich, 1988). Released only two months before *Armageddon*, the 1998 *Godzilla* relocates the monster to New York City. Other films contributing to this cinematic disaster culture were *Independence Day* (Roland Emmerich, 1996) *Twister* (Jan de Bont, 1996), *Dante's Peak* (Roger Donalson, 1997), *Volcano* (Mick Jackson, 1997), and *Deep Impact* (Mimi Leder, 1998)—another sacrificial film, in which an aging astronaut, on board a space shuttle named *Messiah*, gives his life to save the world from an approaching comet.

At the same time that *Armageddon* fixates on the spectacle and entertainment value of catastrophe, this disaster sequence frames cataclysmic loss as rather mundane reality, especially for citizens of New York City. For example, two Japanese tourists, unaware of the asteroid attack, ask their cab driver why traffic is so slow. The rather indifferent cab driver responds, "Well, you know why . . . 'cause this is New York City. Anything coulda happened. Let me see, coulda been a terrorist bomb, dead body—somebody shot, stabbed. And, it's Friday, too, payday . . . somebody's probably jumped . . . didn't get their paycheck." The cab driver portrays disaster as nothing out of the ordinary, just another hazard of modern urbanity. His glib delivery of this laundry list of possible explanations for the gridlock—terrorism, murder, suicide—sounds as if it might be the sprightly speech of an urban tour guide, casually rattling off a list of atrocities that the "lucky" tourist might encounter on a trip to the big city.

Beyond anchoring this disaster scene to historically specific markers—namely, heightened discourse about the threat of terror following such events as the World Trade Center bombing in 1993 and the Oklahoma City bombing in 1995—the cab driver's rhetoric also demonstrates the ubiquity (or banality) of crisis language in public culture in the mid- to late 1990s. Given trauma's privileged position as the "coin of the realm," it makes a certain kind of sense that the cab driver would assume that tragedy was behind the gridlock—as opposed to any number of other less spectacular and less calamitous possibilities, such as road construction or a broken water main. What is more, the glib attitude with which he speculates about what "coulda" caused the traffic jam—homicidal mania or suicidal desperation—evokes the sensibility of a popular term at the time: "going postal."[115] Shorthand for describing extreme loss of self-control resulting in murderous workplace rage, what might be considered the 1990s version of "berserking," this comic phrase implies, with flippancy similar to that of the cabbie, that disaster has become commonplace, if not prosaic.

A paradox results: disaster operates as both a show-stopping spectacle (the narrative *halts* multiple times to *show* scenes of catastrophe and their witnesses) and a banal recurrence (the narrative halts *multiple times* to show scenes of catastrophe and their witnesses.) This paradox also mirrors an unresolved tension at the heart of trauma discourse. On one hand, trauma is framed as an unspeakable shock so anomalous and singular that it annihilates consciousness. On the other hand, at certain moments, trauma discourse pervades public culture so much that it becomes part of vernacular speech, as in Lim's casual, even facetious, description of the film as "pointlessly traumatizing," or as in the popularization of the abbreviation PTSD.[116] This parallel matters for multiple reasons.

First, it lends insight into the logic of trauma discourse. For the notion of traumatic injury to maintain its cultural capital, trauma must be perceived as striking and demanding attention. It must be, like the asteroid, an anomaly. Or, in the language of Harlan and Wade's doctrine of rapid domination, it must produce shock and awe. In order to maintain this discursive hegemony, however, trauma must also assert its own prevalence. Also like the asteroid, it must be capable of striking anywhere at any time, its impacts imagined as inevitable. Striking what Bataille describes as the "double current of panic" and "indifference," this paradox illustrates Seltzer's description of the "abnormal normality of trauma," in which injury is "represented as at once an horrific departure from normalcy and as abnormally normal: wounds to an idealized and intact American culture that is at the same time seen *as* a wound culture."[117]

Second, this parallel also points toward the film's larger conflation of "disaster" (understood here as massive, large-scale catastrophe) and "trauma" that is consistent with the logic of most sacrificial films. As Bataille noted in his essay on Hiroshima, some events (those perceived to be spectacular in size and number) are registered publicly as more traumatic than others (those that happen quietly, commonly, even daily); what results is an implicit hierarchy in which certain experiences or events (and therefore certain victims) are understood to matter more in public discourse.[118] In the logic of trauma discourse, not all traumas are created equal; that is, not all traumas are traumas. As Brown reminds us, this inequity often means that events affecting those in positions of privilege tend to count more than those affecting the disenfranchised or marginalized.[119]

As if to confirm Brown's argument, most of the agreed-upon traumas in *Armageddon* take place in the public eye, for all to see. *Armageddon*'s emphasis on hyperbolic scenes of large-scale disaster implies that the destruction of major centers of global capital should be understood as paramount signifiers of traumatic loss. *Armageddon* offers views of small towns and rural villages only as the *witnesses* of trauma, as in multiple scenes in which rural people are positioned outside the epicenter of trauma, glued to their television sets, and unable to believe their eyes. These scenes of urban catastrophe register not only the quantity of loss but also the perceived quality, or symbolic significance, of loss. Demonstrated by the visual fixation on the destruction of such landmarks as the World Trade Center towers and the Eiffel Tower, these scenes reaffirm the perceived links between modernity, large spectacles, and trauma. Quite literally, *Armageddon*'s comparative calculations insist that for trauma to matter it must be monumental.

Armageddon also sustains Brown's argument that public discourse most often defines "trauma" as it relates to men. Private or inconspicuous traumas seem to matter in this film only when they happen to men. This belief is demonstrated by dialogue that reinforces such hierarchies along normative gender lines. When Harry's only daughter, Grace, reacts to news of the asteroid's trajectory by exclaiming, "This is unbelievable," Truman responds condescendingly, "Actually, this is as real as it gets." In addition to reenacting the concurrent construction of trauma as something that is, on the one hand, shocking and "unbelievable" and, on the other, commonplace and "as real as it gets," this dialogue also reveals the film's gendering of trauma.

Brown argues that "'real' trauma is often only that form of trauma in which the dominant group can participate as a victim rather than as the perpetrator

Figure 14. Horrified but enthralled citizens watching television news about the impending asteroid impact. *Armageddon* (Touchstone Pictures)

or etiologist of the trauma."[120] Catastrophe is something that the young, female Grace just can't "get," but "real" trauma is something that Truman and the mostly male crew he sends to the asteroid understand all too well. While the implications of trauma might be perceived as feminizing—victims are undone and rendered passive or, in the language of Ullman and Wade, impotent—it is an experience that appears to belong only to men and to require the efforts of men to undo.

A Few Not-So-Good Men

Armageddon engages the Bataillean notion of self-loss through the narrative's depiction of a group of wounded and unhinged men who face the pending threat of global destruction and at the same time must manage the wreckage of their own lives. *Armageddon* has an ensemble cast, but this cast is almost exclusively male, figuring men as the primary victims of, witnesses to, and solutions for traumatic suffering. The diverse group of men pulled from Harry's oil rig in the middle of the ocean constantly verges on falling apart and is typically one step away from disasters—both personal and public.

Realizing the asteroid may be a "global killer" that portends "the end of mankind," engineer Dan Truman calls on a group of uninhibited outcasts who are neither trained as astronauts nor disciplined as soldiers but are left largely to their own reckless devices. Lichtenfeld notes that "Truman vetoes anything that sounds like actual science and denigrates anyone who resembles an actual scientist, at least in comparison to the cowboy-soldiers" who will *man* the space shuttles.[121] When the film introduces oilman Harry Stamper, he is hitting golf balls off his oil rig toward Greenpeace activists who are protesting against drilling. Stationed in the South China Sea—near the birthplace of Godzilla—Harry performs himself as a renegade. Although his last name clearly marks the side of the rig, which reads "Stamper Oil" and signals Harry as a successful mogul, this scene also connects Harry's rebellious side to what might be considered rugged working-class machismo. He may be a big name in the oil industry, but he remains one of the roughnecks—not afraid to get his hands dirty or to blow off steam, as demonstrated when he works alongside his employees to control an unexpected gush of oil.

In the next sequence, Harry shoots at his employee and surrogate son A. J. (Ben Affleck), whom he discovers in bed with Grace. Running wildly around the rig, Harry aims to kill A. J. for what he perceives as a violation of his daughter's innocence. This line of action matters for a number of reasons. First, Harry's discovery that Grace has taken up with A. J. signals his potential displacement as the man in her life. Harry has lost his position of patriarchal authority over his daughter; she refuses, for example, to call him "Dad" and declares, "You can't control my life."

As Grace defends her autonomy to her "immature father," she cites the absence of her mother, who left when Grace was a child, as proof of her independence. Later, Grace assures Harry, "I don't blame you for my mother leaving. She left us both." These brief allusions to Harry's status as an abandoned husband and single dad mark him as displaced and alienated, constructing this loss as a trauma that haunts Harry. He may be "the world's best deep core driller," a job description rife with phallic logic, but he appears to have struggled as a husband, a dad, and a boss. Harry's interactions with Grace also introduce his sensitive side, which he displays in tandem with his tendency toward macho bravado.

Second, Harry's violence toward A. J. also marks him as unhinged. Like the "rogue comet" that Truman describes as turning the asteroid belt into "shrapnel" aimed directly at Earth, Harry is out of control and on a collision course with disaster. In "going postal," Harry embodies Farrell's notion of the berserk style and recalls contemporary discourse about workplace rage. Farrell argues that berserk behavior "entails interpretation" and thus becomes "richly ambiguous." While a berserk state might signify "chaotic madness," it can also "signify exceptional valor and stamina."[122] Harry's berserk style is used variably in the film: first, as an amusing sign of Harry's idiosyncrasy, and later, as confirmation of the belief that "in an unjust, rigid society, the lone individual can solve problems only by reckless daring."[123] The scene in which Harry chases A. J. illustrates the former use of the berserk style and, like the cab driver's rather flip attitude toward disaster, is lighthearted in tone, playing *almost* (but not quite) for comic relief.

Armageddon celebrates Harry as an unruly underdog, offering his outburst as evidence of his likeability and suitability as a hero. His droll antics lay the groundwork for interpreting him as a protagonist whose triumph depends upon what Farrell describes as the "heroic defiance of banal inhibitions." Although Harry makes a spectacle of himself—illustrating the berserk style's penchant for "theatricality"—this scene contributes to the film's overall argument that we should expect such risky, defiant behavior from a hero.[124] It is precisely his irreverence and "uncompromising integrity" that make Harry an effective leader when all others around him fail because they play by the rules.[125]

Constructions of Harry as wounded and slightly unhinged mirror depictions of other men in the ensemble cast, including Harry's rowdy team of deep-core drillers and the physically and psychically scarred Truman. Multiple montage sequences highlight the roughnecks' shortcomings. Called "a bunch of retards," labeled "unfit," and told that no "viable subjects" exist among them, the crew has amassed a collection of police records, bad habits, and checkered pasts that might also be called baggage. Rockhound (Steve Buscemi) is an engineer afflicted with what appears to be a sex addiction, Chick (Wil Patton) is a deadbeat dad with a gambling problem, and A. J. is an orphan. The character of Bear (Michael Clark Duncan) crystallizes this construction of the crew members.

The only African American member of Harry's crew, Bear (as his name suggests) appears to conform to traditional expectations for hard-bodied masculinity. Tall, broad, and rippled with muscles, he rides motorcycles through the desert and enjoys danger. But this apparent bastion of traditional masculinity is also the quickest to break down during the medical and psychiatric examinations the crew members are subjected to in order to determine their fitness as astronauts. During his exam (the rectal exam, in particular), Bear strips down to his leopard-print underwear, stands on an exam table, and begins to dance, violating traditional gender norms. Flaunting his muscular physique, Bear adopts a position typically associated with female bodies: an exotic and erotic object on display. Like Harry on the oil rig, Bear makes a spectacle of himself, a scene he will repeat during a psychological exam.

The psychological exam sequence intercuts shots of each crew member with a NASA psychiatrist. The exams provoke discomfort in the would-be astronauts to measure their stability and their capacity for handling stress. Every roughneck fails, with the most dramatic failure belonging to Bear, whose exam produces an emotional meltdown. Sobbing and crying, Bear confesses, "I am not crazy. I'm just a little emotional right now. . . . After this is over, can I get a hug or something?" In speech patterns and mannerisms that pantomime traditionally feminine traits, Bear becomes hysterical. His need to, as his examiner says, "let it out," suggests that, according to NASA's logic, he may not have what it takes to survive in space. Instead of the restraint, discipline, and rather blind adherence to rules that characterize the "real" astronauts, Bear cannot be contained.

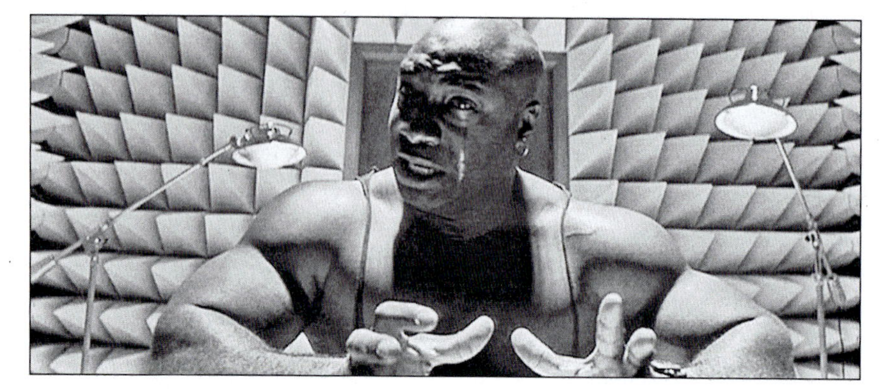

Figure 15. Bear breaking down during his psychological exam. *Armageddon* (Touchstone Pictures)

As much as Bear's conspicuous performance might suggest a departure from the norms that govern hegemonic masculinity, the film's willful objectification of his body and his willingness to "let it go" during his psychological exam recall the impulse in 1990s-era America to emphasize masculinity's alleged injuries and crisis. Although the tone of this film, which addresses the very serious subject of apocalypse with a not-so-serious attitude, comes nowhere near the anguished tenor of Bataille's discussion of his torture photographs, trauma envy saturates *Armageddon*'s fascination with the prospect of these men's undoing. Even though it casts Bear's spectacles as anomalies, *Armageddon* illustrates the extent to which scenes of the male body in pain have become routine in U.S. public culture.

In the culture of sacrificial films, the greatest anomaly in the case of Bear is not his tendency toward breakdowns or "theatricality" but his race, for such films typically fetishize the *white* male body. Bear's breakdown is played entirely for comic relief, while much of the suffering of white men (especially that of Harry) is used for sentimentalized and redemptive ends. Bear's hysteria makes the emotionality of his white male companions seem minimal by comparison. While all of the men might be classified as unfit and at risk for "snapping," none seems *as* unhinged as Bear. Just as Cal's and Rose's breakdowns contrast with Jack's aplomb in *Titanic*, the comedic portrayal of Bear serves as a foil for the other roughnecks, who can lay claim to *some* psychic instability and emotionality without appearing *too* far gone.[126]

Armageddon also contrasts the roughnecks with the impersonal, unfeeling military and NASA personnel. While Harry's men can "let it out," their hyper-disciplined counterparts blindly obey protocol. These purely procedural and mission-oriented figures remain split off from emotions or matters of the heart, as epitomized by Colonel Willie Sharp (William Fichtner). As he leads training exercises prior to the space shuttle launches and commands the mission in space, Sharp strives to manage, discipline, and even eradicate the roughnecks' unruly emotions.

Sharp's training sequences aim to make sure the roughnecks don't "freak out" (or go berserk) on the asteroid, miming the logic of rapid dominance by exposing the crew members to rapid, overwhelming physical and psychological shocks. Describing the crew as the "wrong stuff," Sharp publicly laments, "This is about the sorriest group of people I've seen in all my military career."[127] Later, as if to confirm Sharp's fears and reinforce the cultural fascination with mental instability, Rockhound loses his mind and develops "space dementia." He goes berserk and fires weapons wildly on the asteroid in another (hyperbolic but comedic) example of workplace rage that recalls Harry's earlier violence toward A. J. on the oil rig.

As Sharp prepares the neophytes, he describes what they will experience as a "brutal assault on all your senses." Sharp depicts this training, in Bataillean fashion, as aimed at keeping its subjects in the "orbit of the senses."[128] Warning his trainees, "When you squeal, I'm just gonna go faster and harder," Sharp imagines emotionality and expressiveness as embarrassing displays that deserve punishment. The men in Harry's roughneck crew have very different sensibilities; they take pride in occasionally unleashing their crude and/or emotional selves, which (like the oil discovered on Harry's rig) seem apt to blow at any moment. In fact, the version of masculine subjectivity *Armageddon* advocates counterbalances sensitivity and emotional release with aggressive physicality and salvific authority.[129]

Armageddon mirrors *Titanic*'s construction of working-class masculinity as both tougher and more sensitive than competing versions of the masculine. The film constructs three versions of masculinity: NASA engineers who are all brains (as evidenced by the fact that two NASA scientists are only credited as "Dr. Nerd"), astronauts and military men who are uncompromising and routinized machines, and roughnecks who are robust both physically and emotionally. As in *Titanic*, where only working-class Jack can appropriately (and artistically) express his emotions, in *Armageddon*, the entire roughneck crew is soft around the edges. For example, Harry alternates phallic commands to his crew—"Dig, dig, dig. Chew this iron bitch up"—with plaintive entreaties to a higher power—"Come on, God, just a little help. That's all I'm asking."[130] In contrast, the NASA astronauts and military personnel on the ground remain mechanistic, incapable of expressing emotion or empathy and attentive only to matters of protocol.

This narrative emphasis on the conflicts among various men operates allegorically, animating mid- to late 1990s trauma discourse about the "crisis of masculinity," the threat of national disintegration, and the allegedly fractious implications of identity politics. *Armageddon* performs the nation as "crippled by 'division and resentment,'" as paralyzed by dissent, and as undone by competing world views. In response to such alleged injuries to the collective, *Armageddon* enacts a kind of "repair" for this wounded nation through the dramatization of the men's attempts to come together. As the roughnecks and astronauts learn to work together, the film allegorically dramatizes and fulfills what Biesecker describes as an alleged "need for national reunification."[131] The logic of the narrative mirrors that at work in President Clinton's commemoration of the World War II memorial, which he described as a "permanent reminder of just how much we Americans can do when we work together instead of fighting among ourselves."[132]

In this regard, the use of Heston's voice in the opening narration becomes significant on yet another level. Although Heston was known at the time of *Omega Man*'s release as a left-wing civil rights activist, he was known at the time of *Armageddon*'s release as a conservative figure in the culture wars. Frequently identifying himself as a veteran of World War II, Heston publicly critiqued identity politics, multiculturalism, and affirmative action, which in 1999 he warned would "hijack" Americans' freedom of expression and impose a tyranny of "political correctness."[133] Heston was elected as president of the National Rifle Association in 1998, and, according to Dominic Pulera, often defended "white males as a group."[134] His presence in this film thus invokes a critical attitude toward identity politics, which *Armageddon* constructs as damaging and fracturing the social body.

The roughnecks and astronauts successfully get over their differences and learn to get along. At the film's end, Harry, who once tried to kill A. J., calls him a "son" and sanctions his union with Grace; likewise Harry and Sharp's once violent disagreements about how to handle protocol (they pulled guns on one another in the struggle over whether or not to detonate the nuclear warhead) gives way to mutual trust and admiration, as evidenced by Sharp's later validation of Harry as "the bravest man I know." The joining of this group, therefore, allegorically enacts the reunification of the nation, at the same time that it sets apart—or separates out—the wounded roughnecks as special or ideal citizen-subjects.

The Truman Show

The only NASA expert to bond immediately with Harry is Truman, who demonstrates intelligence, strength, *and* emotionality, differing from his NASA peers because he is wounded. A physical impairment, revealed by a close-up shot of a brace on his foot, prevents Truman from realizing his lifelong dream of becoming an astronaut. Doubly scarred by his physical injury and the psychological hurt of a dream unfulfilled, Truman remains an on-the-ground engineer; but unlike most of the personnel at NASA and in the military,

Truman has heart to accompany his brains. Frequently breaking rules and resisting protocol, Truman mirrors Harry's profound sense of alienation (not to mention impotence) and special wisdom—the kind that Lifton assigned to the Vietnam veteran and that was associated with the veterans of the "Good War."

Truman also has access to the deep emotional wells of his oil-rigging companions. For instance, the night before the shuttle launch, Harry and Truman engage in intimate conversation about their deferred dreams and tough choices. Explaining his unfulfilled longing to experience space and to wear a mission patch, Truman recalls Harry's heartbreak and feelings of abandonment. Truman never overcomes his impotence but achieves restoration and redemption as the renegade engineer behind Harry's salvific mission. When the remaining crew returns from space after successfully diverting the asteroid, A. J. repays Truman's loyalty with a gift from Harry: the sacrificial victim-hero's patch that, through his death, symbolically fulfills Truman's desire for space travel and consummates his recuperative (and homoerotic) bond with Harry.[135] This gesture also ensures the continuation of Harry's sacrificial legacy, creating transgenerational bonds between Harry, A. J., and Truman. Like the final scenes of *Omega Man* and *Poseidon Adventure*, *Armageddon* inaugurates a new lineage of men emboldened, ennobled, and unified by shared experiences of terror and loss. Each text passes on the legacy of traumatic heroism through the spiritual kinship between and exclusive lines of descent among men.

In addition to creating new lineages, *Armageddon* emphasizes cultural memory about previous sacrificial heroism. Rife with historical references to U.S. military history and World War II, *Armageddon* participates in the almost hagiographic treatment of the "Greatest Generation," using narratives about past American sacrifices as frames for making sense of its present-day traumas and struggles for redemption. The first of these references can be found (barely) hidden in the names of the narrative's leading men, Harry Stamper and Dan Truman, whose names—when taken together—suggest an allusion to Harry S. Truman, the thirty-third president of the United States. Although President Truman's decision to drop atomic bombs on Hiroshima and Nagasaki has itself been considered a historical trauma of astronomical proportions (as Bataille himself reminds us), *Armageddon* contributes to the discursive redemption of World War II as the "Good War" by linking the historical figure of President Harry S. Truman to Harry Stamper and Dan Truman—two wounded, irreverent, and selfless heroes that sacrifice their own well-being in order to save others. Before Harry gives up his life to save Earth from the asteroid attack, Dan Truman risks ruining his career (and potentially being charged with treason) to prevent the president of the United States from using nuclear force against the asteroid.

Historical references to and rehabilitations of cultural memory about President Truman, therefore, also shape *Armageddon*'s diegetic president.

Addressing the global community, the president of the United States triumphantly asserts, "Everything that can be done to prevent this disaster is being called into service. All of our combined modern technologies and imaginations—even the wars that we've fought—have provided us with the tools to wage this terrible battle." This speech alludes to cultural memory about President Truman and the decision to use nuclear weaponry. In fact, this speech seems modeled quite precisely on a statement Truman issued only moments after the *Enola Gay* dropped the atomic bomb on Hiroshima, in which he praised the bomb as "the greatest achievement of organized science in history." Celebrating the collaborations of industrialists and scientists under the direction of the U.S. Army, President Truman stated, "It is doubtful if such another combination could be got together in the world."[136]

The rhetorical fetishization of technology also governs the film's heavy reliance on cinematic technology and special effects. While the film's use of combative effects might be understood as undermining spectatorial stability, this use of technology also illustrates the film's totalizing drive toward mastery. Similar to Marita Sturken's discussion of many Hollywood films about the Vietnam War, the "fetishizing of technology in the actual film productio[n]" of *Armageddon* reifies the imagined relationship between "masculinity and technology."[137] These Vietnam war films reinforce the "technological spectacle of combat" in "battle scenes [that] are beautifully and thrillingly staged."[138] Likewise, *Armageddon*'s reliance on big-budget special effects makes disaster a captivating and awe-inspiring sight to be seen and asserts the masculinist authority of cinematic technology.[139]

The president's speech in *Armageddon* also casts trauma as transformative and productive. He claims, "Through all the chaos that is our history, through all of the wrongs and the discord, through all the pain and suffering, through all of our times, there is one thing that has nourished our souls and elevated our species above its origins, and that is our courage." In addition to shots of the "citizens of humanity" that are allegedly united by the courage of the "fourteen brave souls traveling into the heavens," this sequence dramatizes the reunification of the nuclear family. Just as disaster brings Harry and Grace closer, the once-deadbeat dad Chick is reunited with his estranged family. As his son watches the launch on television, his mother reveals his father's true identity. Once a stranger, Chick's willingness to sacrifice himself to save the world proves that he can be a good father.

As much as *Armageddon* relies on history, it also rewrites it, revising President Truman's recourse to nuclear weaponry. After losing contact with the crews on the asteroid, the diegetic president must decide whether or not to detonate the nuclear warhead on the asteroid remotely and, in consequence, kill the space shuttle crews. This decision replays *and* significantly revises Truman's choice to use atomic force during World War II. Like the historical

Truman, the president in *Armageddon* decides to use nuclear weaponry in order to prevent future destruction; but, unlike his extratextual namesake, Dan Truman rejects this decision. Through subterfuge and a potentially treasonous violation of protocol that confirms his likeness to Harry, Truman stops the remote detonation in order to give the roughnecks more time.

When NASA reactivates the remote detonation that Truman had temporarily stalled, *Armageddon* enacts another revision of history, refusing the use of nuclear weapons a second time. With a characteristic combination of masculinist and sentimental rhetoric, Harry convinces Colonel Sharp to disengage the bomb. First, he compels Sharp to give him another try by asserting his professional expertise, claiming, "I have never, never missed a depth that I have aimed for and, by God, I am not going to miss this one." Then Harry makes a pathos-laden appeal, calling on his emotional authority as a father and his promise to his "little girl" that he would be "coming home." Harry's insistence on keeping his promise to his daughter sets the stage for another of *Armageddon*'s many historical allusions.

Harry makes this promise to Grace during an earlier scene shot on location at the launch platform of the ill-fated *Apollo 1*, converted (as it is in reality) into a memorial honoring the mission crew that features two plaques.[140] At this monumental site, Grace absolves her father of his guilt over her mother's absence, and Harry promises to come home to his daughter. Punctuating this highly emotional conversation between father and daughter, a close-up emphasizes the second of the two plaques, which reads, "In memory of those who made the ultimate sacrifice so others could reach for the stars."[141] This reference to the *Apollo 1* matters for two reasons.

First, it illustrates *Armageddon*'s recourse to cultural memory as a frame for making sense of its own narrative. Placing Harry as a beneficiary of this lineage

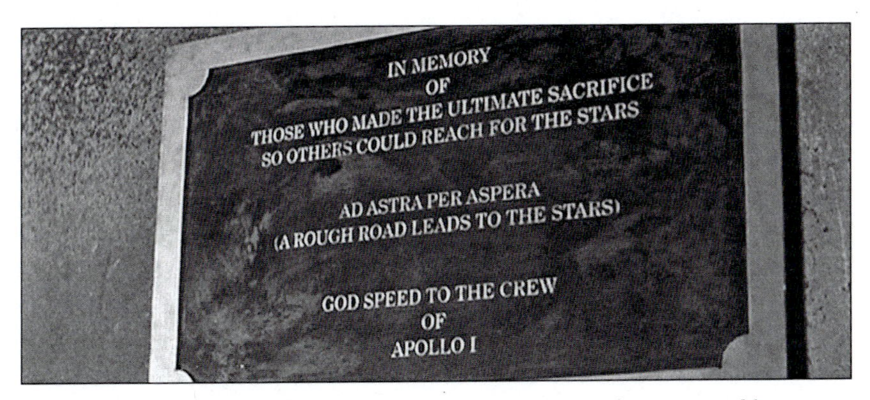

Figure 16. A plaque on the *Apollo 1* memorial honoring sacrifice. *Armageddon* (Touchstone Pictures)

of men who gave their lives for the sake of others, this scene contributes to the contemporary canonization of historical figures as both evidence of U.S. exceptionalism and as grounds for national reunification. Asserting a debt of gratitude to and continuity with these figures from the past, this scene forges bonds between the citizens of today and the heroes of yesterday. Like *Titanic* and *Saving Private Ryan*, *Armageddon* returns to hallowed ground to persuade the nation to forgive past injuries, recognize commonalities, and come together. Second, this scene emphasizes and validates the logic of sacrifice as *the* antidote to trauma. Although it mourns the "memory of those who made the ultimate sacrifice," the plaque also promises that sacrifice will yield productive results: ensuring that "others could reach for the stars." Harry's unexpected mission into space offers proof of such achievement, but his trip into space is also proof that like trauma, sacrifice must also be repeated. This scene foretells not only the inevitability of disaster but also the necessity of sacrifice.

Harry Is the Man

After Harry convinces Sharp to dismantle the nuclear warhead, he and his crew resume digging on the asteroid. When they reach their required depth, they realize that the bomb can no longer be detonated remotely. The remaining members of the crew draw straws to decide who will travel into the belly of the asteroid to engage the bomb manually. Having pulled the shortest straw, A. J. accepts his fate, remarking, "Everybody's gotta die, right? I'm the guy that gets to do it saving the world." Harry escorts A. J. and the nuclear warhead off the space shuttle and then forcibly takes A. J.'s place. Harry directs A. J. to take care of his "little girl" and approves of their marriage, acknowledging his displacement as the most important man in Grace's life and sanctioning a new familial line. Seconds before dying, Harry speaks to Grace via satellite in a conversation that is also broadcast on dozens of screens in mission control. The depiction of Harry's sacrificial death as spectacle to be witnessed confirms the film's treatment of heroic sacrifice as the ultimate, most monumental form of trauma.

Once the space shuttle is safely off the asteroid, Harry detonates the bomb. In that instant, an extreme close-up of his eye precedes a rapid montage of images from Harry's mind. Exaggerating the film's "shock and awe" editing techniques, this sequence of images becomes an almost indecipherable onslaught of fragments (or shrapnel). Combining Harry's past memories of Grace with visions of the future, this sequence performs both the ambivalence of trauma and Bataillean constructions of the sovereign subject. On the one hand, this rapid montage of intrusive, disruptive, disorienting images reenacts the structure of trauma. They come without narrative and seem to possess Harry as if he is (re)experiencing these moments; they also temporarily take the film text hostage, halting its forward progress.

On the other hand, these images also allow Harry to see Grace mature as a woman, glimpsing her on the wedding day he will not actually live to experience. (Harry's imagined picture of his daughter on her wedding day resembles exactly what audiences will see in the final shots of the film.) Harry seems endowed with a heightened (almost supernatural) version of the prescience that Jack enjoys at the end of *Titanic*; so totalizing is his vision that he can actually see into the future. Rapidly intercutting shots of Harry's and Grace's faces, this sequence also asserts that Harry's legacy will continue past his death. Just as Jack lives on through Rose, *Armageddon* implies that Harry will live on through Grace. Transcending the limitations of life and death, past and future, self and other, Harry is everywhere and nowhere at once, in contact with all that exceeds him.

Diegetic witnesses likewise interpret Harry's death as evidence of his unique and authoritative status as a masculinist subject. Watching his death and exalting Harry for his sacrifice, Bear proclaims, "Harry, you the man." This phrase expresses colloquially what Carolyn Dean describes as the masculinist logic of Bataille's theory of self-loss, which "guarantees manhood, paradoxically, through an eroticized castration."[142] Quite overtly, Harry's "loss of self is lived as the constituent moment of selfhood."[143] Harry's death constitutes him as a subject, a man—or, more precisely, *the* subject, *the* man. If before he had merely been a roughneck and an immature father, Harry is now confirmed, through trauma, as a hero beyond reproach and second to none.

Bear's use of this phrase is the second time that Harry receives such a designation by another man marked as racially other. In Harry's first scene, a Japanese investor visits the rig; as Harry and A. J. manage a sudden and unexpected eruption of oil, the Japanese businessman inappropriately declares, "Harry, you a man!" This innocent mistake in a colloquial phrase (substituting "a" for "the") underscores the sacrificial logic at work in the film. Harry may be "a" man all along, but he is not "the" man until he succumbs to (or is subjected to) traumatic heroism.

The global community echoes Bear's reverent response. Audiences around the world watch as the shuttle returns safely to Earth. The crowds cheer, their eyes and hands raised upward to the heavens. Friends, family members, and strangers hug one another, coming together in harmony. Small children celebrate, playing with their own NASA-emblazoned toy shuttles; a shot of a small-town mural adorned with the face of President John F. Kennedy celebrates, "Peace, Life, Hope." These shots of a joyous, unified global population furthers the prevailing discourse that urged Americans to get over their differences and just "get along," and this integrated and synchronous global village confirms fantasies of a collective that is made whole and innocent (again), not despite *but because of* trauma.

Armageddon ends with A. J. and Grace's reunion, and the final shot of the film is a photo finish ending of a kiss between the two lovers (until the credit

Figure 17. The photo-finish ending depicting A. J. and Grace's reunion after Harry's death. *Armageddon* (Touchstone Pictures)

sequence, which depicts home movies from their wedding that mirror exactly what Harry had already predicted). Having received Harry's blessing, A. J. and Grace create something new from the ruins of the past and carry on Harry's legacy. Like *Omega Man*, this final shot, which is itself frozen and fixed in time but nonetheless depicts the survivors' moving-on process, constructs trauma as an end and a beginning and illustrates the concurrent but contradictory impulses in American wound culture to hang on to traumatic loss *and* to let go—to repeat in a "melancholic feedback loop" and mournfully but reverently to "ge[t] time moving again."[144]

Coda

Both *Titanic* and *Armageddon* appeared at the crest of the 1990s wave of sacrificial films, which peaked in 1996–1998 with the successive releases of *Independence Day, Braveheart, Titanic, Armageddon*, and *Saving Private Ryan*. After that, this cycle of sacrificial films gradually waned. Interestingly, *Pearl Harbor* (Michael Bay, 2001), which has been described as a hybrid of *Titanic* and *Armageddon*, appeared as a coda to this cycle of sacrificial films.[145] *Pearl Harbor* merits discussion not only because it compulsively replays its cinematic progenitors but also because of its uncanny timing.

Released in May 2001, *Pearl Harbor* arrived on the eve of the 9/11 attacks, which would themselves be likened to the actual events at Pearl Harbor in December of 1941.[146] Following 9/11, the trauma discourse and crisis rhetoric that characterized so much of the 1990s was simultaneously amplified and recentered, focusing less on a diffuse and pervasive "white male paranoia" and more specifically on fears of terrorism and national emasculation at the hands of an outside Other. If 1990s trauma discourse posited the masculinity of embodied men as being in crisis, then its post-9/11 successor worried about the masculinity of the nation itself. Trauma discourse did not abate in the aftermath of what has been called the worst attack on U.S. soil, but the cinematic trope of sacrifice did recede—at least temporarily—as if the perceived traumas of sacrifice were too close, too raw (or "real") to be redemptive.

Rather than celebrating traumatic heroism, the films released shortly after 9/11 illustrate a more triumphal and masterful tone, as if disavowing the "end of victory culture."[147] Framing violence "in an uplifting and encouraging way," these films make use of the second Bush administration's rhetoric of national resiliency and agency and offer depictions of the nation as unflappable and unharmed.[148] Heroes in such films not only save the world but save themselves as well. Also conspicuously absent from the initial responses to 9/11, as Marcia Landy observes, was any discussion of the Vietnam War, "as if that event were expunged from American history." Instead, public rhetoric favored attention to "national unity" and America's "divine mission" as constructed in relation to the nation's "Good War," not its failed one.[149] Cinematic depictions of self-sacrifice and noble death began to reemerge only belatedly and, significantly, in the midst of increasingly critical public discourse about the nation's response to 9/11 and the controversial "War on Terror." As evidence of national vulnerability met with accusations of overzealous military machismo, the trope of traumatic heroism began to operate once again as a particularly deft tool for negotiating the nation's troubled status as a victim *and* a hero.

CHAPTER 4

REMAKES, RESURRECTIONS, AND SACRIFICIAL RETURNS

"The dominant cultural imaginary of the United States has been shaped, in part, by fantasies of impregnability and invincibility, and, dreadful as these events themselves were, it was also the puncturing of these fantasies that contributed to the shock of September 11." —Susannah Radstone

On the first anniversary of 9/11, the city of New York hosted a series of commemorative events that included speeches by prominent U.S. figures. With the exception of President George W. Bush, who debuted a new speech, mayor Michael Bloomberg asked speakers to deliver canonical texts from U.S. history. New York governor George Pataki recited Abraham Lincoln's Gettysburg Address, New Jersey governor Jim McGreevey delivered the preamble and introduction to the Declaration of Independence, and Bloomberg read excerpts from Franklin D. Roosevelt's Four Freedoms speech.

While Bloomberg framed his decision to mark the occasion in this way as his attempt to "avoid any possibility of politicizing" the memorializations of 9/11, this choice might also be understood as an example of displacement, shifting consideration of the perceived traumas of 9/11 onto memories of past events that are easier to bear as part of national history.[1] Returning to prior experiential frames is a strategy frequently resorted to in U.S. public culture, in this case through events that seek to remember and reconstruct 9/11 and its aftermath.[2]

For instance, rhetoric about Pearl Harbor framed 9/11 as an event that both scarred and unified the nation.[3] Although rhetoric about the Vietnam War was noticeably absent in the immediate aftermath of 9/11, it later resurfaced as a critical frame for discussing 9/11 and the War on Terror, as exemplified by Senator Edward Kennedy's assertion in April of 2004 that "Iraq is George Bush's Vietnam."[4] Post-9/11 Hollywood also performed a return to history, remaking and adapting multiple Vietnam-era films as experiential frames for constructing and interpreting American trauma culture, including *Poseidon* (Wolfgang Petersen, 2006) and *I Am Legend* (Francis Lawrence, 2007), which remake, respectively, *The Poseidon Adventure* (Ronald Neame, 1972) and *Omega Man* (Boris Sagal, 1971).[5]

Poseidon and *I Am Legend* were part of a new wave of sacrificial films that crested around the fifth anniversary of 9/11. Other post-9/11 sacrificial films include *Ladder 49* (Jay Russell, 2004), which focuses on the lives of New York City firefighters but makes no overt reference to 9/11; *King Arthur* (Antoine Fuqua, 2004), which returns to a mythic past to glorify self-loss on the battlefield; *V for Vendetta* (James McTeigue, 2005), which offers a critique of a totalitarian nation-state but valorizes self-sacrifice as a heroic act; *The Omen* (John Moore, 2006), a re-make of a Vietnam-era film, which uses a hero's death to stop the Antichrist; *The Guardian* (Andrew Davis, 2006), which culminates with the final and fatal mission of a beloved but beleaguered coast guard rescuer; *300* (Zack Snyder, 2006), another period film focused on wartime sacrifice and traumatic battlefield heroics; *Blood Diamond* (Edward Zwick, 2006), a drama about a mercenary diamond smuggler who learns compassion and gives up his life; and *30 Days of Night*, (David Slade, 2007), a horror film about a victim-hero that sacrifices himself in a fight against vampires. These sacrificial allegories offer narratives of traumatic loss and recovery as frames for constructing 9/11 and what might be called the nation's "berserk" response via the War on Terror.

Reopening Old Wounds

Almost immediately after the attacks, public discourse figured 9/11 as a national trauma, as exemplified by Wolfgang Schivelbusch's description of the "strike against the twin towers" (in an epilogue aptly titled "On Falling") as "far more traumatic" than a typical military attack, having destabilized the nation's sense of self through the destruction of American symbols of "power, control, hardship, and mastery."[6] The *New York Times* similarly figured the nation itself as injured in dozens of articles. On September 13, 2001, Erica Goode's article "Trauma, Felt Directly or Not, Takes a Psychic Toll" posits a unified and uniform "we," framing American identity as a collective experience. Quoting Dr. Andrew Baum, a University of Pittsburgh professor of psychiatry and psychology, Goode reports, "These events all take a toll on *our* innocence, on *our* sense of vulnerability and on *our* ability to deal with the world."[7]

In another article, Goode, one of the most prolific *Times* writers on the subject of trauma, vividly describes America's devastation. "Some will be unable to grieve normally, their mourning stalled in a mental canyon where screams still echo. Some will be too fearful to walk down the street. Some will take pills. Some will empty bottles of Scotch. Some will simply topple into despair."[8]

Like so much trauma discourse, this picture of the nation's grieving, desperate citizen-subjects summons the image of a fall. Positioning the nation on the edge of a precipice, this image recalls images of the falling Twin Towers, for in the post-9/11 context the already robust significance of "the fall" as a signifier of trauma garnered new force.[9]

If trauma was said to push some citizens over the edge, it was also said to draw others together. For example, one *New York Times* article emphasized the bonds and new communities born of shared suffering. Describing the reunion of two survivors—coming together, embracing one another, and laughing for the first time in weeks—this article recalls Bataille's understanding of anguish as enabling "communication between beings" and the consequent "formation of new beings."[10] The article's image of two women falling into one another's arms, connected and reborn through anguish, resonates with *Time* magazine's description of the city immediately following the attacks: "There were no strangers in town anymore, only sudden friends, sharing names, news and phones."[11]

Another *New York Times* article entitled "The Psychiatrist in the House Feels the Nation's Trauma" (a title that recalls President Clinton's therapeutic "I feel your pain") constructs Representative Jim McDermott of Washington as yet another paralyzed survivor unable to "get his mind off of the image of a plane crashing into the World Trade Center." Citing his own experiential authority as a psychiatrist in Vietnam, McDermott describes himself as suffering from post-traumatic stress disorder after the 9/11 attacks. Similarly diagnosing the nation as a whole, McDermott asserts, "This whole country is going through that horrible experience."[12] McDermott credits his past experiences in Vietnam as enabling him to help others through "community meetings," akin to Vietnam-era "rap groups," aimed at uniting survivors through shared experiences of terror and loss.[13]

Constructions of national trauma also frequently gendered America's alleged injuries. Illustrating Susannah Radstone's contention that "an event's traumatic impact may be linked to its *puncturing* of a fantasy that has previously sustained a sense of identity—national as well as individual," this rhetoric constructs the perceived traumas of 9/11 as disrupting the dominant masculinist fiction of American "impregnability or invincibility" with the metaphorical castration of purported symbols of American superiority and phallic mastery.[14] Examples of such rhetoric abounded in the days and weeks after the 9/11 attacks, figuratively translating the 1990s-era "masculinity crisis" from the (white middle-class) men of the United States to the nation itself.

Two days after the attacks, for instance, psychiatrist Alvin Poussaint appeared on a television special hosted by Peter Jennings and directly linked 9/11 to gendered trauma. Poussaint diagnosed the nation as traumatized, likening the attacks to a rape and to a "kind of symbolic or attempted symbolic castration," in which the terrorists attacked the "towers as phallic symbols."[15] Similarly, an article by William Saletan constructs "the United States as the battered wife to the battering husband of Middle Eastern terrorists."[16] Like the strategy Lorena Bobbitt's defense used in 1994, Saletan used his depiction of the United States as a "battered wife" to justify a strident and militarized response, asserting, "As long as your husband decides which of your acts will earn you a beating, he's the master and you're the slave."[17]

Such rhetoric imagines trauma as a feminizing experience that turns an otherwise intact, masterful national body into fragmented, incomplete, and gaping remains. This rhetoric also encourages the nation to piece itself back together, whatever the cost. Consider, for instance, *Time*'s "moment-by-moment account of the attacks," published on September 14, 2001: after detailing the events of the day, which are cast as "humbl[ing] an empire" through the destruction of its metaphoric cathedrals, the article ends with a sanguine assertion of national rebuilding and rebirth. In response to the question, "What will we do?," the article concludes, "What else but build new cathedrals, and if they are bombed, build some more. Because the faith is in the act of building, not the building itself, and no amount of terror can keep us from scraping the sky."[18]

The emphasis on repairing the nation appropriates the logic of therapy culture. A post-9/11 wave of books offered "how to" guides for healing. Among many others, these books included *The September 11 Syndrome: Seven Steps to Getting a Grip in Uncertain Times* (2002), *September 11: Trauma and Human Bonds* (2003), *Ashes Transformed: Healing from Trauma* (2003), *After the Storm: Healing after Trauma, Tragedy, and Terror* (2006), and *The Posttraumatic Self: Restoring Meaning and Wholeness to Personality* (2006).[19] As their titles suggest, these books reproduce metaphors and assumptions about trauma that reify masculinist fictions of the unified, masterful subject: imagining the healthy self as "getting a grip" (as opposed to falling down or falling apart), constructing trauma as the proverbial ashes from which new subjects and communities are reborn, equating a subject's (or collective's) meaning with wholeness, and defining recovery as a restoration of that imagined wholeness.

Marking trauma's currency as a rhetorical frame for 9/11, an anthology featuring prominent trauma scholars also appeared in 2006. *Mapping Trauma and Its Wake: Autobiographic Essays by Pioneer Trauma Scholars* includes entries from Judith Lewis Herman, Mardi Horowitz, Robert Jay Lifton, Bessel van der Kolk, and John P. Wilson. Edited by Charles Figley, founder of the International Society for Traumatic Stress Studies, this book announces itself as gathering the "pioneers" in the field of traumatology. With a cover featuring photographs of each of the book's contributors, *Mapping Trauma and Its Wake* presents autobiographic essays that address such questions as, "What were the events in your life that led to your interest in trauma?"[20] This book warrants discussion for several reasons.

First, it reproduces the emphasis in trauma discourse on experiential authority and testimony, linking these scholars' expertise to their own encounters with childhood loss or terror and reinforcing constructions of traumatic history as both personal and transformative[21] Second, *Mapping Trauma and Its Wake* also figures traumatic injury as a rather singular event with a definitive before and after—a disruption whose aftereffects are imagined to leave indelible traces. Each author's photograph appears on the first page of his/her essay, while a much earlier snapshot appears at the end, as if each essay has transported the reader (if not the author) back in time—perhaps to a time *before* trauma.[22] This traumatic timeline recalls the commonplace construction of 9/11 as a day that changed everything. Consider, for instance, *Time*'s September 14, 2001, assertion that on 9/11 "some things had changed forever": "The attacks will become a defining reference point for our culture and imagination, a question of before and after, safe and scarred."[23]

Third, despite positing trauma as a rupture with a clear before and after, *Mapping Trauma and Its Wake* also frames trauma as a recurring experience that is always tethered to the past. Suggesting that 9/11 reopened old psychic wounds related to Vietnam, for example, the book maps the transformation of trauma from an experience that is associated primarily with war veterans to one that affects all citizens in a post-terror world.[24] The anthology thus illustrates a paradox central to trauma discourse: although the post-9/11 trauma industry posits 9/11 as a singular, unprecedented day that changed everything, such perceived disturbances are always constructed and interpreted in relation to prior experiential frames.[25]

The tendency to refract tragedies of the present through lenses of the past pervaded post-9/11 rhetoric about national history and identity, as exemplified by the ubiquitous description of Iraq as a "Second Vietnam" and the popular bumper sticker that read "Iraq Is Arabic for Vietnam."[26] Likewise, Schivelbush describes the events of 9/11 as having unearthed the "suppressed remains of Vietnam." Asking whether "America's post–September 11 war fever is really a response to an earlier and unresolved defeat," Schivelbusch reminds us that cultural fantasies and memories always imbricate each another.[27]

Even spokespersons for the U.S. military have acknowledged the convergences between cultural memory about Vietnam, 9/11, and the War on Terror. The belief that mediated representations of the Vietnam War contribute to its troubled place in national public memory, for instance, reportedly motivates the efforts of the Los Angeles division of Army Media Relations to shape Hollywood's depictions of war.[28] Consulting on dozens of Hollywood disaster, action, and war movies, including *I Am Legend*, this division of the army explicitly aims to regulate public opinion and cultural memory about making war. Such efforts stem from the concern that, as the army's former media liaison Lieutenant Colonel J. Todd Breasseale puts it, "Hollywood has created the crazy Nam vet." According to the *Los Angeles Times*, "With the country now enmeshed in another long, unpopular war, Breasseale is hoping to influence a new generation of filmmakers in order to avoid repeating the experience." However, the article reports, "So far, Breasseale feels, most of the movies made about Iraq have really been about Vietnam."[29]

Cultural memory about Vietnam resonates with discourse about the post-9/11 nation for two primary reasons. First, both Vietnam and 9/11 have been figured in largely gendered terms as damaging the stability of the national masculine. Second, both Vietnam and 9/11 have been cast as hypermediated events whose overexposure in the news media has been imagined as contributing to (if not directly causing) national trauma. It is thus not mere coincidence that a wave of self-help and "how to" trauma recovery books saturated the marketplace, a cycle of sacrificial films appeared, and a host of books returned to the subject of Vietnam trauma—all reaching fever pitch on or around the fifth anniversary of 9/11.[30]

It is also not a coincidence that one of the most emblematic iterations of post-9/11 trauma culture comes from Robert Jay Lifton, whose Vietnam-era *Home from War* was reprinted in 2005 with a new preface about the war in Iraq. In a *New York Times* article entitled "We Were Exposed and Raw," Lifton and co-author Charles B. Strozier describe 9/11 as an event that traumatized and irrevocably changed the nation.

> In a flash reality morphed. . . . New Yorkers became vulnerable and very exposed. The mighty towers literally fell before our eyes and thousands died.
>
> The suddenness of the attack also made it traumatic, even for the millions of us who suffered no physical wounds. As we participated vicariously in the violence, it was apparent that there were no words adequate to the experience. People spoke mostly in clichés. The psychological wound to the New York self was very deep. We were exposed and raw, suddenly weakened, even somewhat helpless.[31]

This passage highlights a number of key tensions in 9/11 trauma culture.

First, Lifton and Strozier reproduce constructions of trauma as an unspeakable experience from which survivors may never escape *and* as an experience to be gotten over and learned from. They construct trauma as incommunicable, reducing speakers to mimes with "no words adequate to the experience," stripped down only to "clichés." Imagining trauma as insurmountable, they write, "We will never see those towers again. A part of us has died along with the many victims." This image of survivors as always missing a part of themselves marks the nation as fixed in state of melancholy. Yet Lifton and Strozier also cite the presence of "healing images" that will help the nation "move into a transformed future" that has been fundamentally altered by experiences of terror and loss. They conclude ambivalently, "we will never be the same."[32]

Second, this article marks 9/11 as a trauma particular to New York *and* as an experience shared by the nation. Initially, Lifton and Strozier fetishize New York as a special place: "a bastion of apparent stability" that has "embodied firmness and security" and that has "seemed solid, impenetrable, immutable."[33] This article suggests that tragedy in a place like New York is somehow stranger and more horrific than tragedies experienced elsewhere. This claim naturalizes the assumption that traumas matter more when they happen in certain places (to certain people) than when they happen in other sites (to Others) where terror and loss are imagined as natural or inevitable. This fixation of place also occurs in discourse about Ground Zero, as in Tom Brokaw's description of the site as a "holy place to be enshrined" or Georgian president Eduard Shevardnadze's assertion that "only in New York could such nobility arise from such savagery."[34] Denying Bataille's claim that "horror is everywhere the same," this rhetoric participates, if unwittingly, in the "strategy of comparative trauma calculation."[35]

Even though they single out New York as a singular and exceptional site of trauma, Lifton and Strozier also describe 9/11 as a trauma that happened to everyone in America. Reminiscent of Representative McDermott's assumption that "every one of us" watched as the towers fell, Lifton and Strozier posit the entire nation as "wounded" and caught "vicariously in the violence." Like Bataille, Lifton and Strozer imagine trauma as something that can be shared or directly communicated and imply, consequently, that trauma is something to which all Americans—and the nation itself—can lay claim.[36]

Such assertions about the apparent ubiquity of 9/11 trauma were not without critique, prompting further comparative calculations. (In fact, Goode titles one of her articles, "Calculating the Toll of Trauma.") Felicia Lee acknowledges the prevalence of American trauma culture, claiming, "Whether it is the anniversary of Sept. 11, the continuing threat of terrorism, sexual abuse by the clergy, school shootings or any one of the many other causes of angst, Americans have been inundated with the language of trauma."[37] Lee's article (entitled "Is Trauma Being Trivialized?") describes a "bitter debate" among experts in the field about the value of PTSD as a diagnostic category, a controversy in which many mental health professionals defend their professional territory in the high-stakes trauma industry.

Lee cites the belief that America has "dumbed down PTSD," diagnosing America as a "society that glorifies confession and victimization."[38] Evidence for claims that trauma and PTSD have been banalized can be marshaled from its pervasive presence in popular culture.[39] For instance, on January 7, 2009, MTV's *True Life* documentary series premiered an episode called "True Life: I Have PTSD," which claimed to show viewers "what it's really like to live with PTSD through three young veterans who are struggling to get their lives back on track." Trauma and PTSD also featured prominently in many fictional television shows and novels from 2006 and 2007, centering on damaged protagonists.[40]

Refuting assertions that PTSD has been overused or emptied of any definitive meaning, some psychiatrists insist that the impact of PTSD is widespread. In Lee's article, Bessel van der Kolk defends PTSD as a "good diagnosis" and likens the controversy over trauma to cycles of "backlash" similar to the backlash Vietnam veterans faced. Van der Kolk asserts, "There was backlash against Vietnam veterans when PTSD was first used. In the late 80's and early 90's there was backlash against research on sexual abuse, and in the 90's there was controversy about false memory." Citing "cycles of trauma and then cycles of denial," van der Kolk interprets debates about the value of trauma as symptomatic of larger anxieties, thus reinscribing (using rather circular logic) the language of trauma itself as evidence of its conceptual value and applicability.[41]

Over and Over Exposure

As much as public discourse expressed national concern about how much was being *said about* trauma, this rhetoric also suggested that too much trauma was being seen by U.S. citizens. Post-9/11 trauma discourse lamented the visibility of violence. For example, Lifton and Strozier's article links the traumatic impact of 9/11 directly to its status as a hypervisualized spectacle that citizen-subjects were forced to witness. As Strozier describes standing frozen, "watching the towers collapse," the article positions U.S. citizens, and New Yorkers in particular, as "exposed" on 9/11.[42]

Lifton and Strozier's language suggests multiple interpretations of the word "exposed." They claim that residents of the United States felt exposed—bare, open to the elements, unprotected—as if on 9/11 New York and the rest of the United States became visible and vulnerable in new ways. At the same time, they also implies that U.S. citizens were *exposed to* a violent scene—forced to behold devastating sights. Mirroring Marshall McLuhan's 1968 charge that news coverage of Vietnam was making the American public a "participant in every phase of the war," Lifton and Strozier construct the nation's citizens as having "participated vicariously" in the hyper-visual(ized) spectacle and "violence" of 9/11.[43] Lifton and Strozier thus position Americans both as objects on display *and* as wounded spectators.

Traumatic memory is frequently imagined as a photograph or an image from a movie—for example, one survivor describes traumatic memories as a "Technicolor flashback," while another frames her memories as a "cascade of terrifying mental images, like a movie she cannot turn off." At the same time that many survivors described traumatic memories as being like images, much public discourse about 9/11 trauma blamed images themselves as being the cause of traumatic memory.[44] For example, Representative McDermott mentions news coverage of 9/11 as a potential cause of PTSD, describing U.S. citizens as having been "traumatized by the images and all of what [they've] seen."[45] A 2001 *New York Times* article quotes one neurobiologist who urged news outlets to censor images of the falling towers ("because they are just too strong") and cites research that indicates that the "constant replaying of television images of a disaster may impede recovery."[46] Lance Morrow's editorial for *Time*, "The Case for Rage and Retribution," goes one step further. Describing the 9/11 attacks as producing a "sequence of panic that might have been shot for a remake of *The War of the Worlds* or for *Independence Day*," Morrow declares, "Evil possesses an instinct for theater, which is why in an era of gaudy and gifted media, evil may vastly magnify its damage by the power of horrific images."[47]

Rhetorical constructions of Americans as particularly vulnerable citizen-spectators help explain the frequent recourse to cultural memory about Vietnam as a frame for making sense of 9/11.[48] Both Vietnam and 9/11 have been cast as hypervisualized events whose mediation is said to contribute to (if not cause) national trauma. Called (perhaps erroneously) the "most televised event in history," for instance, 9/11 evokes constructions of Vietnam as an event fought and lost in the media. Robert Hariman and John Lucaites argue that "the inability to lay Vietnam to rest . . . may be due in part to the fact that collective memory of that war was defined by images that are themselves traumatic," including John Filo's photograph of violence at Kent State and Nick Ut's photograph "Accidental Napalm," both of which won the Pulitzer Prize.[49] Just as Vietnam is called the "television" or "living room" war, much recent public rhetoric frames 9/11 as an event that assaulted citizen-spectators and wounded the nation not only *at home* (on U.S. soil) but also *in the home* (via live television).

As much as it casts "exposure" to the scenes of terror as a problem, however, trauma discourse also enlists images as a solution to 9/11 trauma, citing them as a potential tool that may enable survivors to gain mastery over trauma. In addition to a number of cognitive-behavioral techniques heralded in the 1990s, such as exposure therapy and Eye Movement Desensitization and Reprocessing, post-9/11 press coverage about trauma also cited computer-simulated environments as a tool. Echoing Mardi J. Horowitz's Vietnam-era research with stress films, virtual recreations aim to expose survivors gradually to the violent scene so they will be able manage traumatic memory.[50]

Analogous "recovery" work characterizes sacrificial films. Both *Poseidon* and *I Am Legend* deploy the traumatic rhetoric and iconography of 9/11 in their depiction of fictional disaster scenarios. At the same time that these films reopen old wounds, they also revise, rewrite, and remember history. *Poseidon* and *I Am Legend* return to the perceived traumas of history through their reliance on allegorical form and through their status as remakes. Allegory itself might be understood as a post-traumatic form. Characterized by both repetition (a return to a prior tale) and displacement (a refusal to confront that past openly), allegory performs characteristic symptoms of trauma at the same time that it attempts to enact a sense of mastery, as if to prove that something new can be produced from the "ruins" of something old.[51] Robert Hariman contends that "allegory often uses melancholy as a means for perception and interpretation," always carrying with it a "sense of loss regarding whatever it depicts." The creation of new stories engenders what Hariman calls a "richly layered, dynamic liminality" that encourages the reader to imagine new beginnings and the possibility of moving on.[52] Comingling "joy and sadness, hope and mourning," allegorical texts manifest and heal the perceived wounds of the past.[53]

In addition, exemplifying Hariman's claim that allegories offer "multiple layers of meaning" and "a surplus of meaning to signs," *Poseidon* and *I Am Legend* are twice the "twice-told tale."[54] Their compulsion to repeat the past is doubled, not only in the allegorical displacement of 9/11 but also because they are remakes, or repetitions, of prior cultural texts. Although they were produced nearly thirty-five years after their antecedents, *Poseidon* and *I Am Legend* return to their cinematic progenitors rather closely. *Poseidon*, like *Poseidon Adventure*, features a cruise ship capsized by a large wave, depicts passengers trapped in the vessel after receiving poor guidance from the ship's captain, and uses the self-sacrificial death of a male protagonist to enable a handful of survivors to escape. *I Am Legend*, like *Omega Man*, portrays Robert Neville as a military scientist, depicts catastrophic destruction of a major U.S. city wrought by human actions, and insists that Neville must die so a new population can be reborn.

More than coincidence, this repetition replays anxieties about America's identity as an allegedly masculine nation-state, which are, like *Poseidon* and *I Am Legend* themselves, both specific to the post-9/11 context and reminiscent of American culture during and after Vietnam. The restaging of Vietnam-era antecedents reveals efforts to manage unresolved tensions in American cultural memory. Just as memories of Vietnam haunted President George H. W. Bush's push for war in the Persian Gulf and shaped campaign rhetoric in the 2004 battle for the White House, Vietnam's imagined assault on the state of the nation continues to imperil fantasies of American exceptionalism and invincibility and overlaps with public memory about 9/11.[55]

Although *Poseidon*'s and *I Am Legend*'s status as remakes reenacts the repetitive structure of trauma, their recourse to familiar narratives should also be understood as an invitation to let go of anxiety about an event framed (however erroneously) as something no one saw coming. Based on prevailing understandings of testimony as a crucial step toward recovery, *Poseidon* and *I Am Legend* encourage the moving-on process not with a new story but with one that is familiar and predictable. Rather than simply narrativizing trauma, these remakes *re-narrativize* it, offering stories constructed from the ruins of others.

Given Dori Laub's description of 9/11 as an "event without a voice" whose central horror is the lack of any "coherent narrative" about "what it is that has happened to us all," what better way to comfort an uncertain nation than with a story that is known and accessible and has already been given a voice?[56] *Poseidon* and *I Am Legend* manage the paralyzing shocks of 9/11 by asking audiences to move forward with a return to the past. There may be something consoling in knowing exactly what is coming in these films. As Claudia Puig remarks of *Poseidon*, "There's no guessing game as to who will survive and who won't. It's pretty evident from the start who's going to make it (spoiler alert: ethnic minorities don't fare well)."[57]

Although these remakes reenact their cinematic past, they also assert their differences, and the variations in *Poseidon*'s and *I Am Legend*'s repetitions of the past reveal the contemporary trauma culture shaping their narratives. Consideration of how *Poseidon* and *I Am Legend* remember their progenitors and distillation of their differences produce important insights into the changing historical contexts that shape (and are shaped by) each film.

(Not) Rocking the Boat

While 9/11 trauma discourse figured the nation as emasculated, critiques of America's militarized response identified the War on Terror as hypermasculine, overzealous, and overwrought. Vaheed Ramazani argues that while the "collapse of the Towers was experienced as emasculating" because of their "phallic iconicity," the nation's responses have been framed as restoring the "'masculine' health, purity and strength" of the "nation's body." President George W. Bush's rhetoric of American resilience and U.S. military aggression, argues Ramazani, attempted to transform America from "the passive (female) recipient of a violating aggression into the virile progenitor of world solidarity."[58]

A similar sense of machismo pervades Morrow's article "The Case for Rage and Retribution." Recalling his 1994 article on masculinity crises, Morrow both makes use of and belittles the language of trauma in relation to 9/11.[59] He begins, "For once, let's have no 'grief counselors' standing by with banal consolations, as if the purpose, in the midst of all this, were merely to make everyone feel better as quickly as possible." He repeats, "For once, let's have no fatuous rhetoric about 'healing.' Healing is inappropriate now, and dangerous." Instead, Morrow insists, "Let's have rage."[60] Having denounced a therapeutic (or mournful) response, Morrow maintains a traumatic frame, in which he encourages survivors not to move on from loss but to act out in anger against it. Morrow also draws upon the berserk style, inciting "berserk frenzy" and encouraging the nation to "charge into battle in a godlike or beastlike frenzy" and "plunge into emergency action."[61]

Morrow extends this image of the nation in a later article from 2001. Deriding the "Old Paradigm" of the Vietnam-era antiwar movement for thinking "machismo was a fault and the military an archaic and expensive nuisance," he praises the "New Paradigm" for revering "strong men and manly virtues—courage and self sacrifice."[62] Morrow glorifies the post-9/11 context for unifying the nation. He pronounces "hyphen-Americans" a thing of the past, claims that citizens are "Americans, period," and proclaims that there is "nothing like a common enemy to unite and focus all that diversity." From Morrow's perspective, it would seem that if the "Greatest Generation" rhetoric of the 1990s was not enough to bolster and bond the nation, 9/11 had done the trick. Morrow seems thankful that 9/11 brought about "the reinstatement of an older model—a pre-Vietnam perspective."[63]

Morrow's rhetoric illustrates a tension common to 9/11 trauma culture: ostensibly emasculated on 9/11, the American national masculine became aggressive, or berserk, in its wake. While the 9/11 attacks may have imperiled assumptions about American national security and masculinist authority, many around the world perceived America's military response via invasion of Iraq to be excessively violent, vindictive, and misguided, if not illegal. For instance, both former UN secretary-general Kofi Annan and former UN weapons inspector Hans Blix denounced the war in Iraq as illegal, leading one international journalist to call the invasion "a dime novel of farce, fear-baiting manipulation, hubris and hypocrisy."[64]

In the weeks and months surrounding *Poseidon*'s release, such sentiments circulated widely in global discourse. For example, several books published in 2006 critiqued the U.S. invasion of Iraq and President Bush's wartime actions, including Mark Danner's *The Secret Way to War*; Bob Woodward's *State of Denial: Bush at War, Part III*; and *Crimes of War: Iraq*, Richard Falk, Irene L. Gendzier, and Robert Jay Lifton's follow-up to their 1971 critique of the Vietnam War.[65] Similar concern marked the attitude of the American public; in May of 2006, only days before *Poseidon* was released, a CBS poll indicated that 64 percent of Americans disapproved of the president's handling of the Iraq War.

Amid this context of debate and dissent, *Poseidon*'s narrative of survival aboard a fiery, capsizing cruise ship struck by a rogue wave displaces the perceived traumas of 9/11 and its consequences into a fictional account of disaster at sea so it can manage them in an allegorical construction of the past. *Poseidon* initially mimics the traumas of 9/11 in strikingly exact ways, but the film then translates the loss associated with this day into a rhetorically productive re-creation. E. Ann Kaplan argues that Hollywood often addresses historical trauma through depictions of what she calls "quiet" or "common" traumas, but

Poseidon changes course and depicts the unlikely: the spectacular, the unexpected.[66] By focusing on traumatic experience that is constructed as remote and anomalous, this film pushes the past out to sea to be reckoned with safely and contained at a distance.

David Germain's review of *Poseidon* claims that "fictional disaster is an easier sell than stories based on real tragedy." Germain explains that a film such as *United 93* (Paul Greengrass, 2006), a documentary-style drama about the terrorist attack onboard and subsequent crash of United Flight 93, may be uncomfortably close to the "pain" of 9/11, which is "too deep and recent for many movie-goers" and may leave audiences "feeling as though they are reliving that terrible day"—so much so that some audiences reported being traumatized by the film's images, and many theaters pulled *United 93*'s trailer or displayed warnings prior to running it.[67] In contrast to *United 93*'s graphic confrontation with the horrors of 9/11, *Poseidon* offers a less disruptive approach to disaster.

Note that the focus in *Poseidon* on a natural disaster differs remarkably from *The Poseidon Adventure*'s 2005 made-for-television remake, which explicitly links the SS *Poseidon*'s accident to an explosion perpetrated by Islamic terrorists.[68] While the television remake was criticized for its frank confrontation of American anxieties about terrorism and national security, *Poseidon*'s allegorical reenactment of the attacks of 9/11 remains carefully and more comfortably displaced.[69] Depicting an unexpected, unpredictable disaster rather than one that is ordinary, *Poseidon* performs *and* attempts to minimize trauma. Director Wolfgang Petersen explained that "9/11 was and still is a great, great shock for everybody. Just out of nowhere, suddenly disaster strikes. And it could happen to anybody . . . all of a sudden, bang! My world is upside down."[70]

The unforeseen nature of the disaster in the film rhetorically asserts American innocence, suggesting that 9/11, like the wave that hit the *Poseidon* in the film, hit the nation without provocation or warning. As President Bush asserted in April of 2004, "We never really thought America would be a battlefield. We thought oceans would protect us."[71] According to Claire Kahane, claiming to be "blind" to the possibility of the 9/11 attacks facilitates the assumption that the nation shared no responsibility for inciting "acts of retaliation from the margin, from unknown antagonists 'over there.'"[72] *Poseidon*'s narrative about an attack that "blindsides" its victims reproduces 9/11 trauma discourse (offering rather literal proof that the oceans may not protect us) and offers a rhetorical assertion of America's national blamelessness.

The New Wave

Promotion for *Poseidon* encouraged viewers to see the film not as depicting real tragedy but as "pure Hollywood spectacle," or, as its star Kurt Russell describes, "a Hollywood movie, an escape. That's all."[73] Despite such assertions,

Poseidon demonstrates a clear preoccupation with 9/11 and its aftermath.[74] The frequency, specificity, and precision of references to 9/11 in *Poseidon* suggest that, whether consciously or not, this text invites consideration about how the nation should remember 9/11.

Several reviews demonstrate links between *Poseidon* and 9/11, citing as evidence the central character, Robert Ramsey (Russell), a fireman and a former mayor of New York City. Cynthia Fuchs describes Ramsey as a "throwaway reference" capitalizing on a "presumed post-9/11 desire for Heroes."[75] Lisa Schwarzbaum describes Ramsey's identity as "rolling two heroic 9/11 jobs into one."[76] For other reviewers, the film's specific disaster scenario and special effects matrix allude too closely to 9/11. Michael Atkinson dubs the film "simple death porn" with potentially traumatic implications. Asserting that *Poseidon* might "go down better outside of the metro [New York] area than within," Atkinson reminds readers that "fireballs, massive explosions, flying bodies, and architectural obliteration" mean more in a post-9/11 context.[77] Despite suggestions of links between *Poseidon* and 9/11, however, little sustained comment addresses the film's rhetorical contribution to American trauma discourse.

The visual and verbal rhetoric through which *Poseidon* represents the sinking ship conspicuously re-creates the iconography of 9/11. For example, as the ship capsizes, visual attention emphasizes not the threat of water but fires created by a series of explosions in the interior and on the exterior of the vessel. Indeed, fire becomes something of a visual preoccupation of the film; forty-five minutes of *Poseidon* pass before water visibly factors as an imminent threat to the ship's passengers. This is a striking contrast to the original *Poseidon Adventure.*

To illustrate, note how President Bush described what would become the iconic image of the day while speaking on September 11, 2001: "pictures of airplanes flying into buildings, fires burning, huge structures collapsing," which "have filled us with disbelief, terrible sadness, and a quiet, unyielding anger."[78] Five years later, understandings of the event had changed little as he recalled "the horror of watching planes fly into the World Trade Center, and seeing the towers collapse before our eyes. We remember the sight of the Pentagon, broken and in flames."[79] *Poseidon* animates cultural memories of this violent scene with its images of "fires burning" and "huge structures collapsing," which operate like what Freud calls a "memory-trace" that reveals the "point of contact" between a screen memory, a false memory unconsciously created to protect the psyche from recovering a more painful memory that has been repressed, and the trauma it simultaneously refers to and covers over.[80]

Poseidon uses the narrative of the SS *Poseidon* to replay the events of 9/11: the explosions on board the ship and its eventual descent into the sea can be seen as the reenactment of the destruction of the Twin Towers. Symbolically, both the ship and the Towers were structural marvels representing human ingenuity and accomplishment that were, nonetheless, destroyed unexpectedly and almost instantaneously. Underwater shots of the sinking ship emphasize its vertical descent into the ocean, making the cruise liner appear like an underwater tower. The film's depiction of the SS *Poseidon* offers a new icon of phallic mastery to stand in for the Twin Towers, using frequent crane shots and extreme low angles to emphasize the ship's enormousness. The deadly rushing waters that fill *Poseidon*'s mise-en-scène embody the "flood of painful memories" Bush described as rushing back in the days and months prior to the fifth anniversary of September 11.

Likewise, *Poseidon*'s focus on the disbelief, sadness, and anger felt by the passengers on the ship mimics cultural memory about individuals trapped in the Twin Towers. For instance, the sequence depicting the capsizing process emphasizes the sounds of glass breaking, steel groaning, and human screaming; it shows many images of tangled corpses, bodies on fire, survivors dangling high above the ground, and survivors trapped under rubble, including steel beams and bodies. The mise-en-scène resembles that of *World Trade Center*, a film about Port Authority police officers trapped in the wreckage at Ground Zero; even if such similarities are accidental, their presence in a post-9/11 film takes on an additional register of meaning. Moreover, as the blazing ship in *Poseidon* sinks into the ocean, we see men and women jumping from the hull, falling great distances to their deaths in the waters below, and eerily summoning images of those that chose escape from the burning Twin Towers over imprisonment within them.

On September 12, 2001, for instance, the *New York Times* published a photograph of a man falling from the north tower, with a caption reading, "A person falls head first after jumping from the north tower of the World Trade Center. It was a horrific sight that was repeated in the moments after the planes struck

Figure 18. The SS *Poseidon* as an icon of phallic mastery, soon to be upended. *Poseidon* (Warner Bros.)

the towers." On September 19, 2002, The *Chicago Sun Times* also described "people jumping from the building . . . including a man and a woman holding hands as they fell" and "a crowd of hundreds looking up at the gaping hole, then saw bodies tumbling out, one after the other." Consequently, it seems hard (almost impossible) not to find resemblances between these diegetic deaths and those that have become iconic in post-9/11 cultural memory, in which images of falling may function not only as signifiers of the phenomenological structure trauma but also as specific referents to events that took place on 9/11.

Citing Eleanor Kaufman's work on falling as a recurrent traumatic trope, Kahane argues that seeing falling bodies was one of the most "disquieting" experiences of 9/11 not only because "there were actual people jumping, forced from the fire into the abyss," but also because falling specifically signifies traumatic experience: a "signifier of the ultimate loss of control, of loss of agency, of loss of boundaries." The significance of the images of bodies falling from the SS *Poseidon* is thus doubled: referencing the memory of individuals doomed to a literal fall from the towers and the "abyss-like structure of trauma," which, in *Poseidon*, is allegorized by the ship's fall into the depths of the ocean's abyss.[81]

The disaster sequence in *Poseidon* also dramatizes passengers' debates about whether to obey the institutional mandate and remain in the ballroom awaiting rescue or to follow the dissenters' escape plan. This narrative device, within a post-9/11 film, may remind viewers of the fate of individuals advised by Port Authority police to remain in the South Tower compared to the experiences of those who attempted to evacuate.[82] After following the captain's orders not to evacuate the ballroom, almost all passengers on the SS *Poseidon* perish when the lower portion of the ship floods. This scenario, in which a leader fatally advises those in his charge to stay put, may also be understood to reference President Bush's insistence that America "stay the course" in the War on Terror.

Reenacting the devastation of institutional failure, the figure of Captain Bradshaw indicates that collective memory has constructed both the attacks on 9/11 and the nation's response as traumatic to the social body. The national injuries of 9/11, implies *Poseidon*, are attributable not only to the events of that day and their perpetrators but also to their aftereffects and the perceived inefficacies of U.S. leadership structures. While Captain Bradshaw's failure to prevent or understand the magnitude of the attack implies that the nation was too weak, too unprepared, too emasculated on 9/11, I argue below that the subsequent behavior of the renegade heroes in *Poseidon* functions both to atone for such immediate impotence and to assuage anxiety about the nation's post-9/11 hypermasculine retribution.

Offering further evidence that *Poseidon* may be understood as allegorizing 9/11, Captain Bradshaw admits, "Now we're not sure exactly what happened here. But our best guess is that we were struck by what is known as a rogue wave. They're rare, they're unpredictable, and they are lethal." His precise characterization of the wave as "rogue" demonstrates a significant departure from the original film, offering insight into *Poseidon*'s ideological preoccupations with post-9/11 terrorism anxiety. The original *Poseidon Adventure* depicts a disaster caused by a tsunami, not a "rogue wave," which the *American Heritage Dictionary* defines as "an unpredictable, abnormally large wave that occurs on a seemingly random basis in the oceans," which may be alternatively known as a "freak" or "monster" wave.[83]

It is significant that *Poseidon* chooses the term "rogue," a term that is significant in the lexicons of both oceanography and contemporary geopolitics. The latter register is most important as the phrase "rogue state" has been used by the U.S. government since the Cold War to describe perceived threats to western democracies. The second Bush administration applied the term to nations assumed to participate in terrorist activity and/or to possess weapons of mass destruction, including Afghanistan and Iraq.[84] The Bush administration used the term "rogue state," for instance, in 2002 in the *National Security Strategy of the United States of America* to justify the "Bush doctrine" of preventive war, which casts military violence against potential enemies as a kind of self-defense.[85] With this reference, *Poseidon* invites association between the rogue wave and the rogue states linked to the traumas of 9/11 and once identified as the primary enemies of the United States.

The captain's characterization of the wave as "unpredictable" and "lethal" mirrors War on Terror rhetoric that described terrorists as clandestine figures who target random victims with the intent to create chaos, mayhem, and anxiety.[86] In fact, it is precisely allegations of the "inherent unpredictability" of terrorists that have fueled debates about terrorism insurance and justified the far-reaching aims of homeland security and the USA PATRIOT Act, which President Bush reauthorized on March 9, 2006, two months before the theatrical release of *Poseidon*.[87] In a 2004 speech urging the renewal of the act, Bush described terrorists as lurking everywhere: "Now the enemy hides in caves. They lurch [*sic*] in the shadows of the world. They will strike and kill innocent citizens without any conscience, because they have no conscience."[88] Like the rogue wave, terrorists attack suddenly, without warning; and, significantly, both the captain of the SS *Poseidon* and President Bush characterize the enemy as having the capacity to "strike." Captain Bradford's rhetoric thus invites understanding of the catastrophe at sea as a way to make sense of tragedy at home, but from a distance.

Poseidon's escape sequence also suggests connections between the SS *Poseidon* disaster and 9/11, visually framing the cruise liner as a *towering* structure. In addition to frequent extreme low angle shots, this sequence fixates on the passengers' struggle to find what Ramsey calls "vertical access" to an exit at the bottom of the ship. The cinematographic emphasis on the height of the ship is reinforced with recurrent images of elevators and elevator shafts in the mise-en-scène. For example, after escaping the ballroom and traversing fiery passages, the survivors find themselves in an elevator shaft, the setting for the first casualty of a primary character, who falls and is impaled on a steel structure. Soon after, survivors reach the ship's lobby, where viewers are reminded of the many floors of the ship and its multiple elevators, like those of the Twin Towers. It bears noting that as characters marvel at the height of the lobby, a flood of oil bursts through the ceiling, igniting a sea of fire around the survivors. This spectacular effect recalls the incident when jet "fuel flowed across the floors [of the WTC towers] and down elevator and utility shafts, igniting intense fires throughout upper portions of the buildings."[89]

As the group continues to chart its escape, many characters discuss the structural soundness of the SS *Poseidon*, paying special attention to fire safety measures and engineering. For instance, despite the captain's assurance that passengers will be safe from "gas leaks, fires, and flooding," one character responds, "I wouldn't put a lot of faith in what the captain is saying. I'm an architect. These ships weren't designed to stay afloat upside down." Not only does this language provide evidence of concern about the effectiveness of a leader, it also recalls specific findings of the Federal Emergency Management Agency (FEMA) in its *World Trade Center Building Performance Study*. The FEMA report suggests that the towers weren't built to withstand the kind of impact they experienced on 9/11, noting, "Events of this type, resulting in such substantial damage, are generally not considered in building design." Furthermore, phrases like "fireball," "flash fires" and "super-heated" structures are heard frequently in dialogue during *Poseidon*'s escape sequence, mirroring the FEMA report's frequent citations of "fireballs," "intense fires," and "fire-induced reduction of structural strength" and once again suggesting that this disaster film cannot be fully extricated from the traumatic memories its spectacles seem to animate.[90]

As much as *Poseidon* demonstrates a Bataillean investment in spectacular suffering and replays 9/11 trauma discourse, it nevertheless also attempts to manage and negotiate such fears. The allegorical displacement of 9/11 allows its damages and aftershocks to be handled differently. *Poseidon's* re-production of the horrors of 9/11 manages the traumas produced by the constructed status of the United States as a victim and recuperates the nation's subsequent image as vengeful, vindictive, or berserk. In order to understand how this film rewrites traumatic history, we need first to consider the *Poseidon*'s depiction of its hero(es), which marks another significant departure from *The Poseidon Adventure*.

New Dogs, Old Tricks

As noted in chapter 2, *The Poseidon Adventure* transforms Reverend Scott (Gene Hackman) from a beleaguered and figuratively exiled minister to a hero who regains his faith, achieves redemption, and rescues several passengers by sacrificing himself in the film's final scene. Similarly, *Poseidon* culminates in the pregnant death of a victim-hero, Robert Ramsey (Russell), who sacrifices his life to save others, translating traumatic loss into regeneration. Unlike its antecedent, *Poseidon* centers on not just one but two male protagonists: the film has a second protagonist, Dylan Johns (Josh Lucas). Many of the reviews of *Poseidon* interpret Johns as the updated version of Hackman's Scott, given his prominent role as the renegade leader in the film. As Atkinson describes, "Instead of Gene Hackman's bizarrely Nietzschean priest, we get Lucas as a career gambler with a mercenary sense of survival and lots of helpful navy experience as a cliff diver."[91] However, Ramsey's role as Scott's descendant cannot be ignored for two reasons.

At an extra-textual level, parallels exist between the more established actors playing Scott and Ramsey. While Oscar-winner Hackman may have more cultural capital than Russell, their respective roles in two famous sports movies, *Hoosiers* (David Anspaugh, 1986) and *Miracle* (Gavin O'Connor, 2004), link them to one another. Both films feature these actors as coaches whose team leadership engenders redemption for the nation in the wake of historical trauma: *Hoosiers* uses Hackman's role as a basketball coach to reproduce Reagan's paternalistic persona as a U.S. leader and substitutes a story about a basketball team's difficult road to victory for overt consideration of the traumatic history of Vietnam.[92] *Miracle* positions Russell as a surrogate father for a troubled nation, offering a Cold War–era hockey game as what Silk, Schultz, and Bracey would call "a sanitized reconfiguration" of 9/11.[93] Just as *Miracle* performs ideological work similar to that done by *Hoosiers*, Russell's Ramsey resurrects the life and work of Hackman's Scott in *Poseidon*.

Figure 19. Dylan Johns and Robert Ramsey debating if and how they can work together. *Poseidon* (Warner Bros.)

Diegetic similarities also link heroes Scott and Ramsey: in *Poseidon*, Ramsey reproduces Scott's crucial sacrificial gesture, not Johns. It seems more precise to argue that this remake transforms one hero into two: one who lives to move on and one who must die, one who is "delivered from" trauma and one who remains "imprisoned" within it.[94] Responding to the complexities of the post-9/11 context, *Poseidon* doubles its protagonists. While the United States adopted a largely unilateral approach to the War on Terror, *Poseidon* exchanges *The Poseidon Adventure*'s reliance on the discourse of rugged individualism for one that emphasizes cooperation and partnership between leaders who represent significant subject positions in the post-9/11 world: Johns is a former military man and Ramsey is a former NYC mayor and firefighter. This partnership also reinforces the popular assertion that 9/11 trauma unified the nation, echoing, for example, *Time*'s description of the city as containing "no strangers . . . only sudden friends" working selflessly together.[95]

As Johns and Ramsey become better heroes and learn to work together, they reinforce assumptions about the transformative potential of trauma, suggesting that moments of extreme terror or loss clarify what "really matters" and definitively illustrate what "should be done." Johns and Ramsey re-create idealized constructions of 9/11 as a day that galvanized countless heroics. In *Time* magazine, journalist Nancy Gibbs opined, "On a normal day, we value heroism because it is uncommon. On Sept. 11, we valued heroism because it was everywhere."[96] This rather commonplace assertion attempts to make sense of what is imagined as traumatic chaos by endowing extreme terror and loss with meaning, purpose, and redemptive potential.[97] As Johns and Ramsey rise above the fray and become particularly special heroes, they also revise hegemonic constructions of American nationality through their performances of masculinity after trauma: Johns learns compassion and selflessness, and Ramsey acknowledges that his traditional performance of masculinity has been displaced by a new paradigm of heroism.

Johns, a navy veteran, boards the SS *Poseidon* as a loner, interested only in exploiting "desperate, single women" and gambling to "take [people's] money." After the disaster, he changes, trading selfish interests for a sense of obligation to his fellow survivors. For example, the escape efforts position Johns as a surrogate father to Connor, a young boy traveling with his single mother. When Connor is trapped in a rapidly flooding portion of the ship, Johns swims back at his own peril to rescue him. This creates a fatherly bond with Connor, and Johns's consequent connection with the boy's mother is based more on familial devotion or paternal authority than on sexual attraction; the final shots of the film depict Johns embracing mother and son in a rescue boat, suggesting that his transformation has engendered not only a new man but also a new nuclear family.

Johns's transformation suggests a softening of masculinity and begets a regeneration of community, allowing the male hero to maintain a position of authority *and* to perform compassion. So if a Bush-era United States might be accused of considering only its own interests at the expense of the interests of the global community, this military man's evolution might be understood as registering and atoning for such national narcissism. Like the idealized veteran who returns home and successfully abandons his warrior culture, Johns leaves behind his selfish agenda and learns to put others first. Before further addressing the importance of Johns's conversion, it will be helpful to consider the figure of Ramsey, who, as the return of Reverend Scott, most directly addresses the traumas that structure this text.

In many ways, Ramsey re-creates Scott very closely: both are middle-aged men who are estranged from the institutions that once defined them but then forced them to fight conventional wisdom and self-doubt to realize their self-sacrificial destinies. While in *The Poseidon Adventure* Scott explains that his unconventional beliefs led to what he calls professional "banishment" and describes himself as a "renegade stripped of [his] so-called clerical powers," *Poseidon* constructs Ramsey as a traumatized male subject banished from his role as patriarch because his daughter, Jennifer, has found a new love object, Christian. Indeed, the film immediately establishes Ramsey's displacement, introducing him as he awkwardly interrupts an amorous moment between Jennifer and Christian.

Poseidon's revision of its sacrificial victim-hero from a man of the cloth to a New York City civil servant also implies changes in the contested ideological terrain from which the narrative emerges—one in which politics, national security, and the status of the U.S. nation-state have become overtly tied to the problem of patriarchal authority. As noted above, Ramsey's identity collapses two of the most significant iterations of sacrificial masculinity in the 9/11 context, offering displaced figuration of some of the most beloved victim-heroes of 9/11: firefighters and Rudolph Giuliani, the once controversial mayor who became canonized as "America's mayor" for both his decisive responses as a leader and his public expressions of vulnerability as a wounded citizen.[98]

Poseidon implies that Ramsey wasn't just any mayor but was, like Giuliani, one who suffered and longed for redemption. For example, when Ramsey rejects the captain's orders to remain in the ballroom, Captain Bradford tries to persuade Ramsey to stay in the ballroom because of his leadership experience, reminding him, "You *know* disaster scenarios." The captain clearly emphasizes Ramsey's familiarity with disaster, alluding to (though never naming) a catastrophic experience that may have shaped his mayoral term, and given the significance of his identity as New York City's mayor, this allusion can't help but resurrect thoughts of 9/11. A later exchange between Jennifer and another passenger, Elena, also alludes to the traumatic nature of Ramsey's tenure as mayor. Watching Ramsey lead the escape efforts, Elena remarks, "I feel like I know your dad," to which Jennifer responds, "He was mayor of New York for a while when I was a kid." When Elena responds, "Cool," Jennifer counters with a wistful, if not forlorn, response: "It wasn't." Although she never talks about the hardships of her father's mayoral tenure, Jennifer's despondency suggests experiences of perhaps tragic proportions. Only moments after Jennifer establishes the gravity of Ramsey's past, the narrative affirms his sacrality through the punitive death of Lucky Larry, the one character who profanes Ramsey's traumatic history and status as victim-hero.

Drunk and belligerent, Lucky Larry mocks Ramsey: "Big hero. Rescued all those women and children from the fires. Got elected. Man of the people. But you're not the boss anymore. Hmm? You quit. Couldn't hack it. If I can recall correctly, you couldn't even hang onto your wife." Larry's words allude to Ramsey's identity as a displaced hero and his status as a traumatized subject. His notable inflection when he speaks of "*the* fires" seems to reference some past (but unspoken) collective trauma. Inasmuch as Lucky Larry's words signify Ramsey's troubled masculinity—deposed not only from public life but also from his place in the family as patriarch—Ramsey replays discourse about the imagined emasculation of the United States by the 9/11 attacks.

The disdain with which Larry mocks Ramsey's personal and public tragedies foreshadows his death as just punishment for having blasphemed the film's sacrificial victim-hero because, if Ramsey may be understood as a synecdoche for an emasculated nation, the text simply won't tolerate *too* frank a reference to his impotence. Mere seconds after his sacrilege against Ramsey, Larry falls to his death into a fiery pit of oil and water, and given the significance of both fire and falling in cultural memory surrounding 9/11, this punishment seems a particularly forceful object lesson for those who have openly criticized U.S. leaders and/or policies.

Although Ramsey says there is "nothing fair about who lives or dies," *Poseidon* implies otherwise, suggesting that each death is justified by the victim's identity. While Larry dies as punishment for his blasphemy against Ramsey (and by extension, against the traumatized nation), Ramsey dies precisely because of who he is: a traumatized victim-hero, a man who has suffered and been emasculated.[99] His former heroic status renders Ramsey worthy as a sacrificial object, but his past failures also precipitate his sacrifice on two levels. First, Ramsey's death reenacts and rewrites the losses of 9/11, translating tragedy into regeneration, senseless death into productive rebirth. Second, killing Ramsey can also be read as expiatory scapegoating, a purging of his failed masculinity in exchange for new figurations of what the national masculine can and should be.

When the survivors reach the hull of the ship, they discover that moving propellers are blocking their escape. Ramsey's plan to stop the propellers requires him to return to a lower portion of the ship that is flooded and certainly will mean his death. Moments before sacrificing himself, Ramsey speaks with Jennifer and Christian, whom he has recently learned are engaged. As Christian professes his love to Jennifer and offers to swim below, Ramsey steps in and assumes the sacrificial role himself. Committing this final act of salvation and exchanging his life for that of his daughter's future husband, Ramsey makes a sacrifice that not only saves those aboard the ship but also sanctions the new family Jennifer and Christian will presumably create, thus producing new life from the ruins of an old life.[100]

Like Scott, Ramsey acknowledges the need for a new social order and relinquishes his position of patriarchal authority, on which he had only a tenuous grip in the first place. He secures his position as a hero and worthy leader in the logic of the film, confirming the Bataillean paradox of self-loss as the source of new subjects. The salvific nature of Ramsey's death recuperates and retroactively recasts the tragic deaths of 9/11 not as meaningless and senseless but as purposeful and productive. Given *Poseidon*'s attempts to reconcile traditional assumptions about America's perceived masculinity as a nation-state with post-9/11 evidence of its vulnerability and frailty, it is significant to note that *Poseidon* dramatically revises the ending of *The Poseidon Adventure.*

Legends of the Fall

While generally *Poseidon* focuses much more on fire than did *The Poseidon Adventure*, it radically alters one scene from the original, in which fire factors largely. In *The Poseidon Adventure*, Scott falls to his death into a fire-engulfed pool of water. In *Poseidon*, Ramsey neither falls nor dies by fire; instead, he swims back to a flooded portion of the ship where no flames can be seen. It is important that the scenario of Scott's death in *The Poseidon Adventure* was excised from the post-9/11 remake. By declining to depict spectacles of either falling or fire, *Poseidon* offers a defense against, or escape from, the horrors of 9/11 and the images of falling bodies and burning buildings. This narrative revision refuses to subject the film's hero to the exact fate of many on 9/11, offering a less disturbing version of heroic death in a post-9/11 world.[101]

This excision echoes both the eventual move in media coverage of 9/11 to censor images of falling and/or dead bodies and the rather abrupt decision in 2002 to remove Eric Fischl's commemorative sculpture, *Tumbling Woman*, which depicts a woman falling from one of the Twin Towers, from Rockefeller Center in New York.[102] (Building officials removed the sculpture less than a week after its installation because of the number of complaints it drew.) Not unlike photographs of falling bodies and Fischl's sculpture, the ending as filmed in *The Poseidon Adventure* would have risked triggering traumatic

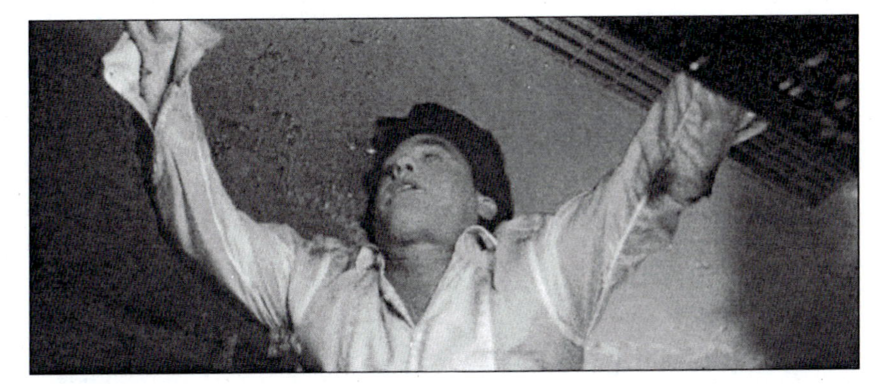

Figure 20. Ramsey dying in the water while saving the other passengers. *Poseidon* (Warner Bros.)

memories in a post-9/11 film. Instead, *Poseidon* substitutes a revised ending that, like the film's allegorical structures, protects viewers from trauma's painful and intrusive return.

Poseidon's final scenes rewrite history: heroes, this film implies, do not die amid fiery chaos and uncontrolled terror. Rather, they move calmly, knowingly to death, strengthened by the consolation of higher purpose. If *Poseidon* reenacts the traumas of 9/11 initially, its ending contains and attempts mastery over them. Both Ramsey's death and Johns's rescue of Connor recall President Bush's 2006 commemoration of "rescue workers who rushed into burning buildings to save lives, knowing they might never emerge again." His death, however, remains at a safe remove from the overt horrors of 9/11 and is further expiated by the installment of Johns and Christian as a new generation of leaders. The film's ending offers, therefore, a comforting assertion of recuperation and redemption, framing 9/11 as, in trauma theorist Kaplan's terminology, "an unhappy event, now safely over."[103]

Ramsey's ultimate demise and abdication of patriarchal authority may also atone for the perceived sins of a post-9/11 America, positioning the suffering, yet salvific masculine body as an "individuated aggregate" for the nation.[104] While, as Susan Jeffords and James William Gibson contend, 1980s hard bodies and warrior culture emulated a Reagan-era politics of aggression and isolation, Ramsey's post-9/11 sacrificial body and Johns's newly softened persona compensate for the image of Bush's post-9/11 America as *too* hard, *too* aggressive, and *too* voracious—in a word, berserk. Ramsey's name suggests both an allusion to and a departure from the hard-bodied masculinity performed by film characters such as Rambo: if Ram*bo* rewrites Vietnam by embodying the fantasy of invulnerability, Ram*sey* reframes the post-9/11 context by performing a national masculinity that is both hard and soft, wounded and redeemed. In this sense, *Poseidon* might be read not only as a healing salve for a wounded nation but also as an apology to the global community.

In contrast to international critiques of the U.S. War on Terror as the unjust and overzealous vengeance of a cold and cruel father, Ramsey's sacrificial death and Johns's conversion perform U.S. identity as compassionate, selfless, and tender.[105] No longer just a father, Ramsey becomes one with *la mer/e* and, in effect, assumes the roles of both father and mother, illustrating Nancy Jay's understanding of sacrifice as a patriarchal appropriation of maternal authority.[106] By replacing Scott's fiery fall with Ramsey's drowning, *Poseidon* invites understanding of his death as regenerative. As America's mythic reconfiguration or even its idealized imagos, Ramsey and Johns perform the nation not as punitive, vengeful, and all powerful but as vulnerable, loving, and life giving. The film constructs the United States, via its synecdochic stand-ins, as a nation that steps in to help and steps aside to make room for others. It is not a nation that causes suffering but one that alleviates pain by assuming it. Within this narrative fantasy, the nation gets recast not as a bloodthirsty action hero but as a kind, benevolent father *and* a laboring, self-sacrificial mother.

The narrative arcs of Ramsey and Johns protect future generations by sacrificing the old guard and its traditional narratives of masculine hegemony. Like Scott, Ramsey surrenders to his failures and shortcomings, trading images of an impenetrable male body for one that is vulnerable, opened up, but neither the sacrifice of the father nor Ramsey's appropriation of the maternal should be read as renouncing U.S. hegemonic privilege, for it is only by becoming a mother that Ramsey truly confirms his status as father, leader, and hero. Like the rhetoric of "compassionate conservatism," Ramsey's and Johns's performances of selfless U.S. masculinity strategically deploy softness in order to shore up the nation's defenses and to use compassion as disavowals of complicity.[107] Ultimately, this post-trauma film repeats the story of the SS *Poseidon* so that once again its sacrificial victim-hero may live, die, and give new life to others, in the process resurrecting the national masculine in the wake of its post-9/11 crucifixion.

Mapping Trauma

I Am Legend depicts a post-apocalyptic world after a virus that was originally created as a cure for cancer mutated and killed most humans or turned them into zombies. Believing himself the plague's sole survivor, military physician Robert Neville (Will Smith) searches for a cure for the disease and battles the infected population, known as Dark Seekers. Neville, who has lost his wife and child, finds temporary solace when he unexpectedly meets other survivors, Anna and a young boy named Ethan, whom he gives his life to save. *I Am*

Legend is the third film to adapt Richard Matheson's 1954 novel of the same name, following *Last Man on Earth* (Ubaldo Ragona, 1964), starring Vincent Price; and *Omega Man* (Boris Sagal, 1971), starring Charlton Heston. *I Am Legend* also references a film that was not based on Matheson's novel, *The World, the Flesh, and the Devil* (Ranald MacDougall, 1959), which focused on the extermination of most of the world's population through chemical warfare.[108]

Of all its antecedents, *I Am Legend* most directly recalls the Vietnam-era *Omega Man*. Both *Omega Man* and *I Am Legend* tell the story of a global epidemic caused by human actions; both films construct Neville as suffering from characteristic symptoms of PTSD; and both films end with Neville's self-sacrificial death. Despite these marked similarities, however, *I Am Legend* does not exactly repeat its forerunner. While *Omega Man*, like its source texts, takes place on the streets of Los Angeles, *I Am Legend* unfolds in New York City, and while *Omega Man* stars a white actor as Neville, *I Am Legend* features a black actor in the lead role.

The translations offered by *I Am Legend*—the repetitions with a difference—suggest rhetorical attempts to reframe and reconstitute more recent history. In particular, translations of both place and race manage post-9/11 discourse about the nation, its leading men, and its prevailing legends, using the discourse of trauma to recuperate the national masculine in the face of anxieties about American vulnerability and critiques of American xenophobia. Operating as a stand-in for the allegedly traumatized nation, Will Smith as Neville fashions his suffering as the basis for collective renewal and redemption. Because of this, the film posits a fantasy of a nation that is post-trauma and post-race.

Without any explicit discussion of 9/11, *I Am Legend* nonetheless refers to cultural memories of this event. Chief among these allusions is the film's updated setting, which does not cite just any version of New York. *I Am Legend* depicts New York as a city in ruins, injured and emptied out by unprecedented loss. In so doing, *I Am Legend* follows such films as *Independence Day* (Roland Emmerich, 1996), which also stars Smith; *Armageddon* (Michael Bay, 1998); and *Fight Club* (David Fincher, 1999), all of which graphically and uncannily anticipate the destruction that transpired on 9/11.[109] In a post-9/11 context, however, images of a fallen New York take on additional registers of political and ideological significance, animating both collective fantasy and cultural memory.

The mise-en-scène engages the traumatic iconography of 9/11: it frequently features the downtown skyline and is filled with dilapidated, uninhabited buildings and streets overrun with dust, debris, and abandoned cars. The buildings, which are marked with red biohazard symbols, appear lacerated and bleeding. The film also features evacuation scenes in which thousands of New Yorkers run for their lives toward bridges to get out of the city. These images of a devastated and abandoned New York City summon memories of the hours, days, and weeks after 9/11 in which everyday life was radically suspended and the landscape was irrevocably changed.

Neville notably designates New York City as "Ground Zero," a phrase that has come to refer to the empty space where the World Trade Center towers once stood; the term borrows from World War II rhetoric that described Hiroshima after the atomic bomb. Frequent references in film dialogue to the date also animate cultural memory of 9/11, indicating that the majority of the film's action takes place between September 4, 2012, and September 9, 2012, just days before the eleventh anniversary of 9/11. These temporal signifiers position *I Am Legend* as offering a fictive "before" and "after" to 9/11, the memory of which is displaced (but not erased) in the text. This film animates the historical context of 9/11 and the language of trauma, constructing 9/11 as a traumatogenic event wounding the nation, its topography, and its people.

The Site/Sight of Trauma

Of special note with regard to memories of 9/11, *I Am Legend* emphasizes mediation in the form of televisions and computer screens, closely recalling the emphasis in *Omega Man* on televisions, movie screens, and surveillance cameras. *I Am Legend*'s attention to mediation demands discussion in the context of the important roles visibility and news media play in cultural memory of and public discourse about 9/11. The film immediately introduces the importance of visuality, opening with a flashback, as television reporters speak in voice-over. In the first shot, a television screen fills the frame as a reporter heralds the discovery of a "miracle cure" for cancer: a genetically engineered strain of the measles virus called Krippin virus (KV). This news footage cuts to New York City three years later, after KV has mutated, spread, and ravaged the planet.

The choice to introduce the fatally mistaken predictions about KV's medical promise through the frame of television news references cultural memory of 9/11 as a hypermediated event whose impacts were intensified by its mediated coverage. The reporter's naïve optimism recalls constructions of the nation before 9/11—a nation unaware of an imminent tragedy. Concern about the nation's blindness and lack of forethought echoes in depictions of infrastructural failures to prevent the spread of KV and to lend aid following its outbreak.[110] As Neville laments, "Nothing happened the way it was supposed to happen. Nothing worked the way it was supposed to work." Instead, "Everything just fell apart."

In contrast to what we see in *Poseidon*, attention to governmental failure to prevent and control the KV outbreak, which was itself the result of human actions and scientific manipulations, unsettles claims of American blamelessness on 9/11. As a military scientist, Neville is professionally connected to the devastation, and *I Am Legend* thus mirrors *Omega Man*'s suggestion that humans are to blame for their own suffering. Both films present a different scenario than Matheson's novel and *Last Man on Earth* do; in those texts, bacteria, not human actions, are to blame. Both *Omega Man* and *I Am Legend* openly confront the perils of modernist progress, and it is no coincidence that both films were produced in the context of U.S. military aggression that deployed new and devastating technologies. Positioning humans as actively producing apocalyptic devastation and suffering—not as passive or innocent bystanders—each film presents a victim-hero who must right a wrong to which he has contributed. In *I Am Legend*, Neville acknowledges his guilt. For example, he defaces an image of himself on a *Time* magazine cover, marking a caption that once read, "Savior. Soldier. Scientist," with a question mark. This expression of self-doubt anticipates his later confession to another survivor, "God didn't do this, Anna. We did."

Introducing the tragic story of KV through the lens of television reporting also implies a causal relationship between the news media's overstated coverage of KV as a "miracle" and the global tragedy that ensued. This frame critiques the role that television news plays in shaping public opinion and policy, echoing widespread discourse about the impact of mediated images as traumatizing to spectators and/or damaging to public opinion. As one of the many films on which the Army Media Relations division has consulted, *I Am Legend* attends acutely to the political, social, and cultural implications of mediation. It is significant that in *I Am Legend*'s fictional news footage a reporter speaks of KV as a miracle full of promise while its creator, Dr. Krippin, appears much more tentative and cautious. This sequence implies that television's tendency toward spectacle and sensationalism is as much to blame for the KV disaster as is the virus itself.

I Am Legend thus anticipates political commentator James Wolcott's 2008 description of news culture as producing an "indiscriminate diet of excitation to keep us permanently on edge," in contrast to what he nostalgically describes as "old-school journalism" that offered a "support bridge though *national trauma*." Wolcott traces this transformation to the Vietnam era, when news coverage of the war "sawed the country into two with its lies and delusions."[111] Hints of cultural memory about the role of media coverage of the Vietnam war also informed President George W. Bush's claim on the fifth anniversary of 9/11 that "we face an enemy determined to bring death and suffering into our homes."[112] This rhetoric frames 9/11 as assaulting the "American home" not just because it involved an attack on U.S. soil but also because of its hypermediation as an event captured live and replayed relentlessly on televisions around the globe.

Television news features prominently throughout the narrative of *I Am Legend* as an organizing element of Neville's lonely existence. In one of his many

Figure 21. Reruns of televised news footage detailing the Krippin Virus disaster and Robert Neville's involvement. *I Am Legend* (Warner Bros.)

repetition compulsions, Neville begins each day watching old news broadcasts recorded before the KV outbreak reached it peak. *I Am Legend* reinforces constructions of 9/11 as an event whose horrors have become inextricably tied to its mediated coverage, producing what Susan Lurie calls a "trauma of spectatorship."[113]

Depictions of Neville's research efforts to find a cure further imply that images may themselves operate as a form of violence. As he experiments on kidnapped Dark Seekers as metaphorical lab rats, Neville visually records his work, taping all of his research trials and using computers to stream videos from his lab. On multiple occasions, *I Am Legend* doubly frames Neville on screen, both within the larger film frame and on the smaller screen of his computer.[114] Frequently, these shots feature Neville looking at his own image on the screen before him. As infected subjects repeatedly die on his table, Neville is forced to see constant and sustained evidence of his impotence, revealing him to be both at the mercy of the disease and a participant in its devastation. Polaroid images of dying and deceased Dark Seekers that line the walls of Neville's lab underscore Neville's participation in this violent, visual economy.

Positioning Neville on both sides of the camera, *I Am Legend* figures him as a victim and complicit witness in ways that recall Lifton and Stozier's ambivalent treatment of 9/11 images. As the object of his own camera's gaze and lone survivor of KV, Neville remains exposed—isolated, unprotected, vulnerable, and on display. As the spectator of his own recordings, Neville also is *exposed to* scenes of violence and devastation, which the film registers as visibly upsetting to Neville. Unlike prevailing constructions of the typical American citizen-spectator as an innocent and unaware bystander on 9/11, however, *I Am Legend* implies that Neville is party to his own trauma of spectatorship, for the images that haunt him are of his own creation.

Figure 22. Anna surveying evidence of Neville's fatal experiments. *I Am Legend* (Warner Bros.)

I Am Legend reinforces this commingling of visibility and violence through a recurrent cinematographic device: as Neville hunts (for food, for infected people), point-of-view (POV) shots reveal Neville's perspective through the scope on his rifle, its targeting apparatus framing the image. In these POV shots, Neville sees life through the literal lens of violence; as audiences share this viewpoint, *I Am Legend* implies that experiences of spectatorship and violence have become inextricably linked. Hence, *I Am Legend*'s emphasis on visual mediation perhaps suggests unease about the almost instantaneous access the world had to the events of 9/11 as they were unfolding and about the implications such experiences have had for American ways of seeing. As I argue later, however, the narrative emphasis on Neville's visual surveillance of his (ultimately successful) hunt for a cure for KV demonstrates the film's efforts to exert mastery over what is imagined as a traumatic past.

An Unmanned World

I Am Legend replays *Omega Man*'s construction of Neville as a traumatized subject. He exhibits textbook symptoms of psychological trauma, including flashbacks, hallucinations, and a repetition compulsion. Neville appears isolated, fragmented, and at his breaking point. Formally, flashbacks operate as a significant editing device throughout *I Am Legend*, like *Omega Man* before it, reiterating the importance of flashbacks as a traumatic trope in Hollywood cinema.

Neville's first flashback occurs moments after the film introduces the KV-infected survivors. Neville and the family dog, Sam, crouch in his bathtub as Dark Seekers screech outside his window. The film cuts to a flashback in which Neville rushes to evacuate his family before the military quarantines the city. Driving his family to the evacuation site but refusing to leave himself,

Neville asserts, "I can still fix this. This is Ground Zero. This is my site." The second flashback occurs as Neville records his latest findings in his search for a cure for KV, cutting from a close-up of Neville's face on his computer screen to continued scenes of the Neville family's attempts to evacuate. Implying that Neville's efforts to cure KV stem directly from his sense of obligation to his family, this structure ties Neville's heroism to his masculinity and patriarchal directives about his paternal responsibilities. As I argue below, his compulsions to kill the Dark Seekers and cure KV suggest a traumatic response to his failure to live up to those directives.

The final flashback occurs after Neville deliberately makes himself vulnerable to an attack by the Dark Seekers, in the hopes that he would not survive the assault. Following brutal violence that renders him unconscious, Neville envisions his last moments with his family. In the flashback, as U.S. military planes bomb the bridges leading in and out of the city, an out-of-control helicopter careens toward the one evacuating Neville's wife and daughter, Marley. Seconds before the fatal impact, the film cuts back to Neville waking up in the present day—like many 9/11 films, *I Am Legend* refuses to show the midair collision.[115]

Auditory and visual hallucinations further reveal Neville's melancholic attachment to his wife and child. For instance, when Neville first discovers other healthy survivors, Anna and a young boy named Ethan, he briefly imagines them to be late wife and daughter; and, in one of the final moments of the film, the whispering voice of his young daughter compels Neville to sacrifice himself to save Anna and Ethan. Neville also frequently speaks to inanimate objects, including store mannequins he has dispersed throughout the city—a device that borrows directly from *The World, the Flesh, and the Devil.* The mannequins never speak, but Neville appears to hallucinate full conversations.

The prominence of family in Neville's flashbacks and hallucinations imply that his trauma relates not only to the large-scale catastrophe that began at "Ground Zero" but also to personal loss. Doubly displaced from his former life, not unlike Ramsey, Neville has lost both his public position of authority as a military scientist and his private position of authority as the patriarch of a nuclear family. His symptoms make clear that much of the damage done to Neville owes to ruptures in his performances of hegemonic masculinity. In the absence of a public sphere in which to act and a private sphere in which to lead, Neville seems uncertain about how to be a man.

Neville also suffers from repetition compulsions; each day of his lonely existence replays the previous one almost exactly. For instance, Neville visits the same video store every day to return a video and rent a new one. He is working through the Blockbuster collection alphabetically and declares himself to be "midway through the 'G's.'" The film Neville returns is *The Godfather* (Francis Ford Coppola, 1972), which many scholars read as negotiating destabilizations of "the family, the nation, and even the integrity of the individual in the Vietnam era."[116] Confirming the routinized nature of his trip to the store, Neville says to a mannequin at the video store, "I'll see you in the morning." Like the watch alarm set consistently to wake him at sunrise and then to alert him to the approach of sunset, these trips to the video store render Neville's days familiar and predictable.

In addition, Neville compulsively broadcasts a radio message every day at noon and waits in the same place, hoping survivors will appear. The message, which is played multiple times throughout *I Am Legend*, makes a plaintive promise to Neville's imagined audience.

> My name is Robert Neville. I am a survivor living in New York City. I will be at the South Street Seaport everyday at midday when the sun is high in the sky. If you are out there, if anyone is out there, I can provide food. I can provide shelter. I can provide security. If there's anybody out there—anybody—please. You are not alone.

This message is significant for a number of reasons.

First, Neville overtly couples his identity as survivor with his location in New York City, emphasizing memories of the city as a central site for loss and as a place that has suffered. It matters that Neville returns incessantly to the South Street Seaport, which is located in Lower Manhattan's financial district, where the World Trade Center towers once stood. Neville's wife and child died at this site, and this is where he returns to attempt suicide. The melancholic Neville remains fixed within his suffering and continues to "act out" his scene of loss, and *I Am Legend* situates downtown Manhattan as the locus of tragedy—the originating point for the traumatic history of its leading man and, by extension, the nation. Just as Neville charts the quadrants of the city, marking spots populated by Dark Seekers, *I Am Legend* maps New York, fetishizing its traumatic topography. Although it never shows Ground Zero, this film maintains the primacy of this wound in the imaginary of the U.S. public.[117]

This emphasis in *I Am Legend* on New York City and Ground Zero as sites (and sights) of great loss reinforces the tendency of 9/11 trauma discourse to mark these places as special and to commemorate their devastation as more significant (more traumatic) than other catastrophic events, recalling Georgian president Eduard Shevardnadze's claim that "only" New York could engender profound responses of "rage" and grief from citizens around the world. Shevardnadze writes, "Today, when I stood in the midst of the utter destruction at ground zero, I was filled with both rage and, ironically, an enormous sense of confidence in the capacity of the human spirit not just to survive such an assault, but to reach a new level of nobility."[118] Extolling the singularity of New York City and the transformative potential of extreme suffering, Shevardnardze's remarks might also be read as a description of Neville's

Figure 23. Robert Neville sitting near downtown Manhattan, enacting a repetition compulsion. *I Am Legend* (Warner Bros.)

gradual conversion from despair and helplessness to his resolute choice "fix" his Ground Zero.

Second, Neville's radio message also reveals his anxiety about his masculinity. He is determined (even desperate) to fulfill the patriarchal injunction to be a provider, insisting on his ability to provide food, shelter, and security. But as much as Neville insists on his abilities as a provider, he also reveals his anxious isolation and fear, ending his message with a forlorn plea for companionship from "anybody." This depiction of Neville constructs trauma as feminizing, having severed him from the social, destroyed his positions of authority, and crippled his ability to obey the directives of hegemonic masculinity. Neville becomes the symbol of the allegedly emasculated nation that was unable on 9/11 to protect its citizens from the terrorist attacks. Echoing rhetoric that posited the nation as emasculated or feminized on 9/11, Neville's radio message reinscribes claims that terror "unmanned" the nation—a fear allegorized in the film's depiction of the last man on Earth. However, as much as *I Am Legend* worries about the post-9/11 national-masculine, it also labors to redeem its fallen hero, recuperating legends of national strength, resilience, and masculinity.

Manning Up

As noted earlier, screens and mediated images play a crucial role in Neville's obsessive and hypervigilant search for a cure for KV. While the emphasis on Neville's visibility—his frequent depiction on computer screens—might be understood as expressing anxiety about the hypermediated post-9/11 context, the simultaneous emphasis on Neville's vision—his ability to see and to use optical technologies—suggests attempts to manage the politics of visibility and spectatorship. By employing images, cameras, and screens in his research process, Neville asserts a totalizing gaze over post-KV chaos and uses media technologies as tools of recovery. This technological control realigns what Isabella Freda describes as typical American politics of spectatorship, placing the citizen-subject once again on the "right" side of the camera—not as its victim-object but as the master of its gaze.[119]

When he is not searching for a cure, Neville hunts Dark Seekers, who take shelter in the darkness of abandoned buildings, closely recalling former president George W. Bush's repeated figurations of terrorists as "shadowy" and hiding in "caves and shadows." Exploiting the nocturnal creatures' vulnerability to light, Neville stalks the Dark Seekers street by street, echoing Bush's insistence on September 20, 2001, that the United States strive "to hunt down, to find, to smoke out of their holes" those he believed to be responsible for the 9/11 attacks. Like Bush, Neville refuses to turn a "blind eye" to his enemies, who become the objects of his active, investigative gaze. The trope of Neville-as-hunter performs a further restabilization of the politics of spectatorship, positioning the nation's cinematic stand-in as an agentive looker rather than as prey. Visual emphasis on Smith's muscular physique and a montage sequence depicting Neville's rigorous exercise routine underscore the gendered nature of this transformation.

If 9/11 has been framed in public discourse as a symbolic castration that unmanned the nation, Neville's strength and resilience assert his ability to "man up" in the face of tragedy. His dedication to curing KV and protecting his site, Ground Zero, performs a version of national identity that is unrelenting in its pursuit of security and justice. *I Am Legend*'s fantasy of unyielding heroism resonates with Farrell's account of the berserk style and reinforces former president Bush's "stay-the-course" rhetoric about the seemingly endless war on terror. Infiltrating the Dark Seekers' hives, Neville affirms Bush's repeated insistence that we "go after" our enemies "where they live"—a positioning mirrored by resemblances between the film's construction of hidden, nocturnal Dark Seekers and Bush's description of terrorists as guided by a "dark vision" and as hiding in "shadowy networks."

Neville's compulsion to "fix" New York illustrates the ambivalence that inheres in the "berserk style," which can elicit both derision (as an act of madness) and praise (as an act of valor).[120] Although *I Am Legend* expresses ambivalence about Neville's complicity in the KV disaster, the narrative ultimately absolves Neville of such guilt, praising his subsequent actions as the result of traumatic loss and the source of the world's recovery. *I Am Legend* carefully manages Neville's guilt through two strategies. First, the film counterbalances Neville's violence—what Morrow might call his commitment to "rage and retribution"—with examples of his vulnerability and compassion. Second, it recuperates evidence of both Neville's weakness (or impotence) *and* his hyper-masculine vigilantism through the logic of self-sacrifice, allowing Neville to undo past losses and atone for transgressions.

Evidence of aggression, hardness, and agency as signifiers of Neville's masculinity coexist with evidence that he is kind, loving, and, sensitive—a characterization supported by Smith's extratextual persona. Throughout the film, his relationship with Sam and memories of his deceased wife and daughter reaffirm Neville's softness. The fact that Smith's own daughter plays his diegetic child adds to constructions of Neville as an attentive father. Registering his woundedness and counterbalancing his resolute pursuit of his enemies with his unflagging love for family, this characterization of Neville echoes the Bataillean assertion that virility belongs not to the strong or invulnerable but to the tragic man.[121] Neville's role may also be read as repairing public narratives about the post-9/11 nation as berserk, inviting understanding of the nation not as vindictive but as compassionate and life-giving.

In the film's final scenes, Neville's paternalistic relationship with his fellow survivors, Anna and Ethan, and his self-sacrificial death firmly establish him as a warm and loving but also strong and resolved victim-hero. After Dark Seekers follow Anna and Ethan to Neville's home, Neville adopts the role of protector. By safeguarding his new companions, Neville rewrites history, atoning for the traumatic loss of his family and his failures as both a public servant and a patriarch. Anna and Ethan, in effect, become his new family, as signaled by the hallucination in which Neville imagines them to be his late wife and daughter. As Dark Seekers rush in, Neville ushers Anna and Ethan into his basement laboratory and hides them in a cement enclosure in a shatterproof cell. While Neville's wife and daughter died publicly in the wide-open expanse of the New York City skyline, Neville sequesters his figurative family underground in the confines of his fortified domestic sphere. Crafting a new ending for his family's narrative, Neville restores home as a safe space. If New York City has been lost, Neville redeems one small corner of his home as a place of refuge in the city.

Neville enjoins Anna and Ethan to deliver salvation to the rest of the world. Having just discovered that his serum is curing his captive Dark Seeker, Neville realizes that her blood may now transmit immunity to others. He draws her blood and gives the vial to Anna to dispense after his death. With Anna and Ethan safely buried in their cement enclosure, Neville (holding a picture of his wife and child) grabs a grenade and pulls the pin, killing himself and the Dark Seekers but sparing Anna and Ethan. Compelled to repeat the sacrificial gesture of his cinematic progenitor from *Omega Man*, Neville gives his own life to beget new ones; a new family is born not from the laboring body of a mother but from the broken body of a "tragic man."[122]

This act of self-sacrificial regeneration simultaneously confronts and contains the trauma of death, subjecting Neville to its finality but affording him mastery nonetheless. While the devastation wrought by KV may have exposed Neville's (and the nation's) ineptitude and weakness, Neville actively and effectively wills this final trauma himself. If at first "everything just fell apart," Neville engineers the final staging of his story. The end of Neville's life becomes the beginning of his legend. This exaltation of redemptive death reaffirms the cultural significance of the "ultimate sacrifice" and the assumption that death (in the trenches or on the battlefield) is the noblest performance of civic duty.

Lost in Translation

The denouement of *I Am Legend* (like that of *Omega Man)* differs sharply from the endings of Matheson's novel and *Last Man on Earth*. These prior texts offer dystopic conclusions, killing both Nevilles tragically, not as an act of salvation.[123] The sacrificial violence of *I Am Legend*'s final scenes also constitutes a revision to the film's original script. In the original ending, Neville neither dies nor kills the Dark Seekers but encourages peaceful coexistence. In this version, Neville recalls the protagonist in Matheson's novel, realizing that as much as the Dark Seekers have become the monsters of his legend, he has become the monster of theirs, hunting down, kidnapping, and torturing the bodies of their people.

In this original ending, Neville understands that his "test subjects" are hostages, his "experiments" forms of torture. The Dark Seekers do not invade his home as animalistic marauders but come to rescue one of them he had taken prisoner. Neville apologetically returns his captive to her people. Without further violence, the Dark Seekers go home, while Neville, Anna, and Ethan leave to find a rumored survivor's colony with the cure for KV in hand. Giving up his quest for mastery over KV, Neville chooses a path of acceptance; and giving up his imperialist desire to control New York, no longer "his" site, Neville cedes the land to its rightful owners.

This original ending to *I Am Legend* offers dramatic potential for revising prevailing narratives about U.S. exceptionalism, imperialism, and cowboy politics, inviting self-reflexive attention to the violence of the nation-state. This ending offers empathy and friendship to the Other and builds rather than burns bridges. This ending did not find its way to the big screen, however; Warner Bros. rejected this ending (and its potential political subversions and ethical demands) and relegated it to the bonus materials on the DVD as an "Alternate Ending" in favor of an ending that revalorizes sacrificial economies of violence, masculinist heroism, and rejection of the Other.

In the ending of the final cut, Neville maintains his misrecognition of the Other as monster. Refusing to bear witness to his own violence, he obliterates all traces of himself and the traumatic history he had helped to create. After Neville detonates the grenade, the screen fades to white, visually signaling the film's attempts to clean up or whitewash an untidy past. Killing the Dark Seekers and himself, Neville creates a new Ground Zero, "ruins" from which a revised legend can be generated and recovery from trauma can be promised. Although *I Am Legend* initially blames Neville for his suffering, its reliance on sacrificial logic undermines this critique, once again positioning the male body as the final solution to traumatic suffering, his martyrdom atoning for and absolving guilt.

Neville's sacrifice thus acts as expiation, both a purging of guilty parties and redemption—a cleansing of guilty hands. As Neville seals off Anna and Ethan and annihilates the remains of KV, *I Am Legend* intimates that traumatic history can indeed be undone and contained, offering a fantasy of moving on that is not based on bearing witness and painful self-reflexivity but is equated with leaving behind and closing off. Killing himself and the Dark Seekers, Neville ensures that evidence of the traumatic past is destroyed, like the virus itself.

This cinematic version of closure and recovery demonstrates Farrell's assertion that trauma often becomes an "enabling fiction," used here to justify Neville's violent rejection of the Other.[124] Constructing KV as a national trauma—compounded by the personal traumas of familial loss—endows Neville with the moral authority needed to legitimate his violent act of erasure. Following his self-sacrifice, what Neville leaves behind is not a history of disease, infrastructural collapse, governmental complicity, and oppression but instead a new story of recovery, rebirth, and redemption. If the story of KV might be understood as an allegory for American loss on and since 9/11, this narrative structure uses the imagined wounds of the nation as both justification for the violence of the nation-state and as evidence that the nation once was and can again be whole, unified, and healthy. And if 9/11, like the KV virus, is to be understood as an anomalous interruption to U.S. life, then Neville's successful quest for a cure offers the possibility of finding closure and moving on from tragic loss.

As she and Ethan escape, Anna recounts Neville's achievements—her words playing in voice-over as they enter a gated survivor's colony after leaving New York City behind. As she enters the gates, Anna praises Neville's "restoration of humanity." The use of voice-over narration resembles survivor testimony and reinforces the film's insistence on closure and moving on. Anna's hopeful words offer the promise of an end to suffering and an "after" following traumatic loss, and the opening and closing of the colony's gates reinforces the film's attempts at closure, with the material evidence of suffering and loss locked safely outside.

Just as *Poseidon*'s setting manages trauma with distance, Anna's conspicuous reference to times and dates further reinforces this notion that trauma can be contained in the past. Anna explains, "On September 9th, 2012, at approximately 8:49 P.M. he discovered that cure and at 8:52 he gave his life to defend it."

Figure 24. Anna and Ethan moving on into the gated survivors' colony. *I Am Legend* (Warner Bros.)

This reference to the temporal specificity of Neville's sacrificial heroism allows the film to compress past, present, and future. Fictively winding back time to those days before September 11th, *I Am Legend* attempts to rewrite traumatic history. The film gets "close" to the temporal signifier of 9/11—almost but not quite touching its memory—in order to erect a new temporal monument, one when the world was reborn. Anna's rhetoric inverts assertions that 9/11 "changed everything," promising rebuilding and new beginnings.

Anna declares, "We are his legacy. This is his legend. Light up the darkness." The film then closes with Bob Marley's "Redemption Song." The use of Marley's music and the repeated iteration of Marley's phrase "Light up the darkness" link Neville to the reggae icon, whom the narrative constructs as an activist for social change and racial equality. At the same time that the film's ending refuses to confront Neville's (and the nation's) history of violence and oppression, *I Am Legend* openly lays claims to promises of racial equality and harmony. These promises, however, prove to be empty ones. Despite the film's overt discussion of racism, its translations of race and place maintain the privilege of both U.S. national identity and whiteness.

Post-Race to the Finish

I Am Legend's most significant departure from *Omega Man* (and from sacrificial films more generally) is its introduction of a black star into the role of sacrificial victim-hero. In this regard, the extratextual significance of Smith's adaptation of Heston's prior role bears noting. At the time of *Omega Man*'s release, Heston was associated with the left. In his first autobiography, Heston describes himself as an opponent of the Vietnam War and as a vanguard supporter of civil rights, having marched in 1963 with Martin Luther King Jr. By the time of *I Am Legend*'s release, Heston was well known as an icon of the right: a former president of the National Rifle Association and a centerpiece of the culture wars, fiercely opposed to affirmative action and identity politics.[125]

If Heston's transformation might be understood as emblematic of the nation's shift from the leftist sixties with its emphasis on collective action to the right-wing eighties and the Reagan-era culture of individualism, then Smith's adoption of Heston's role might be understood as a corrective. The film's conspicuous attention to race might also be understood as, at best, a national apologia for America's histories of racialized violence and xenophobia or, at worst, a disavowal of them, especially given that critiques of the racial politics in the United States became intensely visible in post-9/11 public discourse about the War on Terror.[126]

I Am Legend's choice of leading man seems especially significant because Smith is known as a black actor with great popularity and credibility in cultural spaces traditionally defined as white. Adilifu Nama positions Smith as a "seminal figure in American [science fiction] cinema." Smith's persona makes him an ideal candidate for delicately negotiating tensions in American public culture around the subject of race: a popular and entertaining actor, not known for speaking out politically, Smith can appeal to both black and white audiences without forcing too blunt a confrontation with racial politics.[127]

Citing such films as *Independence Day*, *Men in Black* (Barry Sonnenfield, 1997), and *I, Robot* (Alex Proyas, 2004), Nama contends that Smith has "reinvigorated the status of blackness in [science fiction] cinema" and unseated a "host of white protagonists who confronted the science fiction metaphors of American cultural crisis."[128] Given his striking presence in the science fiction genre, Smith's role as Neville might inspire an uplifting and even redemptive narrative of social progress and change, as if his casting constitutes a kind of victory over histories of racism and inequalities. Interestingly, similar logic reverberated not long after *I Am Legend*'s release during what would eventually become Barack Obama's successful run for the White House.

I Am Legend invites such optimistic interpretations of Smith's role in the film through its construction of Bob Marley, whose album *Legend* plays throughout the film. In fact, Neville repeats the refrain from Marley's "Three Little Birds" ("Don't worry about a thing / 'Cause every little thing is gonna be alright") throughout the film as his survival mantra. Neville describes Marley as asserting a "virologist's idea that you could cure racism and hate—literally cure it—by injecting music and love into people's lives." This rhetorical stance is significant for a number of reasons.

First, at the level of diegesis, this remark overtly links Marley and Neville, the virologist—a link underscored by Neville's decision to name his daughter after the late singer. Although Neville chooses to annihilate (rather than accept) the Dark Seekers, the overt associations with Marley invite understanding of

Neville's violence not as an act of destruction but as an act of salvation. Instead of encouraging reflection on Neville's oppression of and hatred toward the infected population, this reference to Bob Marley positions Dark Seekers as the sources of hate that must be destroyed, marking them, in the rhetoric of George W. Bush, as the "evil-doers." According to such logic, Neville's sacrificial death marks the *end* of racist hatred rather than another instantiation of it. Despite the film's pledge that Neville offers a new hopeful beginning and new ways of seeing, Neville's vision remains tied to economies of violence. This new beginning and the end of darkness still derive from violent and tragic loss; trauma has not been cured or undone. It has simply been displaced.

Second, this reference to Marley's belief that art can operate like an inoculation against racism operates at an extratextual level, positioning both Smith (as artist) and *I Am Legend* (as work of art) as cures to a racist past. *I Am Legend* implies that it might "inject" hope and love into the lives of its audience as an antidote to racism and xenophobia, but the film offers no critical attention to its participation in the ongoing politics of Othering. In fact, this promise operates as a cover for the film's reinscription of racist logics. Articulating a post-race fantasy, *I Am Legend* invites understandings of racism as a problem of history that no longer matters or requires attention, at the same time that it unwittingly betrays this very claim. The doors on that past, the film implies, have been firmly locked shut—as embodied by Neville's impenetrable cell and the sequestered survivor's colony—and audience members should, quite literally, move on.

This rhetorical strategy anticipates remarks made by 2008 Republican presidential nominee John McCain during his concession speech to President-Elect Obama.[129] Addressing the historic election of the first African American president, McCain described the nation as having "come a long way from the injustices that once stained our nation's reputation and denied some Americans the full blessing of American citizenship," as if injustices do not continue in the present day and as if all Americans are granted equal rights to citizenship. Referencing the language of trauma, McCain explained that the "memory" of racism "still had the power to wound"—that is, until now.[130] McCain's use of the past tense implies that these memories no longer carry the power to wound, positing a fictive after or end to the transgenerational traumas of racism.

McCain positioned the nation as a "world away from the cruel and frightful bigotry of *that* time," offering "no better evidence" than the "election of an African American to the presidency of the United States." McCain thus identified Obama's election as a turning point in American history, after which there should be no basis for a critique of legacies of national or civic identity, asserting, "Let there be no reason now . . . let there be no reason now for any American to fail to cherish their citizenship in this, the greatest nation on earth."[131] Like the rhetoric of Heston a decade earlier, McCain's speech asserts that race should no longer operate as a marker of injustice and that oppression can be understood (and forgotten) as belonging to "that time."

The diegetic links between Neville and Marley as virologists similarly imply that Neville's victory over the Dark Seekers and Smith's triumph as a megastar should be understood as a victory over bigotry and that racism, like the KV virus, should be understood as a thing of "that time" against which survivors can be inoculated. The "now" inaugurated by *I Am Legend*—and McCain's speech, only one year later—is constructed as post-race and post-trauma, a world in which racialized violence and suffering should no longer be said to exist. The proof, as implied by *I Am Legend* and McCain, can be seen in the black male bodies on the screen and in the Oval Office.

And yet, despite such promises of hopeful new beginnings and a world where race no longer matters, *I Am Legend* seems somewhat anxious about Neville's status as a legitimate victim-hero, implying that his heroism is compromised by his race, or, more precisely, by his blood. In *Omega Man*, Neville's blood becomes the source of new life in post-apocalyptic Los Angeles as both the serum that cures those infected by the plague and as a symbolic marker of Neville's self-sacrifice. Although this seventies-era film might seem progressive in its depiction of an interracial relationship between Heston and co-star Rosaline Cash, Neville is careful to declare this his redemptive blood is "genuine 160-proof old Anglo-Saxon"—linking the purity and potency of his blood to his whiteness. Smith's Neville can make no such declarations about his blood, which significantly, is *not* the blood that will regenerate the population. Instead of giving his own blood, which boasts immunity to KV, Neville draws blood from his female hostage, the recovering Dark Seeker whom he kills with a grenade only moments later.

Refusing to offer up Neville's blood as the source of new life, *I Am Legend* maintains fantasies about the purity and naturalness of whiteness—such that not one drop of black blood will be used to restore humanity. According to such logic, the rite/right of sacrifice belongs to Neville only provisionally. Thus, even as an exception that introduces a black actor into a white role, *I Am Legend* refuses to sever the hegemony of masculinity from whiteness, reinforces the assumption that traumatic heroism is naturally the province of white men, and reinscribes the privileged position of the white male as the nation's noblest and most valuable citizen-victim. Both *Poseidon* and *I Am Legend* promise new beginnings for the nation and its citizens by returning to a more-than-twice-told tale and reinscribing old legends about sacrifice, the nation, masculinity, and whiteness. Just as they fixate on 9/11 as a singular moment in history, these films also single out the white male subject as uniquely able to make good use of his suffering.

EPILOGUE

BIG-SCREEN MEMORIES

A frozen image of a colossal tower in the midst of collapse suddenly begins to reverse itself. As if by magic, the tower gathers in its scattered pieces and pulls itself together. Smoke and debris, once filling the sky, disappear into the building, which, for a moment, stands in one piece. Then, the building's collapse begins again. This disorienting process of rise and fall—of imagined reconstruction and disintegration—continues in a loop for over three minutes in the YouTube video "9/11 Tower Collapse." Commenting on similar images played and rewound on ABC news coverage on September 11, 2001, Caryn James describes this spectacle as a fantasy of recovery, an antidote for catastrophic loss. Writing in the *New York Times* on September 12, she notes, "We saw history reverse itself; the building appeared whole, as if in a wishful dream."[1] Such footage encapsulates the nation's response to the events of 9/11: on the one hand, incessantly replaying the images of the day, and on the other hand, yearning to undo their memory.

Mass-mediated access to the events of 9/11 was virtually instantaneous; they were witnessed by many as a live event unfolding on television. In the days, weeks, and years that followed, images of the destruction of the World Trade Center were produced ad nauseum as still photographs in newspapers, magazines, and books and as video footage played on television and on the Internet.[2] On anniversaries of 9/11, for instance, networks and cable news stations frequently commemorate the date with continuous coverage of the original event, airing numerous documentaries and news segments about the 9/11 attacks. In some cases, not unlike Robert Neville's repetition compulsions in *I Am Legend*, news outlets rerun original news coverage, actually replaying old footage of the events of 9/11 as they first unfolded on televisions around the world. Joshua Gunn contends that this incessant repetition of images suggests "an obsessive haunting, a cultural performance of witnessing, a longing to return to, and escape from, the violent scene."[3]

In the months leading up to the fifth anniversary of 9/11, this tendency toward repetition became especially pronounced in popular culture. Multiple films during the summer of 2006 explicitly addressed the events of that day, including Paul Greengrass's *United 93*, Danny Leiner's *The Great New Wonderful*, and Oliver Stone's *World Trade Center*. Although the global media landscape included countless productions about 9/11, these commercial films sparked considerable controversy about their timing and the appropriateness of 9/11 as a subject for Hollywood.

As texts that also returned to the violent scene of 9/11, *United 93* and *World Trade Center* became objects of debate because of their alleged potential to cause trauma. Much of the deliberations surrounding these 9/11 films focused on their timing and suitability. For example, audiences in Los Angeles and New York are reported to have chanted "Too soon!" in response to theatrical trailers for *United 93*. In his review of *United 93*, Deroy Murdock wonders if the "four years, seven months, and 17 days" separating 9/11 and the film's release constituted enough temporal distance.[4]

Echoing such concerns, in April 2006, only one month before the release of Wolfgang Petersen's big-budget disaster remake *Poseidon*, a Gallup poll indicated that only 16 percent of Americans were "very likely" to see a film about 9/11 and that almost 42 percent of Americans were "not at all likely" to see such a film. Indeed, with approximately 43 percent of the nation suggesting that a movie about 9/11 was a "bad thing," a film explicitly addressing the events of 9/11 may have seemed a risky bet.[5] The post-9/11 sacrificial allegory *Poseidon* and its contemporary *I Am Legend*, which appeared in December of the following year, avoided this landmine by displacing (rather than confronting) the perceived traumas of 9/11.

The close attention to the meanings and implications of this body of 9/11 films, however, stands in sharp contrast to the fairly flippant public responses to the more usual films of the 2006 summer marketplace: blockbusters.[6] In contrast to critical dismissals of a film such as *The Passion of the Christ* as being overly invested in particular religious doctrines and world views, blockbusters frequently receive censure for an apparent lack of concern about politics, ideology, and history. The summer blockbuster *Poseidon* was no exception. Released on May 12, 2006, *Poseidon* was considered a disaster by many critics, often described as a film long on special effects but short on content—or as one review describes it, "exciting and nerve-wracking in the moment" but empty.[7] *TV Guide* called *Poseidon* "brainless entertainment," and the *Village Voice* disregarded it as "an utterly empty-skulled genre mechanism and nothing more."[8]

One and a half years later, *I Am Legend* experienced similar treatment. Released in anticipation of the Christmas holidays, another movie season notorious for producing big-budget blockbusters, *I Am Legend* was called a "schlocky zombie horror flick."[9] Many critics assessed the film as offering not much more than "kick-back-and-enjoy-the-spectacle pleasure" and "terrific mindless fun."[10] Wesley Morris's review for *Christian Science Monitor* goes even farther, declaring *I Am Legend* to be "apolitical to the bone" and lacking any "allegorical nerve."[11] Kyle Smith's review for *New York Post* actually applauds the film for omitting the "story-clogging despair and political allegory" found in a film such as *Children of Men* (Alfonso Cuarón, 2006), which he jokingly describes as making "apocalypse look like kind of a downer."[12]

In an illustration of the perceived disparity between "serious" films about 9/11 and "empty" blockbusters, *Variety* ran articles about *United 93* and *I Am Legend* on the same page in May 2006. Just days before the release of *Poseidon* and just a few months shy of the fifth anniversary of 9/11, *Variety* described *United 93* as a film with a political agenda and relevance. At the center of the article, a graphic depicting a plane flying over the Statue of Liberty asks, "How are we as Americans supposed to respond?" The article explains that despite the film's potential to "touch too raw an emotional nerve for some moviegoers," conservatives were praising *United 93* in order to galvanize "support for President Bush's war on terrorism." The article notes, for instance, Dennis Prager's belief that "it is just about every American's duty to see this film."[13]

On the same page, *Variety* ran a much smaller article about *I Am Legend* called the "Revival of the Week." Featuring an image of a smiling Will Smith, this industry-oriented article recounts the pre-production difficulties of the film, indicating that Smith had confirmed plans to remake *I Am Legend* after numerous failed attempts.[14] The article begins with the line, "You can't keep a good vampire tale down," and is filled with numerous tongue-in-cheek vampire puns. In contrast to the description of *United 93* as a serious film that offers a "vivid re-creation of the events of Sept. 11," *Variety* frames *I Am Legend* as a lighthearted blockbuster.[15]

The snapshots provided in these two articles—echoed by numerous reviews of both films—suggest that *United 93* and *I Am Legend* could not be less similar. The seemingly incidental spatial proximity occupied by these allegedly dissimilar films within the pages of *Variety*, however, unwittingly mirrors their largely *unacknowledged* ideological propinquity. Although critical treatments of 9/11 remain largely unspoken in *I Am Legend*, this film, like *Poseidon* before it, attempts to reenact, make sense of, and move past what has been constructed as the traumatic memory of that day. Despite being largely written off as empty entertainment, however, *Poseidon* and *I Am Legend* bear a striking resemblance to the heavily scrutinized and allegedly more serious 9/11 films that preceded them.

Gunn argues that "all cultural productions—not simply so-called news, presidential speeches, political talk shows, newspaper columns, and so on—participate in the affective economy of the political," even blockbuster films.[16] To dismiss the films of sacrifice discussed is this book for lacking serious attention to political, social, or cultural issues is to overlook (and underestimate) America's overinvestment in the sacrificial economy. Further, to disregard the rhetorical, allegorical, and cultural significance of sacrificial films is to miss their contribution to America's ongoing trauma culture. *Poseidon* and *I Am Legend*—like the other films discussed in this book—may be exhilarating commercial movies, but they are something *more* than "brainless entertainment" and "mindless fun."

The films addressed in this book rarely, if ever, directly address the histories of trauma to which they seem to respond, relying instead on allegorical displacement, such that even the "emptiest," "schlockiest," and most "brainless" of films may have significant rhetorical weight within a political culture and may play an active role in shaping collective memory and national fantasies. Films such as *Omega Man*, *The Poseidon Adventure*, *Titanic*, *Armageddon*, *Poseidon*, and *I Am Legend* can effectively contribute to trauma discourse and make arguments about cultural memory, the national masculine, and civic duty in large part *because* they appear (and in some cases even claim) to say nothing; and the tendency among reviewers to cast off these films as silly and insignificant may actually contribute to the ideological efficacy of these (big) screen memories.

For Freud, screen memories are inconsequential, or "trivial," memories that displace "objectionable" ones in act of forgetful (mis)remembering meant to offer a defense against, or avoidance of, a traumatic past.[17] To this end, screen memories are largely illusory, "almost like works of fiction" that may hinder a subject's ability to understand his/her own history.[18] Similarly, by substituting a fantasy of redemptive sacrifice for critical attention to the perceived traumas of history, allegorical narratives may, in fact, encumber the nation's ability to confront its complicity in and dependence on its own imagined injuries.

If such films can reaffirm trauma culture without much notice or critical consideration, the nation's fantasy structures may, as a result, be subtly reaffirmed and reinforced. While masculinist fantasies of American resilience and redemption must be constantly reinscribed, they must also be carefully, even delicately, negotiated, especially when they are imperiled or called into question. When spoken too plainly, such fictions of American buoyancy can be (like many of the films considered here) written off as narcissistic jingoism or outdated machismo. When quietly articulated within an allegorical register, these fantasies may be naturalized and normalized as self-evident; and when anchored to the bodies of specific cinematic victim-heroes, these national fantasies may create an identificatory paradigm that invites viewers to imagine themselves as part of an idealized American community. Although these films can never actually undo or repair the perceived wounds of the past, their performances of sacrificial redemption imagine the nation as rising, phoenix-like, from its own ashes and encourage audiences to share in this mythic triumphalism. Allegories turn back time, inviting new understandings of American experiences of terror and loss and providing a fictional cure, or a way to move on, for a wounded collective.

The alleged healing offered by sacrificial films, however, does not encourage critical consideration of national identity or politics. It is built on fantasy and sanitized cultural memory. The efficacy of the allegorical cure stems precisely from its avoidance of any close, unsettling examination of the larger political structures and histories that shape and are shaped by national traumas. It invokes a comforting fiction of therapeutic closure without the painful reflexivity and inspection central to both bearing witness and recovery. This is not to say that mediated texts cannot and should not attempt to provide solace to an injured or grieving collective, but it is a critique of texts that do so by offering cultural anesthesia based on fantasies of recuperation and denials of unresolved suffering.

Indeed, not unlike presidential hopeful John Kerry's 2004 assertion that 9/11 "brought out the best in all of us," the trauma discourse at work within sacrificial films implies that the nation has not only suffered and recovered from tragedy but also has been redeemed and improved in the process. As a result, these allegorical salves may actually forestall public critique of the masculinist assumptions undergirding not only most blockbusters but also much recent American rhetoric and military policy. Although such allegories might not directly implicate national history, they may participate in the construction of cultural fantasies and, as such, help constitute the traumatic rhetorics and sacrificial economies with which the nation rewrites its past, frames its present, and charts its future. Operating somewhere *between* the registers of cultural didacticism and "pure Hollywood spectacle," popular sacrificial films cast national identity and civic duty as dependent on the traumatic heroism of men.[19]

In response, textual criticism can help lay bare national fictions and invite confrontation with America's mythic figurations in order to intervene against their disastrous reinscription—critical work that is uniquely, if not inadvertently, engendered by the nature of allegorical composition. As Robert Hariman argues, allegories are always "iconographic, associational, incomplete."[20] Unlike purely representational discourse, a "richly layered, dynamic liminality" exists between the allegorical text and its "multiple layers of meaning" that engenders multifarious interpretations and requires "active interpretive movement."[21] Implying that a text can say one thing and mean another, allegory inherently affirms the potential of polysemy and agentive reading, rendering the text always open and pliable, never fixed or stable. Like a screen memory, which cannot help but expose the trauma it struggles to conceal, allegory ultimately "defeats the idea that there is one reality or one totalizing design" and thus disallows the closure sacrificial allegories may seek to evoke.[22] Allegories maintain the ambivalence that characterizes both sacrifice and trauma, the drive toward closure always commingled with an impulse toward opening up and falling apart. The allegorical mode thus uniquely enables the critic to offer up new readings that may, in accordance with the logic of sacrifice, stand in for and/or challenge the interpretations the text seems to privilege.

When critics engage this dynamic and liminal space, we also animate our ability to generate inventive, unexpected readings. Doing so allows critics to take up Bonnie Dow's charge to "embrace the vocabulary of creation and art." Dow encourages critics to so "think of ourselves not as investigators of rhetoric but as creators of it." As Dow suggests, critics do not merely discover or respond to texts; we help to create them—to bring them into being through our interpretive work.[23] Allegories lend particular resonance to this creative critical process by giving the critic vast and vibrant space in which to do his/her work and by requiring the critic to articulate the various levels of meaning that exist in and around allegorical texts. The sacrificial films addressed in the book thus reveal how allegorical displacement unwittingly empowers the critic to replay, remember, and remake texts and to generate analyses that envision any number of wishful new beginnings.

NOTES

INTRODUCTION

1. Gibson's film relies heavily on flashback editing, which operates as a chief signifier or embodiment of trauma in the cinema. Flashbacks to prior moments in Christ's life repeatedly interrupt the scene of his crucifixion, returning to such experiences as the Last Supper. In addition to its violent content and emphasis on gore, *The Passion* might also be considered as traumatizing film through the formal interventions of editing.

2. Owen Gleiberman, "Faith Healer? Our Critics Wrestle with the Questions Raised by Mel Gibson's Bloody, Polarizing *The Passion of the Christ*," *Entertainment Weekly*, March 5, 2004, 46. Gleiberman also connects *The Passion* to the genre of horror, calling it "a splatter film in which the victim embraces his own dismemberment." Other critics noted *The Passion*'s use of horror conventions. David Ansen's review for *Newsweek* links *The Passion* to such horror films as *The Exorcist* and *Jacob's Ladder*, suggesting that it is "more likely to inspire nightmares than devotion"; see David Ansen, "So What's the Good News?" *Newsweek*, March 1, 2004, 60. Even the conservative *National Review*, which typically favored the film in its reviews, notes a link to horror; see Thomas Hibbs, "The Horror & *The Passion*," *National Review*, April 9, 2004, http://article.nationalreview.com/?q=OWUoNDIwMTMzNTA5YjA5NmJiMGIxOGE2NDk5YzFkM2U=.

3. Lisa Schwarzbaum, "Faith Healer? Our Critics Wrestle with the Questions Raised by Mel Gibson's Bloody, Polarizing *The Passion of the Christ*," *Entertainment Weekly*, March 5, 2004, 46. Other reviews cite the film as torturous or painful to watch. Ansen describes himself as feeling "abused" by the film, punished "for who knows what sins"; see Ansen, "So What's the Good News?," 60. Leon Wieseltier calls the film a "repulsive masochistic fantasy, a sacred snuff film" that produces a "profoundly brutalizing experience." Consequently, he warns, "Children must be protected from it." See Leon Wieseltier, "The Worship of Blood," *The New Republic*, March 8, 2004, 19. Louise Kennedy's review for *Boston Globe* links the film's "image of macho martyrdom" to its unsettled and unsettling historical context. Noting that "its fixation on suffering and blood, its fascination with public humiliation and torture, and its skillful use of ghastly images to flood the viewer with guilt and horror" make *The Passion* "a genuinely medieval piece

of work," Kennedy argues that the film is a product of its own "fearful and militaristic moment." She ties the film's "immersion in dramatic gore" to particular "unforgettable images on the news"—such as repeated shots of the World Trade Center towers burning on 9/11—that at the time of the film's release were frequently being described as traumatic to the American public. See Louise Kennedy, "Getting Medieval by Stressing Public Suffering, *The Passion* Taps into Pop Culture's Darkest Impulses," *Boston Globe*, March 7, 2004.

4. Ansen describes *The Passion* as the "peculiar, deeply personal expression of the filmmaker's faith," and he connects the film to Gibson's larger body of work, claiming, "There's always been a pronounced streak of sadomasochism and martyrdom running through Gibson's movies, both as an actor and a filmmaker." As a result, Ansen speculates that "on some unconscious level, 'The Passion of the Christ' is, for Gibson, autobiography." See Ansen, "So What's the Good News?" 60.

5. A rhetoric of sacrifice can be found in online fan postings. One reads, "I am so proud of [Gibson] and thankful to him at offering up his career as a sacrifice to advance the message of Christ"; see *www.truthorfiction.com/rumors/g/gibson-passion.htm*. Likewise, the Christian website Beliefnet awarded Gibson a Lifetime Achievement Award in 2006 for his willingness "to sacrifice all that he had for the sake of his mission" of producing *The Passion*. In an interview with Pat Robertson, on his Christian talk show *The 700 Club*, Gibson himself used this language, describing the pain of making this film and the suffering caused by the resulting media fallout as a necessary part of the struggle to bring about change in Hollywood. See Shannon Woodland and Scott Ross, "Mel Gibson Recut," *CBN.com*, http://www.cbn.com/entertainment/screen/passion_gibson_031105.aspx.

6. The term "sacrificial victim-hero" expands upon Sally Robinson's concept of the "victim-hero." See Sally Robinson, *Marked Men: White Masculinity in Crisis* (New York: Columbia University Press, 2000), 220. In the sacrificial variation of this model of wounded masculinity, the male figure does more than redeem himself through injury; he necessarily dies, giving his life in exchange for the salvation of others.

7. Kirby Farrell, *Post-Traumatic Culture: Injury and Interpretation in the Nineties* (Baltimore, Md.: Johns Hopkins University Press, 1998), 44.

8. See Anton Karl Kozlovic, "The Structural Characteristics of the Cinematic Christ-Figure," *Journal of Religion and Popular Culture* 13 (Summer 2006), http://www.usask.ca/relst/jrpc/art8-cinematicchrist-print.html. See also Christopher Deacy, "Screen Christologies: An Evaluation of the Role of Christ-Figures in Film," *Journal of Contemporary Religion* 14, no. 3 (October 1999): 325–337.

9. Numerous works address the significance of Jesus iconography in American culture; for examples, see Richard Fox, *Jesus in America: Personal Savior, Cultural Hero, National Obsession* (New York: Harper Collins, 2005); and Stephen Prothero, *American Jesus: How the Son of God Became a National Icon* (New York: Farrar, Straus, and Giroux, 2003). However, these works address the transformations in and appropriations of the image of the historical Jesus, not the logics of trauma and sacrifice that inform the crucifixion story.

10. Jacinda Read, *The New Avengers: Feminism, Femininity, and the Rape-Revenge Cycle* (Manchester: Manchester University Press, 2000), 11.

11. Throughout history, a privileged mode of sacrifice was the offering of the first-born son, the most cherished child in patriarchal cultures. See Ivan Strenski, "Between

Theory and Speciality: Sacrifice in the 90s," *Religious Studies Review* 22, no. 1 (January 1996): 12.

12. Read, *New Avengers*, 11.

13. The American Psychiatric Association's *Diagnostic and Statistical Manual of Mental Disorders* (DSM-IV) offers a comprehensive and diverse list of experiences that may produce post-traumatic stress disorder: "Traumatic events that are experienced directly include, but are not limited to, military combat, violent personal assault (sexual assault, physical attack, robbery, mugging), being kidnapped, being taken hostage, terrorist attack, torture, incarceration as a prisoner of war or in a concentration camp, natural or manmade disasters, severe automobile accidents, or being diagnosed with a life-threatening illness. For children, sexually traumatic events may include developmentally inappropriate sexual experiences without threatened or actual violence or injury. Witnessed events include, but are not limited to, observing the serious injury or unnatural death of another person due to violent assault, accident, war, or disaster or unexpectedly witnessing a dead body or body parts. Events experienced by others that are learned about include, but are not limited to, violent personal assault, serious accident, or serious injury experienced by a family member or a close friend; learning about the sudden, unexpected death of a family member or a close friend; or learning that one's child has a life-threatening disease." *Diagnostic and Statistical Manual of Mental Disorders-IV* (Arlington, Va.: American Psychiatric Association, 2000), 463.

14. Robinson, *Marked Men*, 5.

15. Ibid., 10.

16. This list relies upon worldwide box office gross incomes as reported by the online database Box Office Mojo. For the complete list, see http://www.boxofficemojo.com/alltime/world/.

17. See Susan Jeffords, *The Remasculinization of America: Gender and the Vietnam War* (Bloomington: Indiana University Press, 1989); Susan Jeffords, *Hard Bodies: Hollywood Masculinity in The Reagan Era* (New Brunswick, N.J.: Rutgers University Press, 1994); and Barbara A. Biesecker, "Remembering World War II: The Rhetoric and Politics of National Commemoration at the Turn of the 21st Century," *Quarterly Journal of Speech* 88, no. 4 (November 2002): 393–409.

18. Roger Luckhurst, *The Trauma Question* (New York: Routledge, 2008), 181.

19. Ruth Leys, *Trauma: A Genealogy* (Chicago: University of Chicago Press, 2000), 2.

20. Ibid., 2. Susannah Radstone offers another summation of canonical understandings of trauma: "From the perspective of trauma theory, such events short-circuit the mind's and the culture's (defensive) sense-making capacities. Instead of passing through processes of narrativization and memory making, [traumatic events] pierce through those defenses, lodging in the mind or in the culture as the shrapnel of traumatic symptomatology"; Susannah Radstone, "The War of the Fathers: Trauma, Fantasy, and September 11," in *Trauma At Home: After 9/11*, ed. Judith Greenberg (Lincoln: University of Nebraska Press, 2003), 118. This understanding of trauma has been widely criticized, particularly by humanities academics, including Judith Butler, Slavoj Žižek, and Leys and Radstone. Nonetheless, this model of trauma continues to inform medical-scientific research and practice and that is the model that has become hegemonic in popular discourse. As such, it is this model of trauma that shapes and is shaped by the films cited in this book.

21. Bessel A. Van der Kolk and Alexander McFarlane, "The Black Hole of Trauma," in *Traumatic Stress: The Effects of Overwhelming Experience on Mind, Body, and Society*, ed. Bessel A. Van der Kolk, Alexander McFarlane, and Lars Weisaeth (New York: Guilford Press, 1996), 4.

22. Patricia Cohen, "The Study of Trauma Graduates at Last," *New York Times*, May 8, 1999, B11.

23. Cathy Caruth, *Unclaimed Experience: Trauma, Narrative, and History* (Baltimore, Md.: Johns Hopkins University Press, 1996), 4.

24. Dominick LaCapra, *Writing History, Writing Trauma* (Baltimore, Md.: Johns Hopkins University Press, 2001), 41.

25. Caruth, *Unclaimed Experience*, 4.

26. Judith Herman, *Trauma and Recovery: The Aftermath of Violence—From Domestic Abuse to Political Terror* (New York: Basic Books, 1992), 1, Herman's italics.

27. Georges Bataille, "Concerning the Accounts Given by the Residents of Hiroshima," in *Trauma: Explorations in Memory*, ed. Cathy Caruth (Baltimore, Md.: Johns Hopkins University Press, 1995), 227, 232.

28. Herman, *Trauma and Recovery*, 3, 175.

29. Dori Laub, "Truth and Testimony: The Process and the Struggle," in *Trauma: Explorations in Memory*, ed. Cathy Caruth (Baltimore, Md.: Johns Hopkins University Press, 1995), 69, 64, Laub's italics.

30. Herman, *Trauma and Recovery*, 175.

31. Ibid., 195.

32. Laub, "Truth and Testimony," 70.

33. Ibid., 69.

34. Maurice Stevens, "Ephemeral Traces: Enigmatic Signification, Race, and the Sciences of Memory," in *Memory, Haunting, Discourse*, ed. Maria Holgren Troy and Elisabeth Wennö (Karlstad, Sweden: Karlstad University Press, 2005), 281.

35. Ibid.

36. Hal Foster, *The Return of the Real: The Avant-Garde at the End of the Century* (Cambridge, Mass.: MIT Press, 1996), 168. Foster is careful to distinguish uses of trauma in popular culture from the humanistic study of trauma, such as the work of Caruth, which address the theoretical and cultural implications of trauma and its representation. I do not make such an absolute distinction; while humanistic theories of trauma might be more complex and nuanced than the discourse of trauma that circulates in Hollywood cinema, I understand academic trauma theory as drawing from and contributing to the same fantasies of subjectivity at work in popular film. Perhaps there is no clearer example of these overlaps than Bataille.

37. Laub, "Truth and Testimony," 63, my italics.

38. Stevens, "Ephemeral Traces," 281.

39. Foster, *Return of the Real*, 168, Foster's italics.

40. Robinson, *Marked Men*, 10.

41. Radstone, "War of the Fathers," 118, 121.

42. Ibid., 120.

43. Farrell, *Post-Traumatic Culture*, 1, 153.

44. Herman, *Trauma and Recovery*, 7. Ivan Strenski argues that the concept of sacrifice also has a cyclical history, eliciting considerable discussion in some moments

and relatively none in others. He contends that the fascination with sacrifice might be understood as symptomatic of larger (but largely unstated) cultural anxieties. Strenski suggests that sacrifice might be "better called a syndrome, rather than an objective 'thing' with its name written on it." Given the variable contexts in which sacrifice emerges and the varying lenses through which it is viewed, Strenski encourages us to see the "sacrificial syndrome" as "conventional, provisional, and constructed for particular purposes." That is, Strenski contends that, not unlike trauma, sacrifice (presumably both the practice and the concept) gets repeatedly constituted and marshaled toward a variety of ends that are always historically, culturally, and discursively shaped. See Strenski, "Between Theory and Speciality," 19.

45. John Mowitt, "Trauma Envy," *Cultural Critique* 46 (Fall 2000): 277.

46. Stephen Keane's survey of the genre, for instance, cites the early to mid-1970s and the mid- to late 1990s as benchmarks for the disaster films. In both periods, large numbers of disaster films were released that had marked success at the box office. See Stephen Keane, *Disaster Movies: The Cinema of Catastrophe* (London: Wallflower Press, 2001), 19, 73.

47. Laura. S. Brown, "Not Outside the Range: One Feminist Perspective on Trauma," in *Trauma: Explorations in Memory*, ed. Cathy Caruth (Baltimore, Md.: Johns Hopkins University Press, 1995), 101–102.

48. Robinson, *Marked Men*, 12.

49. Van der Kolk and McFarlane, "The Black Hole of Trauma," 3–4.

50. In their reviews of *The Passion*, both Leon Wieseltier and Stanley Kauffman note ideological links between the film's exaltation of sacrificial death and the militaristic context in which it was released. Wieseltier, for instance, questions the film's "bloodthirstiness," asking, "is the sanctification of murder really what this country needs now?" Alluding to but never referring to the wars in Afghanistan and Iraq and the controversies over Guantanamo, Wieseltier links *The Passion* to the political use of torture, arguing that the film deploys religious discourse to justify the use of physical abuse for political gain. He writes, "Torture has always been attended by explanations that vindicate it, and justify it, and even hallow it. These explanations, which are really extenuations, have been articulated in religious and in secular terms. Their purpose is to redescribe an act of inhumanity so that it no longer offends, so that it comes to seem necessary, so that it edifies. My victim of torture is your martyr." Noting that religions often mourn those who make the "ultimate sacrifice" as much as they lament the "failures of other individuals to do the same," Wieseltier warns that a film like *The Passion* might do more than merely reflect these proclivities but might also contribute to and perpetuate such violent logic. As a film released in a wartime context *The Passion* seems to claim that "violence is good for America." See Wieseltier, "The Worship of Blood," 19–20. Kauffman understands *The Passion* as a film that reaffirms the usefulness or necessity of violence, suggesting that "the $25 million of his own that Gibson is said to have put into this film" might be interpreted as his "way of saying that violence is not always valueless." See Stanley Kauffman, "Gibson's Offering," *The New Republic*, March 23, 2004, 22.

51. Farrell, *Post-Traumatic Culture*, x, 349.

52. Ibid., 187.

53. Robert Hariman, "Allegory and Democratic Public Culture in the Postmodern Era," *Philosophy and Rhetoric* 35, no. 4 (2002): 268.

54. Cathy Caruth, "Recapturing the Past: An Introduction," in *Trauma: Explorations in Memory*, ed. Cathy Caruth (Baltimore, Md.: Johns Hopkins University Press, 1995),153.

55. Caruth, *Unclaimed Experience*, 4.

56. Ibid., 6.

57. Hariman, "Allegory and Democratic Public Culture in the Postmodern Era," 268–269.

58. Ibid., 270.

59. Caruth, *Unclaimed Experience*, 4.

60. Hariman, "Allegory and Democratic Public Culture in the Postmodern Era," 268, 272.

61. Ibid., 281.

62. LaCapra describes the "impasse of endless melancholy" as an experience in which the "process of working through the past and its historical losses is foreclosed and prematurely aborted." For LaCapra, "acting out" occurs when the subject is "haunted or possessed by the past and performatively caught up in the compulsive repetition of traumatic scenes—scenes in which the past returns and the future is blocked or fatalistically caught up in a melancholic feedback loop." LaCapra, *Writing History*, 46, 21.

63. Sigmund Freud, "Screen Memories," in *Early Psycho-Analytic Publications*, vol. 3 of *The Standard Edition of the Complete Psychological Works of Sigmund Freud*, trans. James Strachey (London: Hogarth Press, 1962), 301. Alison Landsberg argues that "a screen memory is a compromise between two forces: one that recognizes the importance of the event and one that, as resistance, tries to protect the subject from it"; Alison Landsberg, *Prosthetic Memory: The Transformation of American Remembrance in the Age of Mass Culture* (New York: Columbia University Press, 2004), 15.

64. Hariman, "Allegory and Democratic Public Culture in the Postmodern Era," 281. Like allegory, screen memories are fraught and imperfect. At the same time that the screen memory "conceals" trauma, it also "betrays [its] underlying secrets." Freud, "Screen Memories," 301.

65. LaCapra, *Writing History*, 133, 24. Freud also understands sacrifice in relation to trauma. He defines sacrificial practice as an expiatory reenactment of Oedipal trauma, in which the son simultaneously atones for guilt about patricidal fantasies, shows deference to the father, and asserts his own authority over the father. See Sigmund Freud, *Totem and Taboo: Resemblances between the Psychic Lives of Savages and Neurotics*, trans. A. A. Brill (New York: Moffat, Yard, and Company, 1918), 254.

66. Georges Bataille, *Inner Experience*, trans. Leslie Anne Boldt (Albany: SUNY Press, 1988), 88.

67. First depicting Karras as a bystander on a movie set during the filming of an antiwar protest scene, *The Exorcist* invites interpretation of the character's subsequent struggles in relation to the larger social dramas that were understood as damaging the nation. The inclusion of the film subplot within *The Exorcist* exemplifies the use of mise-en-abyme—a device that recurs in a number of the sacrificial films considered here, including *Omega Man*, *Titanic*, and *I Am Legend*. Translated as "placing into infinity" or "placing into the abyss," this literary and artistic device refers to a strategy of internal repetition. In a work of art for instance, mise-en-abyme occurs when an image contains a smaller replica of itself; in literature or film, mise-en-abyme is often known as a story within a story or a film within a film. The use of mise-en-abyme bears

noting for its enactment of traumatic sensibilities, including "repetition, seriality, and stasis." This notion of compulsive, endless repetition as a representational strategy also references the "abyss," which is significant given the recurrent tropological connections I note between trauma and the abyss. See Jonathan Boulter, "The Negative Way of Trauma: Georges Bataille's *Story of the Eye*," *Cultural Critique* 46 (Fall 2000): 156; and Leslie Anne Boldt-Irons, "Sacrifice and Violence in Bataille's Erotic Fiction: Reflections from/upon the Mise-en-Abîme," in *Bataille: Writing the Sacred*, ed. Carolyn Bailey Gill (New York: Routledge, 1995), 91–104.

68. E. Ann Kaplan, *Trauma Culture: The Politics of Terror and Loss in Media and Literature* (New Brunswick, N.J.: Rutgers University Press, 2005), 67.

69. Farrell, *Post-Traumatic Culture*, 18.

CHAPTER 1 — REEL PRESENCE, SACRIFICE, AND THE CINEMA

1. Georges Bataille, *Tears of Eros*, trans. Peter Connor (San Francisco: City Lights Books, 1989), 207.

2. Cathy Caruth, *Unclaimed Experience: Trauma, Narrative, and History* (Baltimore, Md.: Johns Hopkins University Press, 1996), 4; Dominick LaCapra, *Writing History, Writing Trauma* (Baltimore, Md.: Johns Hopkins University Press, 2001), 41.

3. Robert Hariman and John Louis Lucaites, *No Caption Needed: Iconic Photography, Public Culture, and Liberal Democracy* (Chicago: University of Chicago Press, 2007), 182.

4. See Noël Carroll, *The Philosophy of Horror* (New York: Routledge, 1990); Laura Mulvey, "Visual Pleasure and Narrative Cinema," *Screen* 16, no. 3 (Autumn 1975): 6–18; Amos Vogel, *Film as a Subversive Art* (London: Weidenfeld and Nicholson, 1974); and Linda Williams, "Film Bodies: Gender, Genre, and Excess," *Film Quarterly* 44, no. 4 (Summer 1991): 3–16.

5. André Breton, *Manifestoes of Surrealism*, trans. Richard Seaver and Helen R. Lane (Ann Arbor: University of Michigan Press, 1972), 184; Paul Hegarty, *Georges Bataille: Core Cultural Theorist* (London: Sage Publications, 2000), 9. See also Dawn Ades, "Photography and the Surrealist Text," in *L'Amour Fou: Photography and Surrealism*, ed. Rosalind Krauss, Jane Livingston, and Dawn Ades (New York: Abbeville Press, 1985), 153–189. Other frequent topics of discussion related to Bataille's personal life include his troubled childhood and his marriage to Silvia Maklès, who left him to marry Jacques Lacan. See Michael Richardson, *Georges Bataille: Essential Writings* (Thousand Oaks, Calif.: Sage Publications, 1998), 18–21.

6. Ibid., 7.

7. Georges Bataille, *Inner Experience*, trans. Leslie Anne Boldt (Albany: SUNY Press, 1988), 194; Georges Bataille, *Theory of Religion*, trans. Robert Hurley (New York: Zone Books, 1992), 45.

8. Richardson, "Expenditure and the General Economy," in Michael Richardson, *Georges Bataille: Essential Writings* (Thousand Oaks, Calif.: Sage Publications, 1998), 95.

9. Georges Bataille, "The College of Sociology," in *Visions of Excess: Selected Writings, 1927–1939*, trans Allan Stoekl, Carl R. Lovitt, and Donald M. Leslie, Jr. (Minneapolis: University of Minnesota Press, 1985), 251.

10. Georges Bataille, *The History of Eroticism*, vol. 2 of *The Accursed Share*, trans. Robert Hurley (New York: Zone Books, 1991), 109.

11. Nancy Jay, *Throughout Your Generations Forever: Sacrifice, Religion, and Paternity* (Chicago: University of Chicago Press, 1992), 17.

12. Georges Bataille, *Consumption*, vol. 1 of *The Accursed Share*, trans. Robert Hurley (New York: Zone Books, 1991), 59.

13. Bataille, *Visions of Excess*, 70.

14. Bataille, *The History of Eroticism*, 109.

15. Bataille, *Visions of Excess*, 73.

16. LaCapra, *Writing History*, 2–3.

17. Carolyn Marvin and David Ingle, *Blood Sacrifice and the Nation: Totem Rituals and the American Flag* (Cambridge: Cambridge University Press, 1998), 4.

18. Georges Bataille, *Literature and Evil*, trans. Alastair Hamilton (New York: Marion Boyars, 2001), 50.

19. Bataille, *The History of Eroticism*, 106.

20. Bataille, *Literature and Evil*, 177, 52.

21. Gil Bailie, "Cinema and Crisis: The Elusive Quest for Catharsis," *Image: A Journal of the Arts* 20 (Summer 1998): 17–18.

22. Bataille, *Literature and Evil*, 66–67.

23. Ibid., 49.

24. Bataille, *The History of Eroticism*, 109.

25. It is not entirely surprising that Bataille speaks the language of trauma only indirectly. Although he reportedly underwent psychoanalysis and was familiar with the work of Freud, whose writings on trauma largely influenced the model of trauma that operates obliquely in Bataille's work, Bataille typically figured himself as an outsider or a dissident with regard to more established or conventional discursive cultures. See Michel Surya, *Georges Bataille: An Intellectual Biography*, trans. Krzysztof Fijalkowski and Michael Richardson (New York: Verso Books, 2000), 76–80. To rely directly on a Freudian lexicon would have endangered Bataille's interest in creating new and radical ways of thinking about subjects, pleasure, and desire. Nonetheless, there are striking resemblances between Bataille's and Freud's theorizations of subjectivity, especially in relation to the subject's desire for undoing, or what Freud would call the death drive, and for his/her conflicting need for self-preservation or mastery.

26. Jonathan Boulter, "The Negative Way of Trauma: Georges Bataille's *Story of the Eye*," *Cultural Critique* 46 (Fall 2000): 156.

27. Georges Bataille, *Erotism: Death and Sensuality*, trans. Mary Dalwood (San Francisco: City Lights Books, 1986), 104.

28. Boulter, "The Negative Way," 163, 154.

29. Bataille, "Concerning the Accounts Given by the Residents of Hiroshima," 230.

30. Ibid., 226, 229.

31. Bessel A. Van der Kolk and Alexander McFarlane, "The Black Hole of Trauma," in *Traumatic Stress: The Effects of Overwhelming Experience on Mind, Body, and Society*, ed. Bessel A. Van der Kolk, Alexander McFarlane, and Lars Weisaeth (New York: Guilford Press, 1996), 3.

32. Bataille, "Concerning the Accounts Given by the Residents of Hiroshima," 228.

33. Laura S. Brown, "Not Outside the Range: One Feminist Perspective on Trauma," in *Trauma: Explorations in Memory*, ed. Cathy Caruth (Baltimore, Md.: Johns Hopkins University Press, 1995), 101–102.

34. Boulter, "The Negative Way," 166; Bataille, *Inner Experience*, 194.

35. Bataille, *Erotism*, 59.

36. Bataille, *Inner Experience*, 119, my italics.

37. Janet Maslin, "Titanic," *New York Times*, December 19, 1997, E1. Boulter notes that similar ambivalence characterizes Bataille's description of a fatal accident in his novella *Story of the Eye*, which exemplifies the "basic dialectic of attraction-repulsion to the scene and sight of trauma"; Boulter, "The Negative Way," 158.

38. LaCapra, *Writing History*, 133.

39. Bataille, *Tears of Eros*, 206; Georges Bataille, *Guilty* (Venice: Lapis Press, 1988), 32; Kaplan, *Trauma Culture*, 2.

40. Bataille, *Guilty*, 35.

41. Bataille, *Inner Experience*, 120.

42. Ibid. LaCapra suggests that notions of the "unrepresentability of the sublime," as in the case of trauma, "would seem to parallel, if not to displace, early modern debates about the Eucharist"; LaCapra, *Writing History*, 190. In those debates, the question was whether or not the Mass should be understood as a sacrifice—a reenactment of Christ's death, as is suggested by the doctrine of transubstantiation—or if it should be understood as a representation.

43. Amy Hollywood, *Sensible Ecstasy: Mysticism, Sexual Difference, and the Demands of History* (Chicago: University of Chicago Press, 2002), 57, 86.

44. Ibid., 95, 91.

45. Bataille, *Guilty*, 36; Bataille, *Inner Experience*, 194, Bataille's italics.

46. Hollywood, *Sensible Ecstasy*, 93.

47. Boulter, "The Negative Way," 155.

48. Hollywood, *Sensible Ecstasy*, 91.

49. Bataille, *Inner Experience*, 194.

50. Boulter, "The Negative Way," 166; Hal Foster, *The Return of the Real: The Avant-Garde at the End of the Century* (Cambridge, Mass.: MIT Press, 1996), 166.

51. John Mowitt, "Trauma Envy," *Cultural Critique* 46 (Fall 2000): 283. Foster similarly suggests that in much "contemporary culture[,] truth resides in the traumatic or abject subject," whose "diseased or damaged body" is fetishized as providing unique access to the real; Foster, *Return of the Real*, 166.

52. LaCapra, *Writing History*, 190–191.

53. Hollywood, *Sensible Ecstasy*, 83. Bataille might address this conundrum by explaining that what he celebrates is self-loss rather than self-sacrifice in which the subject is destroyed but not necessarily offered up. But in both Bataille's writings and the film culture discussed in this book, this distinction gets obscured—or even elided—as the loss of self becomes a means by which the subject can be regenerated. For more on this difference and Bataille's failure to maintain the distinction between self-loss and self-sacrifice, see Carolyn Dean, *The Self and Its Pleasures: Bataille, Lacan, and the History of the Decentered Subject* (Ithaca, N.Y.: Cornell University Press, 1992), especially 228–231.

54. Bataille, *Inner Experience*, 120.

55. Hollywood, *Sensible Ecstasy*, 93; Bataille, *Inner Experience*, 119. This notion that pain might be communicated (or transmitted directly) between a victim and a witness also mirrors what Leys describes as Caruth's mimetic understanding of trauma. Leys writes, "Inherent in Caruth's theory of trauma is the belief that the trauma experienced by one person can be passed on to others" through their witnessing of the trauma. She continues, "The result is that individuals or groups who never experienced trauma directly themselves are imagined as 'inheriting' the traumatic memories of those who died long ago." Leys addresses the hazards of such a perspective, suggesting that it

risks turning trauma into a commodity that can be owned, borrowed, or appropriated. Inasmuch as this logic "makes the trauma of one person always appertain or belong to someone else as well," it also makes "victimhood unlocatable" and able "to migrate or spread contagiously to others." See Leys, *Trauma*, 284, 296.

56. Joan Scott, "Experience," in *Feminists Theorize the Political*, eds. Judith Butler and Joan W. Scott (New York and London: Routledge, 1992), 24.

57. Bataille, *Inner Experience*, 79.

58. Ibid., 53–54.

59. Bataille, *Erotism*, 90; Bataille, *Inner Experience*, 79.

60. Bataille, *Inner Experience*, 131.

61. Georges Bataille, *Sovereignty*, vol. 3 of *The Accursed Share*, trans. Robert Hurley (New York: Zone Books, 1991), 222.

62. Bataille, *Visions of Excess*, 236.

63. Dean, *The Self and Its Pleasures*, 244.

64. Ibid., 228.

65. Ibid., 242.

66. Carolyn Dean, "Introduction," *Diacritics* 26, no. 2 (1996): 3–4.

67. Ibid., 4.

68. Dean, *The Self and Its Pleasures*, 245.

69. Bataille, *Inner Experience*, 134.

70. Dean, *The Self and Its Pleasures*, 245. Bataille's recurrent description of women and heterosexual sex as engendering masculine self-loss also evince masculinist fantasies of subjectivity. He describes women as able to overwhelm, undo, and even "unman" his subjectivity, writing, "Desire for a woman's body, for a tender, erotically naked woman" creates within him "a sort of hallucinatory darkness [that] pushes me slowly over the edge towards craziness . . . in which I escape the illusion of any solid connection between me and the world." Bataille, *Guilty*, 12.

71. Bataille, *Visions of Excess*, 244; Richard B. Ullman and Doris Brothers, *The Shattered Self: A Psychoanalytic Study of Trauma* (Hillsdale, N.J.: Analytic Press, 1988), 5.

72. Jonathan Shay, *Achilles in Vietnam: Combat Trauma and the Undoing of Character* (New York: Scribner, 1994), 180, 188.

73. Julia Kristeva, *Black Sun: Depression and Melancholia*, trans. Leon S. Roudiez (New York: Columbia University Press, 1992), 222–223; Kirby Farrell, *Post-Traumatic Culture: Injury and Interpretation in the Nineties* (Baltimore, Md.: Johns Hopkins University Press, 1998), 185.

74. Farrell, *Post-Traumatic Culture*, 18; Bataille, *Inner Experience*,134.

75. Farrell, *Post-Traumatic Culture*, 18; Eleanor Kaufman, "Falling From the Sky: Trauma in Perec's 'W' and Caruth's 'Unclaimed Experience,'" *Diacritics* 28, no. 4 (Winter 1998): 49; Bataille, *Visions of Excess*, 238. The trope of falling, which expresses ambivalence about trauma as a source of both loss and hope, recurs throughout much of Bataille's work. For example, he writes, "He alone is happy who, having experienced vertigo to the point of trembling in his bones, to the point of being incapable of measuring the extent of his fall, suddenly finds the unhoped-for strength to turn his agony into a joy capable of freezing and transfiguring those who meet it"; Bataille, *Visions of Excess*, 236.

76. Foster, *Return of the Real*, 159–160. Chris Kraus offers a similar critique, noting that female artists who encourage abjection, such as Simone Weil, get frequently censured or marked as pathological, while men operating within similar paradigms

earn praise for being avant-garde or transgressive. See Chris Kraus, *Aliens & Anorexia* (Brooklyn: Semiotext(e), 2000).

77. Gregory Orr, *Poetry as Survival* (Athens: University of Georgia Press, 2002), 121.

78. Bataille, *Inner Experience*, 53–54.

79. Naomi Klein, *The Shock Doctrine: The Rise of Disaster Capitalism* (New York: Picador, 2007), 8; "Text of John Kerry's Acceptance Speech at the Democratic National Convention," *Washington Post*, July 29, 2004.

80. Jay, *Throughout Your Generations Forever*, xxiii.

81. Ibid., xxiii, 147.

82. Ibid., 112.

83. Marvin and Ingle, *Blood Sacrifice*, 4, 6. The use of the term "fallen" to describe soldiers who have died (and likewise firefighters and police officers) not only refers to the loss of life but also connotes that such a loss is noble. See Eleanor Kaufman, "Falling from the Sky: Trauma in Perec's 'W' and Caruth's *Unclaimed Experiences*," *Diacritics* 28, no. 4 (Winter 1998): 49.

84. Marvin and Ingle, *Blood Sacrifice*, 66.

85. Ibid., 24.

86. Ibid., 69.

87. Shay also suggests a specific link between war, sacrifice, and trauma, noting that military training often reiterates the discourse of Christian self-sacrifice, in which soldiers are encouraged to "hold the lives of their comrades dearer than their own." What results, argues Shay, is a "willingness for self-sacrifice [that] is endemic in combat," as is "evidenced by thousands of unambiguously sacrificial deaths in war." Shay contends that despite the "strongly positive view of such self-sacrifice" espoused in religious, militaristic, and nationalist sites, this valorization of sacrifice in combat has traumatic consequences when the sacrificial gesture doesn't accomplish what is intended. "What happens," he asks, "when the sacrifice, or the sincere willingness to sacrifice does not 'work'?" Shay contends that when sacrifice is not achieved or is not perceived as efficacious or purposeful, the survivor may experience feelings of guilt, failure, "spiritual abandonment[,] and meaninglessness" that he links directly with PTSD. Put another way, he indicts the rhetoric of sacrifice as a potential cause of or contributor to combat trauma. Shay, *Achilles in Vietnam*, 74–75.

88. Kaplan, *Trauma Culture*, 24. See also Tom Gunning, "Modernity and Cinema: A Culture of Shocks and Flows," in *Cinema and Modernity*, ed. Murray Pomerance (New Brunswick, N.J.: Rutgers University Press, 2006); Wolfgang Schivelbusch, *The Railway Journey: Trains and Travel in the Nineteenth Century*, trans. Anselm Hollo (New York: Urizen Books, 1979); Lynne Kirby, *Parallel Tracks: The Railroad and Silent Cinema* (Durham, N.C.: Duke University Press, 1997).

89. Kaplan, *Trauma Culture*, 69.

90. Steven Shaviro, *The Cinematic Body* (Minneapolis: University of Minnesota Press, 1993), 45.

91. Ibid., 43.

92. Bataille, *Tears of Eros*, 207.

93. Linda Williams, "Film Bodies: Gender, Genre, and Excess," *Film Quarterly* 44, no. 4 (Summer 1991): 4.

94. Bataille, *Guilty*, 35, Bataille's italics.

95. Shaviro, *Cinematic Body*, 54, 57.

96. Ibid., 42.

97. Penley writes about the relationships *Star Trek* fans form with the franchise's characters, suggesting that female fans of *Star Trek* often find themselves identifying not with a single character but with a multiplicity of characters, including its two male protagonists, Captain Kirk and Mr. Spock. Penley argues that fans of this show may also find themselves identifying not just with individual characters but with the whole of the *Star Trek* universe and its diverse characters and values. Her work stresses the spectator's ability to manage multiple subject positions at once and to tolerate a significant amount of contradiction and fragmentation surrounding his/her identities and identifications. See Constance Penley, *NASA/Trek: Popular Science and Sex in America* (New York and London: Verso, 1997). Clover's work on the horror film emphasizes spectatorial positioning as fluid, shifting, and potentially marked by inconsistencies. She offers a gendered analysis of the modern horror film, attempting, not unlike Shaviro, to complicate feminist film theory's focus on sadism and active looking, critiquing its "repeated denial or avoidance" of spectatorial masochism "in contrast to the wealth of attention lavished on male sadism." Clover's research indicates that the typical male viewers of the horror genre, who are frequently assumed to identify with the killer/monster (also assumed to be male), also find themselves identifying with "screen females in fear and pain." See Carol Clover, *Men, Women, and Chainsaws: Gender in the Modern Horror Film* (Princeton, N.J.: Princeton University Press, 1992), 225, 5. Like Penley, Clover notes the possibility of cross-gender identifications as male viewers may find themselves in "communication" with female characters. Clover also argues that identifications may shift over the course of a film—as in the spectator that begins by rooting for the psycho-killer but eventually aligns him/herself with the female victim-hero. Likewise, it is also possible that spectators may hold multiple identifications simultaneously, taking pleasure in both the crimes of the killer and the struggles of the hero.

98. Janet Walker, "Trauma Cinema: False Memories and True Experience," *Screen* 42, no. 2 (Summer 2001): 214.

99. Hollywood, *Sensible Ecstasy*, 109.

100. Ibid., 109.

101. Boulter, "The Negative Way," 157.

102. Ibid., 158, 174.

103. Roland Barthes, *The Responsibility of Forms* (Berkeley: University of California Press, 1991), 34, Barthes's italics.

104. Hariman and Lucaites, *No Caption Needed*, 183.

105. Bataille, *Tears of Eros*, 207.

106. LaCapra, *Writing History*, 54.

107. Shay, *Achilles in Vietnam*, 188.

108. Ibid., 191.

109. Thomas Laqueur, "Lost Causes," *The Nation*, November 23, 2003, 25.

110. Marita Sturken, *Tangled Memories: The Vietnam War, the AIDS Epidemic, and the Politics of Remembering* (Berkeley: University of California Press, 1997), 85.

111. LaCapra, *Writing History*, 52–53.

112. Gil Bailie, "Cinema and Crisis," 18.

113. Jay, *Throughout Your Generations Forever*, 17. Of the overlapping functions of joining and separating, Jay writes, "Communion sacrifice unites worshippers in one

moral community and at the same time differentiates that community from the rest of the world" (19).

114. Bailie, "Cinema and Crisis," 20. Girard argues that sacrificial practice regulates tensions in a social body: when mimetic desires lead to conflict and the potential for violence emerges, the scapegoating of a sacrificial victim moderates discord and deflates hostility by projecting them outward. The rite of sacrifice, then, aims to restore order and unity to the community. See René Girard, *Violence and the Sacred* (Baltimore: Johns Hopkins University Press, 1979); and Girard, *The Scapegoat* (Baltimore: Johns Hopkins University Press, 1986).

115. Bailie, "Cinema and Crisis," 20.

116. Farrell, *Post-Traumatic Culture*, 24.

117. Shaviro, *Cinematic Body*, 25.

118. Bataille, *Erotism*, 141.

119. Dean, *Self and Its Pleasures*, 243.

120. Shaviro, *Cinematic Body*, 65.

121. Dean, *Self and Its Pleasures*, 244.

122. Tania Modleski, *Feminism without Women: Culture and Criticism in a "Postfeminist" Age* (New York: Routledge, 1991), 7.

123. David Savran, *Taking it Like a Man: White Masculinity, Masochism, and Contemporary American Culture* (Princeton, N.J.: Princeton University Press, 2001), 9.

124. Robinson, *Marked Men*, 125.

125. Ibid., 125.

126. Ibid., 9.

127. Farrell, *Post-Traumatic Culture*, 47.

128. Ibid., 47.

CHAPTER 2 — UNHINGED HEROES AND ALPHA TRAUMAS

1. In 1968, the ratings system of the Motion Picture Association of America replaced the Hays Production Code, which had regulated the content of Hollywood films for over thirty years. Under the new system, which categorizes films according to potentially offensive or disturbing content, films with PG or R ratings have more freedom to depict graphic violence than films aimed at younger audiences. The increase in violence and special effects is also connected to the economic woes of the industry in the late 1960s, when it was near bankruptcy. In response, the industry strove to attract larger audiences with heightened big-screen thrills.

2. Marita Sturken, *Tangled Memories: The Vietnam War, the AIDS Epidemic, and the Politics of Remembering* (Berkeley: University of California Press, 1997), 15–6.

3. Tom Engelhardt, *The End of Victory Culture: Cold War America and the Disillusioning of a Generation* (Amherst: University of Massachusetts Press, 1995), 14–15.

4. Philip Windsor, *Strategic Thinking: An Introduction and Farewell* (New York: Lynne Rienner Publishers, 2002), 181.

5. Judith Herman, *Trauma and Recovery: The Aftermath of Violence—From Domestic Abuse to Political Terror* (New York: Basic Books, 1992), 26, 9.

6. Boyce Rensberger, "Delayed Trauma in Veterans Cited," *New York Times*, May 3, 1972, 19.

7. Ibid.; Robert Jay Lifton, "A Re-Examination," *New York Times*, August 20, 1973, 31.

8. Rensberger, "Delayed Trauma in Veterans Cited," 19.

9. Ibid.; Chaim Shatan, "Post-Vietnam Syndrome," *New York Times*, May 6, 1972, 35.

10. Herman, *Trauma and Recovery*, 27.

11. Shelby Coffey, "Back Home with Three Vietnam Casualties," *Washington Post*, July 19, 1970, 12, 9. Coffey ends the article by mentioning the countless others whose stories of trauma will never be told. He also offers a critique of war as an enterprise built on illusions about the dignity and power of sacrificial death, ending with a quotation from André Malraux's *The Temptation of the West* (1926). After observing a plaque that reads, "He who sacrifices himself joins in the grandeur of a cause," a character from Malraux's novel responds, "But the only grandeur I can see here is that which it owes to sacrifice" (19). Coffey concludes that this paradox is rarely discussed in American public culture because it "depresses the paying customers" to whom war is marketed.

12. Jon Nordheimer, "Post-War Shock Besets U.S. Vets," *New York Times*, August 21, 1972, 1, 24.

13. Susan Jeffords, *The Remasculinization of America: Gender and the Vietnam War* (Bloomington: Indiana University Press, 1989), 116; Engelhardt, *The End of Victory Culture*, 254.

14. Kirby Farrell, *Post-Traumatic Culture: Injury and Interpretation in the Nineties* (Baltimore, Md.: Johns Hopkins University Press, 1998), 44.

15. Jeffords, *The Remasculinization of America*, 120.

16. Robert Jay Lifton, *Home from the War: Learning from Vietnam Veterans* (Boston: Beacon Press, 1973), 39.

17. Ibid., xvii, 35.

18. Ibid., 36.

19. John Mowitt, "Trauma Envy," *Cultural Critique* 46 (Fall 2000): 283.

20. Robert Hariman and John Louis Lucaites, *No Caption Needed: Iconic Photography, Public Culture, and Liberal Democracy* (Chicago: University of Chicago Press, 2007), 21.

21. "Some Ex-GI's Feel Alienated," *Washington Post*, March 16, 1972, H6; Cynthia Robb, "A Nation Wounded," *New York Times*, August 20, 1973, 30. Lifton also applies the term "post-Vietnam syndrome" to the nation as a description of America's failure to acknowledge both the plight of veterans and the nation's complicity in producing such pain. Positing the existence of "powerful war-linked residuum in the American people" related to feelings of "confusion, guilt, rage, and betrayal," Lifton argues, "We have become a nation of troubled survivors of a war not yet over and still just distantly perceived"; Lifton, *Home from the War*, 447–448.

22. Engelhardt, *The End of Victory Culture*, 203–204.

23. Kirby Farrell, "The Berserk Style in American Culture," *Cultural Critique* 46 (Autumn 2000): 191, 193. Following Nixon, President Ronald Reagan began his term of office in 1980 by appropriating the already circulating phrase "Vietnam Syndrome" and using medical language to "diagnose" (what conservatives perceived to be) the negative side effects of the Vietnam War for American morale and national security. While Lifton uses this cultural diagnosis to critique the war effort and to challenge the nation-state's reliance on violence, Reagan's use of this diagnostic rhetoric promotes enhanced militarization of the nation, having attributed the nation's "syndrome" not to the traumas of *war* but to the alleged traumas of *defeat*.

24. Paul Zimmerman, "Moral Midnight," *Newsweek*, June 16, 1975, 76.

25. Mardi Horowitz, "Psychic Trauma: Return of Images after a Stress Film," *Archives of General Psychiatry* 20, no. 5 (1969): 553, 559.

26. J.C. Bozzuto, "Cinematic Neurosis following *The Exorcist*: A Report of Four Cases," *Journal of Nervous and Mental Disease* 161, no. 1 (1975): 43–48. The concept of cinematic neurosis prompted a number of similar studies, including Robinson and Barnett's study of neurosis in relation to *Jaws* (Steven Spielberg, 1975). See J. A. Robinson and A. Barnett, "Letter: Jaws Neurosis," *New England Journal of Medicine* 293, no. 22 (November 27, 1975), 1154–5.

27. Engelhardt, *The End of Victory Culture*, 15

28. Farrell, *Post-Traumatic Culture*, 155.

29. Sturken, *Tangled Memories*, 45.

30. Yvonne Tasker, *Spectacular Bodies: Gender, Genre, and the Action Cinema* (New York: Routledge, 1993), 50.

31. Ibid., 49.

32. Lifton, *Home from the War*, 35. The image of deer hunting plays a major role in Michael Cimino's 1978 film *The Deer Hunter*, which tells the story of young friends damaged by their time in Vietnam. The image was also later used in Francis Lawrence's 2007 remake of *Omega Man*, *I Am Legend*, which features Will Smith-as-Neville hunting deer in an abandoned downtown New York.

33. Ibid., 45.

34. Sturken, *Tangled Memories*, 104.

35. Jonathan Shay, *Achilles in Vietnam: Combat Trauma and the Undoing of Character* (New York: Scribner, 1994), 86.

36. Lifton, *Home from the War*, 35.

37. A similar strategy of anonymity was used almost thirty years later in *Saving Private Ryan* (Steven Spielberg, 1998). One of the earliest scenes of the film depicts a group of unidentified men storming the beaches of Normandy and facing gruesome and graphically depicted deaths before we learn of their individual histories. This anonymity "effectively promotes our patriotic identification with *all* of them while blocking our subjective identification with any *one* of them"; Barbara A. Biesecker, "Remembering World War II: The Rhetoric and Politics of National Commemoration at the Turn of the 21st Century," *Quarterly Journal of Speech* 88, no. 4 (November 2002): 396.

38. Cathy Caruth, *Unclaimed Experience: Trauma, Narrative, and History* (Baltimore, Md.: Johns Hopkins University Press, 1996), 2.

39. Caruth, "Trauma and Experience: Introduction," in *Trauma: Explorations in Memory*, ed. Cathy Caruth (Baltimore, Md.: Johns Hopkins University Press, 1995), 5.

40. Hariman and Lucaites, *No Caption Needed*, 182.

41. Ibid.

42. Maureen Turim, "The Trauma of History: Flashbacks upon Flashbacks," *Screen* 42, no. 2 (Summer 2001): 209.

43. Nordheimer, "Post-War Shock Besets U.S. Vets," 24.

44. Two years after *Omega Man*, *The Stone Killer* (Michael Winner, 1973) reenacted this depiction of the Vietnam veteran as unable to leave behind the violence of war, positioning returning vets as killers for hire.

45. Adam Lowenstein, *Shocking Representation: Historical Trauma, National Cinema, and the Modern Horror Film* (New York: Columbia University Press, 2005), 112.

46. Sturken, *Tangled Memories*, 115, 106.

47. Farrell, *Post-Traumatic Culture*, 175–176. It is interesting to note that one of the earliest documented examples of psychological trauma was attributed to trains and

railway accidents. A condition known as railway spine was documented in survivors of railway accidents in the nineteenth century who developed phantom symptoms even though they had suffered no physiological injuries. See Stevens, "Ephemeral Traces," 277.

48. Andrew Hoskins, *Televising War: From Vietnam to Iraq* (London: Continuum, 2004), 15. Hoskins questions the veracity of claims that television shaped the outcome of the war, citing the greater influence of newspapers; but he notes that whatever the reality, the public attributed more blame to television. Accordingly, I read *Omega Man* not in relation to any alleged reality about the impact of television news coverage but in relation to the assumptions that were circulating at the time and that have become commonplace within the U.S. culture's memory of that war.

49. Marshall McLuhan, *War and Peace in the Global Village* (Ann Arbor: University of Michigan Press, 1968), 134.

50. Steven Shaviro, *The Cinematic Body* (Minneapolis: University of Minnesota Press, 1993), 54.

51. Presenting a film within a film, the scene in which Neville watches *Woodstock* recalls mise-en-abyme. Miming the repetitive nature of trauma and invoking the interminable qualities of the abyss, the recurrence of this device in multiple sacrificial films demonstrates the structuring role the logic of trauma plays in this body of films.

52. Mark Sample, "There Goes the Neighborhood: The Seventies, the Middle Class, and *The Omega Man*," in *Shocking Cinema of the Seventies*, ed. Xavier Mendik (Hereford: Noir Publishing, 2002), 35.

53. Georges Bataille, *Erotism: Death and Sensuality*, trans. Mary Dalwood (San Francisco: City Lights Books, 1986), 59. Understandings of the abject as both attractive and repellent also inform Julia Kristeva's understanding of the abject, which she describes as "simultaneously beseech[ing] and pulveriz[ing] the subject." See Julia Kristeva, *Powers of Horror: An Essay on Abjection* (New York: Columbia University Press, 1982), 5.

54. Sample, "There Goes the Neighborhood," 34.

55. Georges Bataille, *Inner Experience*, trans. Leslie Anne Boldt (Albany: SUNY Press, 1988), 119.

56. Sample, "There Goes the Neighborhood," 30–31.

57. Lifton, *Home from the War*, 226.

58. Ibid., 226–227.

59. Ibid., 238.

60. Such a generous reading of *Omega Man* would suggest its consonance with the film's 1954 source novel, *I Am Legend*, by Richard Matheson. Matheson's novel, in which Neville discovers his likeness to the infected plague victims and chooses understanding of them over violence against them. At the end of the novel, for instance, Neville recognizes that he is the monster of the infected people's legends. Realizing he has become "a scourge even worse than the disease they had come to live with," Neville declares himself "anathema and black terror to be destroyed" and commits suicide so that the world's new population may live in peace without being tormented by him. The novel thus articulates a critical stance toward Neville's prior acts of violence against the infected population, compelling its protagonist to see his similarity to his alleged enemies. After "he understood what they felt and did not hate them," Neville took his life silently, without "butchery before their eyes," by taking pills and simply slipping away. Richard Matheson, *I Am Legend* (New York: Bantam Books, 1954), 151.

61. Ibid., 238.

62. Ibid., 239.

63. Sample, "There Goes the Neighborhood," 35.

64. Sturken, *Tangled Memories*, 131.

65. Michel de Certeau, *The Practice of Everyday Life*, trans. Steven Rendall (Berkeley: University of California Press, 1984), 93, 92.

66. Shaviro, *Cinematic Body*, 25.

67. Lisa rescues Neville on two occasions. First, Lisa and Dutch help Neville escape from the stadium where The Family is preparing his public execution. Flipping on the stadium lights, Lisa and Dutch blind the photosensitive population long enough to hoist Neville onto the back of Lisa's motorbike and drive away. Later, when members of The Family ambush Neville's home and trap him in their line of machine-gun fire, Lisa suddenly appears and shoots Neville's attackers. In both cases, Lisa uses technologies (a motorcycle and a machine gun) effectively, perhaps implying that she has a greater degree of (phallic) mastery of her equipment than Neville has of his own.

68. Sturken, *Tangled Memories*, 113.

69. Bataille, *Erotism*, 91.

70. Nancy Jay, *Throughout Your Generations Forever: Sacrifice, Religion, and Paternity* (Chicago: University of Chicago Press, 1992), xxiii.

71. Ibid., 90; Bataille, *Inner Experience*, 79.

72. Georges Bataille, *Sovereignty*, vol. 3 of *The Accursed Share*, trans. Robert Hurley (New York: Zone Books, 1991), 222, Bataille's italics.

73. This choice of title illustrates the film's key difference from both Matheson's novel and *Last Man on Earth*, neither of which relies on sacrificial death or endows its protagonist with sacrosanct authority. In *I Am Legend*, Neville kills himself not in a salvific act of self-sacrifice but out of despondency and recognition of his own monstrosity. In *Last Man on Earth*, Neville is murdered by the infected people who take over the world in the film's dystopic and largely unresolved ending.

74. Victor Turner, *Dramas, Fields, and Metaphors: Symbolic Action in Human Society* (Ithaca, N.Y.: Cornell University Press, 1974), 69.

75. Sample, "There Goes the Neighborhood," 29. It is significant that Neville falls into a fountain, a symbol frequently used in Christian discourse to describe Christ's blood as nourishing and cleansing. For example, based on biblical references to Christ as "living water" and to Christ's believers as "washed in the blood of the lamb," Christian rhetoric often refers to Christ as the "fountain of life." This image has existed in Christian devotional literature, iconography, and music since the Middle Ages. It is also this image of Christ as a fountain of "living water" that underpins the Christian rituals of baptism, in which participants are said to be reborn through Christ after having been sprinkled with water from a font or submerged in a baptistery. See Ulla Hasstrup, R. E. Greenwood, and Soren Kaspersen, *Images of Cult and Devotion: Function and Reception of Christian Images of Medieval and Post-Medieval Europe* (Copenhagen: Museum Tusculanum Press, 2004).

76. Sample, "There Goes the Neighborhood," 31.

77. Hariman and Lucaites, *No Caption Needed*, 182.

78. Lowenstein, *Shocking Representation*, 128. Lowenstein's discussion of photo finishes derives from the work of Garrett Stewart. Citing such films as *Butch Cassidy and the Sundance Kid* (George Roy Hill, 1969), Stewart argues that the still photo as the final shot of a film works to convey death. Lowenstein extends this analysis in his reading of *Last House on the Left* (Wes Craven, 1972), noting that such images offer political

critiques about the war by referencing and making use of the iconography of photojournalism. Garrett Stewart, "Photo-Gravure: Death, Photography, and Film Narrative," *Wide Angle* 9, no. 1 (1987): 11–31.

79. Ibid., 129.

80. Georges Bataille, *Tears of Eros*, trans. Peter Connor (San Francisco: City Lights Books, 1989), 207.

81. Farrell, *Post-Traumatic Culture*, 18.

82. Hariman and Lucaites, *No Caption Needed*, 244.

83. Kai Erikson, *Everything in Its Path: Destruction of Community in the Buffalo Creek Flood* (New York: Simon & Schuster, 1976), 254. On February 26, 1972, a coal slurry impoundment dam burst, flooding the Buffalo Creek hollow in southern West Virginia with millions of gallons of black wastewater. For a detailed description of the disaster and its aftermath, see Kai Erikson, *Everything in Its Path: Destruction of Community in the Buffalo Creek Flood* (New York: Simon & Schuster, 1976), 28–46.

84. Lowenstein, *Shocking Representation*, 115.

85. Ibid., 115–116.

86. Farrell, *Post-Traumatic Culture*, 18, my italics.

87. Jackie Orr, *Panic Diaries: A Genealogy of Panic Disorder* (Durham, N.C.: Duke University Press, 2006), 21.

88. Eleanor Kaufman, "Falling from the Sky: Trauma in Perec's 'W' and Caruth's *Unclaimed Experience*," *Diacritics* 28, no. 4 (Winter 1998): 44, 49.

89. Shaviro, *Cinematic Body*, 54.

90. Ibid., 54.

91. McLuhan, *War and Peace in the Global Village*, 134.

92. Shaviro, *Cinematic Body*, 53. The effectiveness of *Poseidon Adventure* in encouraging such participation is demonstrated by its prominent fan culture, which, decades after the film's release, is marked by active participation with the text, including role-playing, reunions, and reenactments. Documentation and examples of the film's fan culture can be seen in the 2003 documentary *Cult and Culture: Poseidon Adventure.*

93. Lifton, *Home from the War*, 137.

94. Ibid., 39, 35.

95. Scott also closely resembles another cinematic contemporary, Father Karras, the sacrificial victim-hero of *The Exorcist*. Like Scott, Karras is torn—between his training as a priest and a psychiatrist, between his commitments to his biological family and his congregation, between his faith in God and his fear of the suffering he witnesses every day—and searches desperately to find meaning and purpose in his life. Also like Scott, Karras battles with the Church, doubting his place within the institution, and a significant portion of the diegesis in *The Exorcist* is devoted to Karras's identity crisis. But it is precisely Karras's marginalization and frustration with Church policies that enable him to save Regan MacNeill from demonic possession, and it is the disquietude in his personal, spiritual, and professional life that compels him to give it all up in order to save others. This is also the case with Scott.

96. Joan Scott, "Experience," in *Feminists Theorize the Political*, eds. Judith Butler and Joan W. Scott (New York and London: Routledge, 1992), 24–25.

97. Ibid., 25.

98. Bataille, *Literature and Evil*, 177.

99. Shay, *Achilles in Vietnam*, 180.

100. Engelhardt, *The End of Victory Culture*, xi.

101. Lowenstein, *Shocking Representation*, 115–116.

102. Scott's language as he prepares to sacrifice himself anticipates, almost exactly, the final words uttered by Father Karras in *The Exorcist*. Commanding the devil to leave young Regan's body and enter his own, Karras yells, "Take me!"

103. Jonathan Boulter, "The Negative Way of Trauma: Georges Bataille's *Story of the Eye*," *Cultural Critique* 46 (Fall 2000): 166–167, Boulter's italics.

104. Carolyn Dean, *The Self and Its Pleasures: Bataille, Lacan, and the History of the Decentered Subject* (Ithaca, N.Y.: Cornell University Press, 1992), 244.

105. The importance of falling is reiterated in *The Exorcist* as well. After having commanded the devil to leave Reagan's body and enter his own, Karras hurls himself out of Regan's bedroom window and down a flight of stairs. His corpse remains broken and bloodied on the concrete after his fatal fall.

106. Kaufman, "Falling from the Sky," 49–50.

107. Neville's and Scott's interment in watery graves also illustrates what Jay identifies as the gendered work of ritualized sacrifice as a means to remedy human origins in maternal bodies and offer rebirth through male ones; see Jay, *Throughout Your Generations Forever*, xxiii. As Klaus Theweleit argues, a symbolic link exists between bodies of water and female bodies, especially maternal ones, as in the linguistic connection between *la mer* (the sea) and *la mère* (the mother). See Klaus Theweleit, *Male Women, Floods, Bodies, History*, vol. 1 of *Fantasies* (Minneapolis: University of Minnesota Press, 1987), 292. If we accept Theweliet's analysis, the heroes' final and fatal submersion in water suggests a symbolic return to the maternal matrix, making rather explicit what Jay describes as the appropriative logic of the sacrificial economy in which fathers are positioned to replace mothers as a new originary site, abjected so that they may become the alpha and the omega, father and mother, hero and victim, life and death. Jay, *Throughout Your Generations Forever*, xxiii.

108. Sample, "There Goes the Neighborhood," 40, 31.

CHAPTER 3 — FREE FALLS IN THE 1990S

1. David Margolick, "Lorena Bobbitt Acquitted in Mutilation of Husband," *New York Times*, January 22, 1994, 7.

2. Mark Seltzer, *Serial Killers: Death and Life in America's Wound Culture* (New York: Routledge, 1998), 1.

3. Margolick, "Lorena Bobbitt Acquitted," 7.

4. In the universe of sacrificial films, *Independence Day* is somewhat anomalous. It is not the chief male protagonist that dies but a more minor character. What also distinguishes this film from its peers is the position of an African American actor (Will Smith) in the lead role. Given the prevailing whiteness of the sacrificial victim-hero, it seems significant that the hallowed rite of sacrificial death is displaced onto a more minor character (Randy Quaid), whose whiteness endows him with a certain kind of redemptive authority that is denied to the film's black protagonist, as if his lack of what *Omega Man* might call "genuine 160-proof old Anglo-Saxon" blood denies him the credibility or privileged status to be offered up as a cherished object. This rule was broken in *I Am Legend* (the 2007 remake of *Omega Man*), which does allow a black character (also played by Will Smith) to offer up himself as a sacrificial victim-hero but not by sharing his blood. I discuss the issue of race and blood more fully in chapter 4.

5. Seltzer, *Serial Killers*, 6, 22.

6. Ibid., 22.

7. Ibid.

8. Ibid., 254. As another useful illustration of this wound culture and the fascination with catastrophe, a 1994 article from *Time* details the "rise and fall" of "crisis rhetoric." See "The Rise and Fall of the Political Catchphrase," *Time*, February 14, 1994, 14.

9. E. Ann Kaplan, *Trauma Culture: The Politics of Terror and Loss in Media and Literature* (New Brunswick, N.J.: Rutgers University Press, 2005), 32–33. Grady relies primarily on a study by Dr. Joseph A. Boscarino that traced the experiences of soldiers who had served in Vietnam for many years. Grady considers Boscarino an authority on the subject of PTSD not because of his education or professional credentials (or even the specifics of his research) but because of his authority as a Vietnam veteran. Grady quotes him as saying, "I know what combat veterans went though and saw some of it personally." Denise Grady, "War Memories May Harm Health," *New York Times*, December 16, 1997, F9.

10. Kaplan, *Trauma Culture*, 33.

11. A search of the *New York Times* database from 1980 to 1989 yields 93 matches for the search term "post-traumatic stress disorder." From 1990 to 1999, this number jumps to 288.

12. Other examples of 1990s-era books that examined trauma in relation to Vietnam include Wilbur Scott, *The Politics of Readjustment: Vietnam Veterans Since the War* (New York: Aldine De Gruyter, 1993), Eric T. Dean, *Shook over Hell: Post-Traumatic Stress, Vietnam, and the Civil War* (Cambridge: Massachusetts, 1997), H. W. Chalsma, *The Chambers of Memory: PTSD in the Stories of U.S. Vietnam Veterans* (Northvale, New Jersey: Jason Aronson, 1998), and Ron Zaczek, *Farewell, Darkness: A Veteran's Triumph over Combat Trauma* (Annapolis: Naval Institute Press, 1994).

13. Kaplan, *Trauma Culture*, 33–35.

14. John Mowitt, "Trauma Envy," *Cultural Critique* 46 (Fall 2000): 274, 283. Trauma Studies was not without its critics. As Kaplan explains of such critiques, "what seemed increasingly like a 'faddish' aspect to humanities trauma research soon produced strong objections from some literary and film scholars in the late 1990s." As an example of this critical literature, Kaplan cites Michael Roth's "Why Trauma Now?," a lecture he delivered at the Humanities Institute in Stony Brook, New York, in 1998. This work builds upon Roth's earlier critical work on the relationship between history, memory, and mourning in Michael S. Roth, *The Ironist's Cage: Memory, Trauma, and the Construction of History* (New York: Columbia University Press, 1995). See Kaplan, *Trauma Culture*, 34. Mowitt's work also critically addresses when, why, and how trauma studies developed within the humanities. Mowitt sees the development of the field as in part a response to the culture wars of the late 1980s and the 1990s. See Mowitt, "Trauma Envy," 284.

15. Patricia Cohen, "The Study of Trauma Graduates at Last," *New York Times*, May 8, 1999, B9.

16. Ibid.

17. Georges Bataille, "Concerning the Accounts Given by the Residents of Hiroshima," in *Trauma: Explorations in Memory*, ed. Cathy Caruth (Baltimore, Md.: Johns Hopkins University Press, 1995), 229.

18. Cohen, "The Study of Trauma Graduates at Last," B9.

19. Mowitt, "Trauma Envy," 283.

20. Jane Brody, "After the Disaster Comes the Trauma," *New York Times*, April 26, 1995, B9. Brody, like Cohen, assumes that trauma is universal and asserts that clinicians had only recently "come to realize just how widespread and potentially crippling the disorder can be." Stating that PTSD "is more common than even most experts believe," she cites a survey by Dean G. Kilpatrick that suggests that PTSD may have affected over 12.3 million women in the United States alone. In contrast, *Washington Post* reporter Dan Brown was more skeptical about the prevalence of trauma, stating that the "burgeoning industry of books, videotapes and seminars offering counselors help in diagnosing cult abuse victims . . . has helped popularize what is, in fact, an extremely rare set of traumatic circumstances, namely child abuse organized around Satanism." See Dan Brown, "Halloween Can Haunt Troubled Personalities," *Washington Post*, October 31, 1991, A16.

21. Claims about trauma's ubiquity resonate in a 1994 letter to the editor of the *New York Times*. The author writes, "It is likely that a significant number of your readers have been trauma patients, have been touched by trauma or will feel the ripple of trauma at some time in their lives." Meg Kallman O'Connor to Editor of *New York Times*, *New York Times*, September 4, 1994, NJ9.

22. Cohen, "The Study of Trauma Graduates at Last," B9.

23. Ibid., B11, B9.

24. "How to Heal Psychological Wounds," *New York Times*, September 28, 1993, B9. Many newspaper articles describe specific treatment protocols to help trauma survivors repair their damaged subjectivities. For instance, Brody describes "systematic desensitization," in which traumatized individuals are "gradually exposed to the circumstances that provoke their trauma-induced symptoms, at first through their imagination and eventually in the real world." See Brody, "After the Disaster Comes the Trauma," C9. Sharon Linsker describes Eye Movement Desensitization and Reprocessing (EMDR). In this process, a clinician guides a patient's eye movements from left to right as he/she tries to recall a traumatogenic experience. These left-to-right motions are understood as enabling the brain to integrate and process otherwise fragmentary and intrusive memories so that a survivor might be able to "remember an experience as unpleasant, but not relive it again and again." Sharon Linsker, "Eye Motions That Limit Trauma," *New York Times*, December 10, 1995, WC10. Similar to Mardi J. Horowitz's 1969 work on "stress films," such cognitive-behavioral therapies assume that manageable doses of traumatic imagery can enable survivors to master their trauma and control intrusive symptoms, such as flashbacks, nightmares, and repetition compulsions. See Mardi Horowitz, "Psychic Trauma: Return of Images after a Stress Film," *Archives of General Psychiatry* 20, no. 5 (1969): 553, 559.

25. Cathy Caruth, "An Interview with Robert Jay Lifton," in *Trauma: Explorations in Memory*, ed. Cathy Caruth (Baltimore, Md.: Johns Hopkins University Press, 1995), 137.

26. Ibid. Lifton understands trauma to produce a "doubling of self," in which a traumatized person's subjectivity splits. The new subjectivity threatens to take over the original self and must therefore be eliminated. It is, therefore, striking that themes of trauma (and restorative sacrifice) recur in films about demonic possession. Just as trauma frequently is described as possessing survivors, *The Exorcist* depicts a subject whose body (quite literally) had been possessed and taken hostage, requiring elimination of the evil other and reintegration of the victim's subjectivity after her possession.

27. For example, President George H. W. Bush asserted, "The specter of Vietnam has been buried forever in the desert sands of the Arabian peninsula." George H. W. Bush, "Radio Address to United States Armed Forces Stationed in the Persian Gulf Region," March 2, 1991, in *Public Papers of the Presidents of the United States: George H. W. Bush: 1991*, Book 1 (Washington, D.C.: Government Printing Office, 1991), 207. He is also quoted as saying, "By God, we've kicked the Vietnam syndrome once and for all!" Maureen Dowd, "War Introduces a Tougher Bush to the Nation," *New York Times*, March 2, 1991, 1. For a full discussion of the Gulf War as a "spectacular orchestration of a new ending for the Vietnam War," see Marita Sturken, *Tangled Memories: The Vietnam War, the AIDS Epidemic, and the Politics of Remembering* (Berkeley: University of California Press, 1997), 125–144.

28. Brent Mitchell, "Medical Lessons of Vietnam Pay Off for Wounded in Persian Gulf War," *Washington Post*, June 30, 1991, A4.

29. Ibid.

30. The 1993 coverage of the World Trade Center bombings also reproduces the assumption that the nation has learned from the mistakes of Vietnam. See Jon Nordheimer, "For Blast Survivors, Shock Waves of Stress," *New York Times*, March 10, 1993, A1, B4.

31. Daniel Goleman, "Why Some Overcome Trauma and Others Do Not," *New York Times*, May 8, 1996, C10.

32. See Carole Paquette, "Adults Recall Suffering Abuse," *New York Times*, May 14, 1995, LI10+; Christian Berthelsen, "Women Are Speaking Out to Heal Trauma of Rape," *New York Times*, April 4, 1999, 19. Another key example of feminist work in the 1990s connecting rape to the study of trauma is Judith Herman's *Trauma and Recovery: The Aftermath of Violence—From Domestic Abuse to Political Terror* (New York: Basic Books, 1992).

33. Sally Robinson, *Marked Men: White Masculinity in Crisis* (New York: Columbia University Press, 2000), 6, 125. In *Misery*, a white male novelist suffers bodily trauma and psychological torture at the hands of a crazed female fan, while in *Disclosure*, the story of a white male business executive who is systematically stalked and sexually assaulted by female co-worker bears traces of contemporary discourse about gendered violence and rape. Even more noteworthy, the protagonists of both *The Prince of Tides* and *Falling Down* bear hallmark signs of PTSD: in the former, an unemployed schoolteacher seeks therapy to help recover memories of childhood physical and sexual abuse; in the latter, an unemployed defense worker "snaps" and violently "berserks" on the streets of Los Angeles. Note also the recurrence of "falling" as a descriptor of traumatic experience in *Falling Down*, whose tagline was "The adventures of an ordinary man at war with the everyday world."

34. See also P. Marin, "The Prejudice against Men," *The Nation* 253, no. 2 (July 8, 1991): 46–51; R. A. Shweder, "What Do Men Want? A Reading List for the Male Identity Crisis," *New York Times Book Review*, January 9, 1993, 3; and D. Stillman, "The Trouble with Male Bashing," *Los Angeles Times Magazine*, February 27, 1994, 32–38.

35. David Gates, "White Male Paranoia: Are They the Newest Victims or Just Bad Sports?" *Newsweek*, March 29, 1993, 48. In Pat Conroy's 1986 *Prince of Tides*, the novel that inspired Streisand's film, the narrator, Tom Wingo, describes himself in strikingly similar terms as Gates's figuration of men in the 1990s. He recounts being caught "outside and undefended" by the civil rights movement, "spit on by peace demonstrators" during Vietnam, and "bushwacked" by feminism; all in all, he surmises, "I seem to

embody everything that is wrong with the twentieth century," which by his account was not "an easy century to endure." Pat Conroy, *The Prince of Tides* (New York: Random House, 1986), 9.

36. Gates, "White Male Paranoia," 52.

37. Kirby Farrell, *Post-Traumatic Culture: Injury and Interpretation in the Nineties* (Baltimore, Md.: Johns Hopkins University Press, 1998), 161.

38. Lance Morrow, "Men: Are They Really That Bad?" *Time*, February 14, 1994, 54, 55.

39. Ibid., 55–56.

40. Robinson, *Marked Men*, 5–6.

41. Morrow, "Men: Are They Really That Bad?" 56, my italics.

42. Ibid., 58.

43. Ibid., 57–58.

44. Ibid., 58.

45. Mowitt, "Trauma Envy," 283.

46. Laura. S. Brown, "Not Outside the Range: One Feminist Perspective on Trauma," in *Trauma: Explorations in Memory*, ed. Cathy Caruth (Baltimore, Md.: Johns Hopkins University Press, 1995), 101.

47. Ibid., 102.

48. Ibid., 107.

49. Mowitt, "Trauma Envy," 273.

50. Ibid., 274.

51. Robinson, *Marked Men*, 8.

52. Ibid.; Gates, "White Male Paranoia," 52.

53. Kai Erikson, "Notes on Community and Trauma," in *Trauma: Explorations in Memory*, ed. Cathy Caruth (Baltimore, Md.: Johns Hopkins University Press, 1995), 186–187.

54. Georges Bataille, "The College of Sociology," in *Visions of Excess: Selected Writings, 1927–1939*, trans. Allan Stoekl, Carl R. Lovitt, and Donald M. Leslie Jr. (Minneapolis: University of Minnesota Press, 1985), 251.

55. Nancy Jay, *Throughout Your Generations Forever: Sacrifice, Religion, and Paternity* (Chicago: University of Chicago Press, 1992), 17.

56. Some public discourse about Vietnam veterans as a band of brothers united by suffering circulated at the same time that veterans of World War II were being cast in this way. For example, a 1990 article from the *Washington Post* suggests "common bonds" between Vietnam veterans from the United States and Soviet veterans of the war in Afghanistan. These groups, the article suggests, were united by their similar experiences of "unpopular wars" and "common struggles." See Fern Shen, "Soviet, U.S. Veterans Share Bond of Unpopular Wars," *Washington Post*, August 9, 1990, C1.

57. Barbara A. Biesecker, "Remembering World War II: The Rhetoric and Politics of National Commemoration at the Turn of the 21st Century," *Quarterly Journal of Speech* 88, no. 4 (November 2002): 394.

58. Ibid.

59. Ibid., 396.

60. Ibid.

61. Patricia Leavy, *Iconic Events: Media, Politics, and Power in Retelling History* (Lanham, Md.: Lexington Books, 2007), 18.

62. Almost a year before the release of Cameron's epic, on November 17, 2006, a made-for-television movie version of the *Titanic* story aired on CBS. Directed by Robert

Lieberman, *Titanic* focuses on relationships and conversations between passengers before the ship's accident. Although this much less successful and less famous version of the story is not a sacrificial film, it is certainly infused with trauma discourse. For instance, the film depicts the rape of a passenger traveling in steerage by one of the ship's employees (played by Tim Curry).

63. Maureen Turim, *Flashbacks in Film: Memory & History (New York and London: Routledge, 1989)*, 17.

64. Joan Scott, "Experience," in *Feminists Theorize the Political*, ed. Judith Butler and Joan W. Scott (New York and London: Routledge, 1992), 24.

65. Bataille, *Visions of Excess*, 239.

66. Caruth, "An Interview with Robert Jay Lifton," 131.

67. Ibid., 135.

68. Cameron explained that the "Old Rose" frame story "is about the transference of dynamic energy from one person to another to another. The greatest loves in a person's life are the ones that have a transformative effect." See Justine Elias, "The Taskmaster Who Made Titanic," *New York Times*, December 14, 1997, 26.

69. Vivian Sobchack, "Bathos and Bathysphere: On Submersion, Longing, and History in *Titanic*," in *Titanic: Anatomy of a Blockbuster*, ed. Kevin Sandler and Gaylyn Studlar (New Brunswick, N.J.: Rutgers University Press, 1999), 191.

70. Ibid., 192.

71. Ibid., 193.

72. Biesecker, "Remembering World War II," 398.

73. Bill Clinton, "Remarks at a Veterans Day Wreath-Laying Ceremony in Arlington, Virginia," November 11, 1995, http://www.va.gov/opa/vetsday/speakers/1995remarks.asp.

74. Eleanor Kaufman, "Falling from the Sky: Trauma in Perec's 'W' and Caruth's *Unclaimed Experience*," *Diacritics* 28, no. 4 (Winter 1998): 49.

75. Similar to Robert Neville's screening of *Woodstock* in *Omega Man*, this virtual reenactment of the *Titanic*'s sinking within *Titanic* suggests another instance of *mise-en-abyme* approximating the repetitive nature of trauma.

76. Steven Shaviro, *The Cinematic Body* (Minneapolis: University of Minnesota Press, 1993) 9.

77. Ibid.

78. Ibid., 33.

79. Ibid., 46.

80. Ibid., 48, Shaviro's italics.

81. Todd McCarthy, "Spectacular 'Titanic' a Night to Remember," *Variety*, November 3–9, 1997, 7; Stephen Hunter, "Titanic's Unsinkable Saga," *Washington Post*, December 19, 1997, D1; Janet Maslin, "Titanic," *New York Times*, December 19, 1997, E1.

82. Shaviro, *The Cinematic Body*, 57.

83. Ibid., 49, 65.

84. Hunter, "Titanic's Unsinkable Saga."

85. Cal accuses Jack of stealing the Heart of the Ocean Diamond, which he hides in Jack's coat pocket. Cal is motivated by his jealousy of Jack's relationship with Rose, implying that what Jack has "really" stolen is Rose, whom Cal imagines to be property.

86. Brenton J. Malin, *American Masculinity under Clinton: Popular Media and the Nineties "Crisis of Masculinity"* (New York: Peter Lang, 2005), 7.

87. Ibid., 7–8. Lehman and Hunt similarly argue that *Titanic* celebrates a "refreshingly different kind of masculinity while recuperating conventional masculinity"; Peter Lehman and Susan Hunt, "'Something and Someone Else': The Mind, the Body, and Sexuality in *Titanic*," in *Titanic: Anatomy of a Blockbuster*, ed. Kevin Sandler and Gaylyn Studlar (New Brunswick, N.J.: Rutgers University Press, 1999), 102.

88. Malin, *American Masculinity under Clinton*, 63.

89. Ibid., 80–81.

90. Mowitt, "Trauma Envy," 287.

91. Biesecker, "Remembering World War II," 398; Maslin, "Titanic."

92. Lehman and Hunt, "Something and Someone Else," 101.

93. Ibid., 101, 104.

94. Ibid., 104.

95. Ibid., 105.

96. Elias, "The Taskmaster Who Made Titanic," 17, 26.

97. Ibid., 17.

98. Lehman and Hunt, " Something and Someone Else,'" 106.

99. Ibid.

100. Rose's use of repetition acts as a self-hypnotic mantra that allows her "to quit a place where bad thoughts are happening." Psychiatrist Lenore Terr notes that self-hypnosis is a common strategy that trauma survivors, especially young ones, use to dissociate through such strategies as "counting, focusing on objects . . . visualizing another place, or repeating certain phrases over and over." Lenore Terr, *Unchained Memories: True Stories of Traumatic Memories, Lost and Found* (New York: Basic Books, 1995), 78, 71.

101. Kaufman, "Falling from the Sky," 49.

102. Freud distinguishes melancholy from mourning as a pathological response to loss. The melancholic internalizes characteristics of the lost love object, losing sight of him/herself in the process. Freud wrote, "In mourning, it is the world that has become poor and empty; in melancholia, it is the ego itself." The pathology of melancholy lies in the fact that "an object-loss was transformed into an ego-loss." So while Freud casts successful mourning as a healthy moving on (or letting go), he understands the melancholic to be stuck. See Sigmund Freud, "Mourning and Melancholia," in *The Standard Edition of the Complete Psychological Works of Sigmund Freud* trans. James Strachey (London: Hogarth Press, 1974), 14:246, 249.

103. Morrow, "Men: Are They Really That Bad?" 56.

104. The asteroid attack also destroys the astronaut's aptly named space shuttle, *Atlantis*, alluding to disaster in the literal abyss of the ocean. Like *Poseidon Adventure*, *Titanic*, and *Poseidon*—all films in which disaster takes place at sea—this reference treats the sea as a signifier of what Kaufman calls the "abysslike structure of trauma." See Kaufman, "Falling from the Sky," 49.

105. Shaviro, *Cinematic Body*, 32.

106. Walter Benjamin, *Illuminations*, ed. Hannah Arendt, trans. Harry Zohn (New York: Schocken Books, 1968), 238.

107. Eric Lichtenfeld, *Action Speaks Louder: Violence, Spectacle, and the American Action Movie* (Santa Barbara, Calif.: Greenwood Publishing Group, 2004), 220, my italics.

108. Michael O'Sullivan, "'Armageddon's' Big Bang Theory," *Washington Post*, July 3, 1986, N46. Roger Ebert's review of *Armageddon* similarly writes, "The movie is an assault on the eyes, the ears, the brain, common sense and the human desire to be entertained." He also quotes promotional materials for the film that depict the film as a violent attack, claiming it will "obliterate your senses" and "suck the air right out of your lungs." Roger Ebert, "Armageddon," *Chicago Sun Times*, July 1, 1998, http://rogerebert.suntimes.com/apps/pbcs.dll/article?AID=/19980701/REVIEWS/807010301/1023.

109. Lichtenfeld, *Action Speaks Louder*, 220.

110. Harlan K. Ullman and James P. Wade, *Shock and Awe: Achieving Rapid Dominance* (Washington, D.C.: National Defense University, 2006), xxv.

111. Naomi Klein, *The Shock Doctrine: The Rise of Disaster Capitalism* (New York: Picador, 2007), 16.

112. This scene's conspicuous attention to the American fascination with the destruction of New York City proved to be uncanny when three years after the release of *Armageddon*, the 9/11 attacks centered on the spectacular destruction of the Twin Towers.

113. Robert Hariman and John Louis Lucaites, *No Caption Needed: Iconic Photography, Public Culture, and Liberal Democracy* (Chicago: University of Chicago Press, 2007), 244.

114. See Colette Balmain, *Introduction to Japanese Horror Film* (Edinburgh: Edinburgh University Press, 2008), 31; Tom Perrine, *Film and the Nuclear Age: Representing Cultural Anxiety* (London: Taylor & Francis, 1998), 89; and Yomata Inuhiko, "The Menace from the South Seas: Ishirô Honda's *Godzilla*," in *Japanese Cinema: Texts and Contexts*, ed. Alastair Phillips and Julian Stringer (New York and London: Routledge, 2007), 105.

115. In the 1990s, multiple incidents of workplace rage took place in large urban post offices; as a result, popular culture frequently depicted the postal worker as a potentially damaged and dangerous subject. See Seltzer, *Serial Killers*, 22. The prevalence of the "berserk style" also characterizes other phrases that became popular in the 1990s, including "workplace rage" and "road rage." Noting, for instance that the phrase "going postal" had become a "staple of comedy routines," Farrell argues that popular rhetoric "compared job stress to combat trauma and viewed downsizing as a kind of battlefield injury"; Kirby Farrell, "The Berserk Style in American Culture," *Cultural Critique* 46 (Autumn 2000): 187, 198.

116. PTSD garnered attention by comedian and social commentator George Carlin on his 1990 album *Parental Advisory: Explicit Lyrics*. In a track called "Euphemisms," Carlin laments what he describes as the dilution of terms describing combat trauma, which changed from "shell shock" to "battle fatigue" to "operational exhaustion" and eventually to the abbreviation "PTSD," which he understands as "soft language" that tries to "conceal reality" and minimize the violence and brutality of war.

117. Bataille, "Concerning the Accounts Given by the Residents of Hiroshima," 222; Seltzer, *Serial Killers*, 254, 6.

118. Bataille, "Concerning the Accounts Given by the Residents of Hiroshima," 226.

119. Brown, "Not Outside the Range," 101–102.

120. Ibid., 102.

121. Lichtenfeld, *Action Speaks Louder*, 225.

122. Farrell, "Berserk Style," 184, 182.

123. Ibid., 186.

124. Ibid.,182, 191.

125. Ibid., 182.

126. Such balance is also achieved by Lev, a Russian cosmonaut the roughnecks meet on their journey into space. Having been alone in space for over a year, Lev is delusional and nonsensical, alienated and detached—much more damaged than his American counterparts. Like Bear-as racial-Other, Lev-as-cultural-Other makes the unstable roughnecks seem sane and well balanced by comparison.

127. Sharp's description of the crew as the "wrong stuff" is a reference to the film *The Right Stuff* (Philip Kaufman, 1983), which told the story of the crew of the *Mercury 7*. Set during the Cold War and released during the Reagan era, *The Right Stuff* affirms traditional constructions of American exceptionalism and masculine heroism.

128. Shaviro, *Cinematic Body*, 32.

129. The choice to refer to the crew's expressions of discomfort as squealing suggests an intertextual allusion to *Deliverance* (John Boorman, 1972), a Vietnam-era film in which a man being raped is told to "squeal like a pig." Like *Armageddon*, *Deliverance* centers on a group of men on an uncertain journey, fixates upon scenes of the white male body in pain, and is full of crisis rhetoric. In contrast to *Deliverance*'s argument that men suffer from emotional "inexpressivity," *Armageddon* insists that "real" men shed tears. The sensitive man was celebrated in the 1990s in the men's movement and in such organizations as the Promise Keepers. See Robinson, *Marked Men*, 165, 179; David Savran, *Taking It Like a Man: White Masculinity, Masochism, and Contemporary American Culture* (Princeton: Princeton University Press, 1998), 295–296; and Kelly Oliver, *Subjectivity without Subjects: From Abject Fathers to Desiring Mothers* (Lanham, Md.: Rowman & Littlefield, 1999), 3–24.

130. Almost as if the characters are aware of their own extratextual position in a sacrificial lineage that links ancient Greek theater to contemporary cinema, one character describes the disastrous attempts to drill on the asteroid as a "goddamn Greek tragedy."

131. Biesecker, "Remembering World War II," 394.

132. Ibid., 394.

133. Charlton Heston, "Winning the Cultural War," speech delivered at Harvard Law School, February 16, 1999, http://www.americanrhetoric.com/speeches/charltonhestonculturalwar.htm.

134. Dominic Pulera, *Sharing the Dream: White Males in Multicultural America* (London: Continuum International Publishing Group, 2006), 255.

135. The relationship between the impotent and grounded Truman and the reckless and high-flying Harry mirrors the relationship between John McClane and his police buddy, Sergeant Al Powell, in *Die Hard* (John McTiernan, 1988), suggesting yet another intertextual reference at work in *Armageddon*. Both films feature Willis as an unhinged and rugged protagonist whose tendency toward uncontrollable recklessness is managed by an intimate and redemptive relationship with another wounded man.

136. Harry S. Truman, "Statement by the President Announcing the Use of the A-Bomb at Hiroshima," August 6, 1945, http://millercenter.org/scripps/archive/speeches/detail/3820.

137. Sturken, *Tangled Memories*, 107.

138. Ibid.

139. Ibid.

140. The *Apollo 1* mission was aborted when the command module was destroyed during a training exercise in 1967, killing the mission's crew members. The launch platform was subsequently turned into a memorial.

141. The other plaque reads, "Launch Complex 34, Friday, 27, January 1967, 1831 Hours. Dedicated to the living memory of the crew of the Apollo 1: USAF. Lt. Colonel Virgil I. Grissom, USAF. Lt. Colonel Edward H. White, II, U.S.N. Lt. Commander Roger B. Chafee. They gave their lives in service to their country in the ongoing exploration of humanity's final frontier. Remember them not for how they died but for those ideals for which they lived."

142. Carolyn Dean, *The Self and Its Pleasures: Bataille, Lacan, and the History of the Decentered Subject* (Ithaca and London: Cornell University Press, 1992), 241.

143. Ibid., 244.

144. LaCapra, *Writing History*, 21; Hariman and Lucaites, *No Caption Needed*, 183.

145. *Pearl Harbor* recalls *Titanic* as a "historical narrative [that] is subsumed by a banal love story." In addition, both also feature images of "ships keeling over with sailors desperately fighting gravity to hang on" and exalt heroic death; Robert Waters, "Bruckheimer at War: Two Takes on *Pearl Harbor*," *Film & History* 31, no. 2 (2001): 72.

146. Marcia Landy, "'America under Attack': Pearl Harbor, 9/11, and History of the Media," in *Film and Television after 9/11*, ed. Wheeler Winston Dixon (Carbondale: Southern Illinois University Press, 2004), 79.

147. Tom Engelhardt, *The End of Victory Culture: Cold War America and the Disillusioning of a Generation* (Amherst: University of Massachusetts Press, 1995).

148. Rebecca Bell-Metereau, "The How-To Manual, the Prequel, and the Sequel in Post-9/11 Cinema," in *Film and Television after 9/11*, ed. Wheeler Winston Dixon (Carbondale: Southern Illinois University Press, 2004), 144, 146.

149. Landy, "'America under Attack,'" 86.

CHAPTER 4 — REMAKES, RESURRECTIONS, AND SACRIFICIAL RETURNS

1. Janny Scott, "The Silence of the Historic Present," *New York Times*, August 11, 2002, 29.

2. Isabelle Freda, "Survivors in the West Wing: 9/11 and the United States of Emergency," in *Film and Television after 9/11*, ed. Wheeler Winston Dixon (Carbondale: Southern Illinois University Press, 2004), 227.

3. Marcia Landy, "'America under Attack': Pearl Harbor, 9/11, and History of the Media," in *Film and Television after 9/11*, ed. Wheeler Winston Dixon (Carbondale: Southern Illinois University Press, 2004), 79. *Time* magazine exemplifies the rhetorical evocation of Pearl Harbor. In a special issue, produced just three days after the attacks, it featured multiple articles that described 9/11 as a "day of infamy." In an open letter to the readers, the *Time* staff writes, "Thus began for all of us a day that will live as much in infamy as December 7, 1941." See "To Our Readers," *Time*, September 14, 2001, 1.

4. Edward Kennedy, "A Critique of Administration Policy on Health Care, Education, and the Economy," speech delivered at the Brookings Institute, April 5, 2004, http://www.brookings.edu/events/2004/0405health-care.aspx.

5. Other post-9/11 films that remade Vietnam-era films include *The Texas Chainsaw Massacre* (Marcus Nispel, 2003), *Amityville Horror* (Andrew Douglas, 2005), *The Hills Have Eyes* (Alexandre Aja, 2006), *When a Stranger Calls* (Simon West, 2006), and *Halloween* (Rob Zombie, 2007).

6. Wolfgang Schivelbusch, *The Culture of Defeat: On National Trauma, Mourning, and Recovery*, trans. Jefferson Chase (New York: Metropolitan Books, 2001), 291–292.

7. Erica Goode, "Trauma, Felt Directly or Not, Takes a Psychic Toll," *New York Times*, September 13, 2001, A1, my italics.

8. Erica Goode, "Stress from Attacks Will Chase Some into the Depths of Their Minds, and Stay," *New York Times*, September 18, 2001, B1.

9. See also Andrew Jacobs, "For Haunted Survivors, the Towers Fall Again and Again," *New York Times*, September 30, 2001, B1+.

10. Ibid., B10; Georges Bataille, "The College of Sociology," in *Visions of Excess: Selected Writings, 1927–1939*, trans. Allan Stoekl, Carl R. Lovitt, and Donald M. Leslie Jr. (Minneapolis: University of Minnesota Press, 1985), 251.

11. Nancy Gibbs, "If You Want to Humble an Empire," *Time*, September 14, 2001, http://www.time.com/time/magazine/article/0,9171,1000761,00.html.

12. McDermott quoted in David E. Rosenbaum, "The Psychiatrist in the House Feels the Nation's Trauma," *New York Times*, October 1, 2001, A16. *Time* also characterized New York City as paralyzed and later as a kind of mental patient, asserting, "Hysteria was gripping the city." See Gibbs, "If You Want to Humble an Empire."

13. Rosenbaum, "The Psychiatrist in the House Feels the Nation's Trauma," A16. This debriefing strategy is not without critics. In the days following 9/11, a number of medical professionals spoke out against community meetings, alleging that such gatherings may produce trauma without offering sufficient therapeutic response. Such an approach is described as "open[ing] up the wound" without offering a plan for repair. As one psychologist explains, "If we tell people there is a severe danger that they will fall from a precipice, we should not be surprised that some of those people end up on the rocks." See Erica Goode, "Some Therapists Fear Services Could Backfire," *New York Times*, September 16, 2001, 21.

14. Susannah Radstone, "The War of the Fathers: Trauma, Fantasy, and September 11," in *Trauma at Home: After 9/11*, ed. Judith Greenberg (Lincoln: University of Nebraska Press, 2003), 121.

15. Landy, "'America under Attack,'" 82.

16. Brenton J. Malin, *American Masculinity under Clinton: Popular Media and the Nineties "Crisis of Masculinity"* (New York: Peter Lang, 2005), 162.

17. Ibid.

18. Gibbs, "If You Want to Humble an Empire."

19. Other similar books include Steven Gold, Alberto Kai Fai Shayo, and Jan Faust, *Trauma Practice in the Wake of September 11, 2001* (Binghamton, N. Y.: Haworth Maltreatment and Trauma Press, 2002), Jane Webber, Debra Bass, and Richard Yep, *Terrorism, Trauma, and Tragedies: A Counselor's Guide to Preparing and Responding* (Alexandria, Va.: American Counseling Association Foundation, 2005), John Briere and Catherine Scott, *Principles of Trauma Therapy: A Guide to Symptoms, Evaluation, and Treatment* (London: Sage Publications, 2006), Yuval Neria, Raz Gross, Randall Marshall, and Ezra Susser, *eds., 9/11: Mental Health in the Wake of Terrorist Attacks* (Cambridge: Cambridge University Press, 2006), and Barbara Rubin Wainrib, *Healing Crisis and Trauma with Mind, Body and Spirit* (New York: Springer Publishing Company, 2006). Although this wave of books begins almost immediately following 9/11, the increased frequency of releases in 2006, near the fifth anniversary of 9/11, bears noting. This timing also coincided with the appearance of *Poseidon* in U. S. movie theaters.

20. Charles Figley, ed., *Mapping Trauma and Its Wake: Autobiographic Essays by Pioneer Trauma Scholars* (New York: Routledge, 2006), 132.

21. Matthew Friedman links his interest in the study of trauma to his Jewish heritage and firsthand experience of anti-Semitism; he also cites the suicide of his only sibling as a transformative experience. Mardi Horowitz describes both witnessing and experiencing acts of violence as a young child as influences on his work. Henry Krystal defines childhood illness as a formative trauma in his own life. Beverley Raphael names childhood experiences of World War II in Australia as factors in her study of trauma. Zahava Solomon discusses being the descendent of Holocaust survivors as influential. Bessel van der Kolk describes himself as coming by the study of trauma "honestly," having experienced "enough trauma in [his] family's background," including World War II and poverty, "to warrant taking a serious look at what this was all about." Bessel Van der Kolk, "The Body Keeps the Score: Brief Autobiography of Bessel Van der Kolk," in *Mapping Trauma and Its Wake: Autobiographic Essays by Pioneer Trauma Scholars*, ed. Charles R. Figley (New York and London: Routledge, 2006), 211. Lars Weisaeth connects his work to childhood experiences in Nazi-occupied Norway. Many other scholars cite intimate connections with Holocaust survivors and the resulting guilt as influential; others also frame Vietnam—either personal experience in the war or connections to veterans—as shaping their life's work. Many of these essays also frame 9/11 as a more recent, but traumatic, catalyst for new investigations of trauma.

22. It is worth noting that of the seventeen "before" photographs included in the book, fifteen were taken during or in the immediate aftermath of the Vietnam War, as if this fictive winding back of time identifies this historical context as the origin of its authors' (work on) trauma.

23. Gibbs, "If You Want to Humble an Empire."

24. Figley, *Mapping Trauma*, 47–61. Similar logic informs much public rhetoric about the Iraq War as having animated prior traumas. See Anemona Hartocollis, "New Fears Rise, Old Fears Stir," *New York Times*, April 13, 2003, CY1.

25. Freda, "Survivors in the West Wing," 227. Another example of prior experiential frames can be seen in the cinematic proclivity toward depictions of destruction in New York City, including the fall of the World Trade Center towers. As demonstrated in chapter 3, *Armageddon* and *Fight Club* visualized the towers' collapse, only a few short years before the 9/11 attacks. As Claire Kahane argues, despite the prevailing assertion that the nation did not "see it coming," much of the horror of 9/11 stems from "preexisting anxieties." Citing Slavoj Zizek, Kahane notes that the "most deeply unsettling traumas are not those that are entirely unexpected but those that are anticipated in fantasy." See Claire Kahane, "Uncanny Sights: The Anticipation of the Abomination," in *Trauma at Home: After 9/11*, ed. Judith Greenberg (Lincoln: University of Nebraska Press, 2003), 107–108. That the actual events of 9/11 were interpreted through these prior cinematic lenses has been demonstrated by the frequency with which survivors and witnesses likened the events to "watching a movie." See Wheeler Winston Dixon, "Introduction: Something Lost—Film after 9/11," in *Film and Television after 9/11*, ed. Wheeler Winston Dixon (Carbondale: Southern Illinois University Press, 2004), 9.

26. Tony Grajeda, "The Winning and Losing of Hearts and Minds: Vietnam, Iraq, and the Claims of the War Documentary," *Jump Cut: A Review of Contemporary Media* 49 (Spring 2007), http://ejumpcut.org/archive/jc49.2007/Grajeda/index.html.

27. Schivelbusch, *The Culture of Defeat*, 293. Rosenbaum similarly connects Representative McDermott's response to 9/11 to the congressman's experiences in Vietnam, suggesting that McDermott's expertise on 9/11 trauma owes to experiential authority earned by having witnessed an earlier historical trauma. See Rosenbaum, "The Psychiatrist in the House Feels the Nation's Trauma," A16.

28. Almost immediately following 9/11, the Bush administration also attempted to influence media representations of terrorism, war, and the nation-state. Movie executives were summoned to the White House twice for discussions of how to best represent—or, as Susan Faludi puts it, "market"—the War on Terror. See Susan Faludi, *The Terror Dream: Fear and Fantasy in Post-9/11 America* (New York: Metropolitan Books, 2007), 6–7.

29. Breasseale quote in Julian E. Barnes, "Calling the Shots on War Movies," *Los Angeles Times*, July 7, 2008, http://articles.latimes.com/2008/jul/07/nation/na-armyfilms7.

30. Post-9/11 books about Vietnam trauma include David W. Powell, *My Tour in Hell: A Marine's Battle with Combat Trauma* (Ann Arbor, Mich.: Modern History Press, 2006), Raymond Monsour Scurfield, *War Trauma: Lessons Unlearned from Vietnam to Iraq* (New York: Algora Publishing, 2006), Penny Coleman, *Flashback: Posttraumatic Stress Disorder, Suicide, and the Lessons of War* (Boston: Beacon Press, 2006), and Ronald Dawe and William Shroder, *Soldier's Heart: Close Up Today with PTSD in Vietnam Veterans* (Westport, Conn: Greenwood Publishing Group, 2007). Slightly earlier books include Jonathan Shay, *Odysseus in America: Combat Trauma and the Trials of Homecoming* (New York: Simon and Schuster, 2002) and Gregory A. Helle, *The Enemy Within: One Vietnam Veteran Helps Others Cope with PTSD* (Bloomington, Ind.: AuthorHouse, 2004).

31. Robert Jay Lifton and Charles Strozier, "We Were Raw and Exposed," *New York Times*, September 16, 2001, CY7.

32. Ibid.

33. Ibid.

34. Landy, "'America under Attack,'" 86; Eduard Shevardnadze to the Editor of the *New York Times*, *New York Times*, October 5, 2001, A26.

35. Georges Bataille, "Concerning the Accounts Given by the Residents of Hiroshima," in *Trauma: Explorations in Memory*, ed. Cathy Caruth (Baltimore, Md.: Johns Hopkins University Press, 1995), 228; John Mowitt, "Trauma Envy," *Cultural Critique* 46 (Fall 2000): 283.

36. Lifton and Strozier, "We Were Raw and Exposed," CY7. Understandings of trauma as transmittable were replicated, rather literally, in 2005 by a number of articles citing a study published in the *Journal of Clinical Endocrinology and Metabolism*, demonstrating the "transgenerational transmission" of PTSD from women who were pregnant during 9/11 to their fetuses. See "Babies Show Ripple Effects of Mothers' Stress from 9/11 Trauma," *Women's Health Law Weekly*, May 29, 2005, 79.

37. Felicia Lee, "Is Trauma Being Trivialized?" *New York Times*, September 6, 2003, B9. Lee's sentiment accords with psychiatrist Robert Rosenheck's belief that Americans have been primed to interpret experience through the frame of trauma. Robert Rosenheck asserts, "It's ingrained in our culture to express the horror of something by saying it's so bad that it causes mental illness." Quoted in Goode, "Calculating the Toll of Trauma," New York Times, September 9, 2005, F5.

38. Lee, "Is Trauma Being Trivialized?" B9. Similarly, Sally Satel critiques the banalization and overuse of trauma, arguing that a "culture of trauma has blossomed" and has contributed to potentially fraudulent claims of PTSD; Sally Satel, "For Some, the War Won't End," *New York Times*, March 1, 2006, A19.

39. Consider the language of trauma visible in this spate of titles of articles published in *Time* between September 24 and October 15, 2001: "Attack on the Spirit," "Tending the Wounds," "The Anxious Skies," "A Crisis of Faith," "Nation on the Couch," and "Even Soldiers Hurt."

40. Another indicator of trauma's continued valence in American public discourse can be seen in its recurrence in popular culture. On television, for example, ABC launched the serial drama *The Nine* in 2006, which relies heavily on flashback editing to depict the traumatic memories and experiences of a group of hostages in a bank robbery. The TNT drama *Saving Grace*, which premiered in 2007, takes place in Oklahoma City and features a number of subplots related to the bombings of the Alfred P. Murrah Federal Building, centering on a protagonist haunted by the childhood trauma of sexual abuse by a priest. One year later, HBO premiered *United States of Tara*, which is about a women with dissociative identity disorder brought on by repressed memories of childhood trauma. PTSD and trauma culture related to such events as the Columbine shootings in 1999, 9/11, and Hurricane Katrina also structure the plots of such novels as Jonathan Safran Foer, *Extremely Loud and Incredibly Close* (New York: Houghton Mifflin, 2006), Philip Roth, *Exit Ghost* (New York: Vintage House, 2007), Rudolph Delson, *Maynard and Jennica* (New York: Houghton Mifflin Harcourt, 2007), and Wally Lamb, *The Hour I First Believed* (New York: Harper Perennial, 2008).

41. Lee, "Is Trauma Being Trivialized?" B9.

42. Lifton and Strozier, "We Were Raw and Exposed," CY7.

43. Marshall McLuhan, *War and Peace in the Global Village* (Ann Arbor: University of Michigan Press, 1968), 134; Lifton and Strozier, "We Were Raw and Exposed," CY7. A similar image informs an article written by the staff of *Time* magazine for the special issue on September 14, 2001. Reproducing, by its very form, the notion that trauma bands together survivors, this collectively written essay asserts, "It was strange that a say of war was a day we all stood still. We couldn't move—that must have been the whole idea—so we had no choice but to watch." See Gibbs, "If You Want to Humble an Empire."

44. Abby Ellin, "Personal Business: Traumatized Workers Look for Healing on the Job," *New York Times*, September 30, 2001, BU10; Erica Goode, "Treatment Can Ease Lingering Trauma of September 11," *New York Times*, November 20, 2001, F1. Another of Goode's articles refers to a psychologist who links "the course of a traumatic memory to developing a photograph." Explaining the ways that traumatic memories may emerge slowly or even belatedly, Goode writes, "Light hits the film. Chemicals are added. But the image is not set until the fixative is applied." See Goode, "Stress from Attacks Will Chase Some into the Depths of Their Minds, and Stay," B11.

45. Rosenbaum, "The Psychiatrist in the House Feels the Nation's Trauma," A16.

46. Erica Goode, "Traumatic Moments End, but the Reminders Linger," *New York Times*, November 6, 2001, F7.

47. Lance Morrow, "The Case for Rage and Retribution," *Time*, September 14, 2001, http://www.time.com/time/nation/article/0,8599,174641,00.html.

4849. Freda, "Survivors in the West Wing," 242.

49. Robert Hariman and John Louis Lucaites, *No Caption Needed: Iconic Photography, Public Culture, and Liberal Democracy* (Chicago: University of Chicago Press, 2007), 172.

50. See Maggie Lake, "Virtual Reality Heals 9/11 Wounds," CNN, April 29, 2005.

51. Robert Hariman, "Allegory and Democratic Public Culture in the Postmodern Era," *Philosophy and Rhetoric* 35, no. 4 (2002): 280.

52. Ibid., 280–281, 290.

53. Ibid., 280.

54. Ibid., 272.

55. As noted in chapter 3, President George H. W. Bush explicitly framed the Gulf War as form of recovery from Vietnam Syndrome, which he described as being kicked and buried in the desert sands. George H. W. Bush, "Radio Address to United States Armed Forces Stationed in the Persian Gulf Region," March 2, 1991, in *Public Papers of the Presidents of the United States: George H. W. Bush: 1991*, Book 1 (Washington, D.C.: Government Printing Office, 1991), 207. Over a decade later, the presidential race between John Kerry and George W. Bush frequently engaged Senator Kerry's status as a Vietnam veteran in debates about the war in Iraq and his qualifications as a candidate. For more on the role of collective memory about Vietnam in this election, see Hariman and Lucaites, *No Caption Needed*, 171.

56. Dori Laub, "September 11, 2001—An Event Without a Voice," in *Trauma at Home: After 9/11*, ed. Judith Greenberg (Lincoln: University of Nebraska Press, 2003), 204.

57. Claudia Puig, "'Poseidon' Will Have You Rooting for the Big Wave," *USA Today*, May 12, 2006, E5.

58. Vaheed Ramazani, "September 11: Masculinity, Justice, and the Politics of Empathy," *Comparative Studies of South Asia, Africa, and the Middle East* 21, nos. 1–2 (2001): 118–119, 121.

59. Morrow, "Men: Are They Really That Bad?" *Time*, February 14, 1994, 58.

60. Morrow, "The Case for Rage and Retribution." Despite his distaste for the discourse of trauma, Morrow deploys the logic of trauma in his call for the "nourishment of rage." Explicitly citing Pearl Harbor, Morrow invites understanding of 9/11 as a day that should "live in infamy" and encourages the development of a "unified, unifying, Pearl Harbor sort of purple American fury." This rhetorical strategy might be understood as using the logic of trauma for two reasons. First, Morrow's return to history and another violent scene in America's past recalls the compulsive repetition that is thought to characterize posttraumatic behavior. Second, Morrow's call for "unified, unifying" anger reproduces constructions of trauma as an experience with the power to draw people together.

61. Kirby Farrell, "The Berserk Style in American Culture," *Cultural Critique* 46 (Autumn 2000): 181–182.

62. Lance Morrow, "Has Your Paradigm Shifted?" *Time*, November 29, 2001, 152.

63. Ibid.

64. Kamrul Idris, "American Credibility Damaged," *New Straits Times*, January 26, 2004, 10.

65. Mark Danner, *The Secret Way to War: The Downing Street Memo and the Iraq War's Buried History* (New York: New York Review Books, 2006); Bob Woodward, *State of Denial: Bush at War, Part III* (New York: Simon & Schuster, 2006); Richard Falk,

Irene Grendzier, and Robert Jay Lifton, eds., *Crimes of War: Iraq* (New York: Nation Books, 2006).

66. E. Ann Kaplan, *Trauma Culture: The Politics of Terror and Loss in Media and Literature* (New Brunswick, N.J.: Rutgers University Press, 2005), 69. Kaplan argues that melodramas often serve as a generic site for managing cultural anxiety about historical trauma. Instead of telling stories about war and combat trauma and confronting public events, such films feature more personal narratives of familial and/or romantic loss as a "screen" for negotiating cultural trauma and for reaffirming public narratives. See, for example, Kaplan's reading of Alfred Hitchcock's *Spellbound* (1945).

67. David Germain, "Audiences Love a Fictional Disaster Flick," *Buffalo News*, May 14, 2006, E1.

68. *The Poseidon Adventure*, directed by John Putch and written by Paul Gallico and Bryce Zabel, was first broadcast on November 20, 2005, on NBC—just six months before Petersen's *Poseidon* was released into theaters.

69. The critical reception of this film was largely poor, often because of its focus on terrorism. Robert Bianco, "NBC Turns This 'Poseidon' into True Disaster," *USA Today*, November 18, 2005; Michelle Tauber, review of *The Poseidon Adventure*, *People Weekly*, November 28, 2005, 55.

70. James Hebert, "Turning Hollywood Upside Down: Forget the Fluff: Poseidon Echoes a Time When Disaster Can Strike without Warning," *San Diego Union-Tribune*, May 7, 2006, F1.

71. George W. Bush, "Information Sharing, Patriot Act Vital to Homeland Security," speech at Kleinshans Music Hall, Buffalo, New York, April 20, 2004, http://georgewbush-whitehouse.archives.gov/news/releases/2004/04/20040420-2.html, my italics.

72. Kahane, "Uncanny Sights," 109.

73. Scott Bowles, "Graphic 'Poseidon' Could Upset Audiences," *USA Today*, May 11, 2006, D1.

74. Paramount's publicity for *World Trade Center* was similarly careful to differentiate Stone's docudrama from the disaster genre. Michael Shamberg, one of the film's producers, asserted that the film would not be "the *Towering Inferno-Titanic* version"; Karina Longworth, "9/11 Movie Won't Be 'Towering Inferno' Remake," *Cinematical*, October 31, 2005.

75. Cyntha Fuchs, "Don't Tell Me We're Trapped!" *PopMatters*, May 8, 2006, http://www.popmatters.com/pm/review/poseidon-20061/.

76. Lisa Schwarzbaum, "Rocking the Boat," *Entertainment Weekly*, May 19, 2006, 53.

77. Michael Atkinson, "Just Add Water," *Village Voice*, May 10–16, 2006, C50.

78. George W. Bush, "Statement by the President in Address to the Nation," September 11, 2001, http://georgewbush-whitehouse.archives.gov/news/releases/2001/09/20010911-16.html

79. George W. Bush, "President Discusses Global War on Terror," September 5, 2006, http://georgewbush-whitehouse.archives.gov/news/releases/2006/09/20060905-4.html

80. Freud, "Screen Memories," in *Early Psycho-Analytic Publications*, vol. 3 of *The Standard Edition of the Complete Psychological Works of Sigmund Freud*, translated by James Strachey (London: Hogarth Press, 1962), 318. Freud explains that traces of a displaced memory can be found within screen memories, revealing what has been covered over by the psychic substitute.

81. Kahane, "Uncanny Sights," 110. The portion of the ocean that is between approximately 4,000 and 6,000 meters deep is known as the abyss.

82. Transcripts of radio and telephone transmissions between individuals in the towers and emergency responders revealed that many callers were advised to remain in the South Tower after the North Tower was struck. See "Transcripts Chronicle 9/11 Terror," *CNN.com*, January 15, 2004.

83. *The American Heritage Dictionary of the English Language*, 4th ed., s.v. "rogue wave." This revision also deviates from Paul Gallico's source novel for *The Poseidon Adventure*, which calls the wave a tsunami.

84. Robert Litwak argues, "The term 'rogue state' is an American political rubric without standing in international law that has gained currency since the end of the Cold War." Litwak continues, "Until the late 1970s, the term 'pariah' or 'rogue' was used to describe regimes whose internal system or behavior toward its own people was viewed as abhorrent." This usage shifted, argues Litwak, following the 1979 report by the U. S. State Department on state-sponsored terrorism, at which point "the criterion for rogue state shifted from internal to external behavior." Under the Clinton administration, the term referred primarily to "the pursuit of WMD, the use of terrorism as an instrument of state policy, and the perceived threat to Western interests in key regions." The Clinton administration developed criteria for defining nations as rogue states but later changed the phrase to "state of concern." President George W. Bush resumed use of the phrase "rogue state" and also introduced the phrase "Axis of Evil." Robert S. Litwak, *Rogue States and U. S. Foreign Policy: Containment after the Cold War* (Washington, D. C.: Woodrow Wilson Center Press, 2000), 3, 7.

85. National Security Council, "Prevent Our Enemies from Threatening Us, Our Allies, and Our Friends with Weapons of Mass Destruction," *National Security Strategy* (September 2002), http://georgewbush-whitehouse.archives.gov/nsc/nss/2002/nss5.html. The phrase "rogue state" also was used in a National Security Council report that identifies Afghanistan and Iraq as rogue threats. See National Security Council, *9/11 Five Years Later: Successes and Challenges* (September 2006), http://georgewbush-whitehouse.archives.gov/nsc/waronterror/2006/.

86. *Time* magazine demonstrates such depictions of terrorists, calling one of the hijacked planes used to attack the towers a "rogue plane"; Gibbs, "If You Want to Humble an Empire."

87. Aluyah Imoisili, "Quantifying the Ever-Present Danger," *Best's Review* 108, no. 4 (August 2007): 68.

88. Bush, "Information Sharing, Patriot Act Vital to Homeland Security."

89. Federal Emergency Management Agency, *World Trade Center Building Performance Study: Data Collection, Preliminary Observations, and Recommendations* (Washington, D.C.: Federal Insurance and Mitigation Administration, 2002), 1.

90. Ibid., 2, 1.

91. Atkinson, "Just Add Water," C50.

92. Ron Briley, "Basketball's Great White Hope and Ronald Reagan's America: *Hoosiers* (1986)," *Film & History* 35, no. 1 (2005): 17.

93. Michael Silk, Jaime Schultz, and Bryan Bracey, "From Mice to Men: Miracle, Mythology, and the 'Magic Kingdom,'" *Sport in Society* 11, nos. 2–3 (2008): 279.

94. Georges Bataille, *Tears of Eros*, translated by Peter Connor (San Francisco: City Lights Books, 1989), 207.

95. Gibbs, "If You Want to Humble an Empire."

96. Ibid.

97. An analogous assumption that trauma transforms and redeems sufferers and witnesses operates in Roger Rosenblatt's declaration that 9/11 killed the "Age of Irony" by giving American direct access that what is real and what really matters. Rosenblatt writes, "When the white dust settles, and the bereaved are alone in their houses, there will be nothing but grief around them, and nothing is more real than that. . . . The kindness of people toward others in distress is real. There's nothing to see though in that. Honor and fair play? Real. And the preciousness of ordinary living is real as well." Rosenblatt concludes the article by conflating the nation's suffering, fury, and eminence, asserting, "The greatness of the country: real. The anger: real. The pain: too real." See Rosenblatt, "The Age of Irony Comes to an End." *Time*, October 1, 2001, 79.

98. Oprah Winfrey dubbed Giuliani "America's mayor" in 2002. See Fred Siegel, "America's Mayor; Rudolph Giuliani," *Economist*, July 28, 2005, 80.

99. The significance of Ramsey's sacrifice can also be seen in its contrast to another punitive death: Valentine dies as punishment for harboring an illegal immigrant.

100. This plot device replays almost exactly the scene from *Armageddon* in which Harry Stamper spares A. J. from sacrificial death as a gift to his daughter.

101. *Poseidon*'s refusal to show mirrors both *United 93* and *World Trade Center*, which fade to black rather than depicting the planes' collisions. *United 93* ends seconds before the plane crashes on the ground in Stoneycreek Township, Pennsylvania, and *World Trade Center* depicts the time before and after the World Trade Center attack but not the attack itself.

102. Associated Press, "Complaints Force Removal of Graphic September 11 Statue," *Chicago Sun-Times*, September 19, 2002, 32. See Barbie Zelizer, "Photography, Journalism, and Trauma," in *Journalism after September 11*, ed. Barbie Zelizer and Stuart Allan (New York and London: Routledge, 2002), 65.

103. Kaplan, *Trauma Culture*, 85.

104. Hariman and Lucaites, *No Caption Needed*, 21.

105. See also Susannah Radstone, "The War of the Fathers: Trauma, Fantasy, and September 11," in *Trauma At Home: After 9/11*, ed. Judith Greenberg (Lincoln: University of Nebraska Press, 2003), 117–123; and Joshua Gunn, "Father Trouble: Staging Sovereignty in Spielberg's War of the Worlds," *Critical Studies in Media Communication* 25, no.1 (March 2008): 1–27.

106. Klaus Theweleit, *Male Women, Floods, Bodies, History*, vol. 1 of *Fantasies* (Minneapolis: University of Minnesota Press, 1987), 258–259; Nancy Jay, *Throughout Your Generations Forever: Sacrifice, Religion, and Paternity* (Chicago: University of Chicago Press, 1992), xxiii.

107. George W. Bush, "President Promotes Compassionate Conservatism," speech at Parkside Hall, San Jose, California, April 30, 2002, http://georgewbush-whitehouse.archives.gov/news/releases/2002/04/20020430-5.html.

108. One month before the theatrical release of *I Am Legend*, Global Asylum released a straight-to-DVD remake of Richard Matheson's novel called *I Am Omega* (Griff Furst, 2007). In this version of the story, the Robert Neville character is renamed Renchard (Mark Dacascos), one of few humans immune to a virus that has destroyed New York City, turning most of its inhabitants into cannibals.

109. Kahane, "UnCanny Sights," 107–108. See also Radstone, "War of the Fathers," 117–121.

110. These narrative devices, coupled with the iconography of a devastated city that Neville must "loot" in order to survive, might also operate as references to Hurricane Katrina and the devastation in New Orleans.

111. James Wolcott, "The News Blues," *Vanity Fair*, November 2008, 126, my italics. Wolcott's chronology of his own encounters with history, which he overtly frames as traumatic and which he argues "the media are only making worse," links 1968—the year of the Tet offensive and massive napalm campaigns in Vietnam—and 9/11 as two of the most monumental moments of his life (124). Philip Roth's 2007 novel, *Exit Ghost*, also frames experiences of 9/11 in relation to memories of Vietnam. For example, the novel's protagonist describes himself as scarred by the images of 9/11 and driven out of the city by fear. This "malaise," the narrator argues, recalls the terror he felt watching images of war during the Vietnam era.

112. McLuhan, *War and Peace in the Global Village*, 134; George W. Bush, "President's Address to the Nation," September 11, 2006, http://georgewbush-whitehouse.archives .gov/news/releases/2006/09/20060911-3.html.

113. Susan Lurie, "Falling Persons and National Embodiment: The Reconstruction of Safe Spectatorship in the Photographic Record of 9/11," in *Terror, Culture, Politics: Rethinking 9/11*, ed. Daniel J. Sherman and Terry Nardin (Bloomington: Indiana University Press, 2006), 46.

114. This doubling of Neville might be interpreted as producing an effect of seriality that mimes the repetitive nature of trauma.

115. For example, in both *United 93* (Paul Greengrass, 2006) and *World Trade Center* (Oliver Stone, 2006)—two docudramas about the 9/11 attacks—the camera fades to black seconds before showing the crashing of hijacked planes. It is also interesting to note that the helicopter crash reproduces a plot device from *Omega Man*, although with significant differences. In *Omega Man*, Neville's helicopter crashes after the pilot develops plague symptoms, preventing Neville from disseminating the vaccine. However, this film, which was produced at a time when plane crashes didn't carry the specific weight that they do in the post-9/11 imaginary, shows the full impact of the helicopter's fiery crash. *I Am Legend*'s refusal to show the crash demonstrates a strategy of displacement, in which references that are *too* specific or *too* close to 9/11 are frequently tempered or covered over.

116. Nick Browne, "Violence as History in the *Godfather* Films," in *Francis Ford Coppola's Godfather Trilogy*, ed. Nick Browne (Cambridge: Cambridge University Press, 2000), 19. Vera Dika similarly reads *The Godfather* as offering a "collective fantasy of legitimized violence" in response to perceptions of America as "the perpetrator of unjust acts." See Vera Dika, "The Representation of Ethnicity in *The Godfather*," in *Francis Ford Coppola's Godfather Trilogy*, ed. Nick Browne (Cambridge: Cambridge University Press, 2000), 78.

117. During his trips to the Seaport, Neville climbs aboard the USS *Intrepid*, an aircraft carrier famous for its use in combat tours in World War II and Vietnam, which further links Neville's personal tragedy with transgenerational histories of both national trauma and recovery.

118. Eduard Shevardnadze to the Editor of the *New York Times New York Times*, October 5, 2001, A26.

119. Freda, "Survivors in the West Wing," 242.

120. Kirby Farrell, "The Berserk Style in American Culture," *Cultural Critique* 46 (Autumn 2000): 182.

121. Carolyn Dean, *The Self and Its Pleasures: Bataille, Lacan, and the History of the Decentered Subject* (Ithaca, N.Y.: Cornell University Press, 1992). 244.

122. Ibid.

123. In Matheson's novel, Neville realizes that in a world dominated by the infected he is of the "old race," the "abnormal one." He understands that, to his enemies, he is the source of terror and "shrinking fear." The novel ends with Neville's suicide after his realization that he is the monster who will haunt the legends of generations to come. See Richard Matheson, *I Am Legend* (New York: Bantam Books, 1954), 149–151. In *Last Man on Earth*, Neville also realizes that he has been a source of fear for his enemies—his final words repeat, "They were afraid of me"—but he does not relinquish his scorn toward them or his imagined position of privilege as a human. He calls the infected men and women "freaks" and "mutations," insisting that it is they who are sick, not he. In this adaptation, Neville fails to triumph over his enemies, who kill him with a spear, leaving his body prostrate on the altar of a church. Despite this sacred setting, however, *Last Man on Earth* does not offer a sense of salvation or redemption but ends at the tragic moment of Neville's death with no hope for reconciliation between the warring factions or regeneration of a healthy world. Neville simply dies, and the plague victims remain to repopulate the world on their own terms.

124. Farrell, *Post-Traumatic Culture*, x.

125. Charlton Heston, *In the Arena: An Autobiography* (New York: Simon & Schuster, 1995), 261.

126. For example, at the fifth anniversary of 9/11, MSNBC published a series of articles and testimonials published on its website on the subject of race after 9/11. See "Scorched by the Scourge of Post-9/11 Racism," MSNBC, *www.msnbc.msn.com/id/14587965/*. Also, in 2006 and 2007, multiple publications directly linked U.S. policies on terrorism to racism, including Steven Salaita, *Anti-Arab Racism in the USA: Where it Comes From and What It Means for Politics* (London: Pluto Press, 2006); Mary Bosworth and Jeanne Flavin, *Race, Gender, and Punishment: From Colonialism to the War on Terror* (New Brunswick, N. J. and London: Rutgers University Press, 2007); and Amaney Jamal and Nadine Christine Naber, *Race and Arab Americans before and after 9/11: From Invisible Citizens to Visible Subjects* (Syracuse: Syracuse University Press, 2007).

127. Adilifu Nama, *Black Space: Imagining Race in Science Fiction Film* (Austin: University of Texas Press, 2008), 39.

128. Ibid.

129. Senator McCain referred to *I Am Legend* during the 2008 presidential campaign. He described himself as metaphorically rising from the dead on multiple occasions. For example, in 2007, he said, "I've been declared dead in this campaign on five or six occasions. I won't refer to a recent movie I saw, but I think I am legend"; Holly Ramer, "McCain: I Am Legend," *New York Post*, December 30, 2007, 7.

130. John McCain, "Concession Speech," delivered in Phoenix, Arizona, November 4, 2008. For a full transcript, see "McCain's Concession Speech," *New York Times*, November 5, 2008, http://www.nytimes.com/2008/11/04/us/politics/04text-mccain.html.

131. Ibid., my italics.

EPILOGUE

1. Caryn James, "Live Images Make Viewers Witnesses to Horror," *New York Times*, September 12, 2001, A25.

2. Such feature films include *The Guys* (Jim Simpson, 2003), *11'09"01* (Youssef Chahine and Amos Gitai, 2002), *Fahrenheit 9/11* (Michael Moore, 2004), and *Reign Over Me* (Mike Bender, 2007). Television movies include *9/11*, first broadcast on March 10, 2002, on CBS, directed by James Hanlon and Rob Klug and written by Tom Forman and Greg Kandra; *Flight 93*, first broadcast on January 30, 2006, on A&E, directed by Peter Markle; *9/11: The Twin Towers*, first broadcast on September 3, 2006, on Discovery Channel, directed by Richard Dale and written by Andrew Bampfield and Ed Fields. Many television shows also addressed 9/11 and/or the War on Terror, including *The West Wing*, *Law & Order*, *Without a Trace*, and *Bones*.

3. Joshua Gunn, "Mourning Speech: Haunting and the Spectral Voices of Nine-Eleven," *Text and Performance Quarterly* 24 (2004): 97–98.

4. Deroy Murdock, "United 93 Comes at the Right Time," *Human Events*, April 24, 2006, 20.

5. Joseph Carroll, "Public Divided Over Appropriateness of 9/11 Movies," Gallup News Service, April 26, 2006, http://www.gallup.com/poll/22552/Public-Divided-Over-Appropriateness-911-Movies.aspx.

6. While Christy Lemire described *United 93* as a film with "simplicity and dignity" grounded by "accuracy" and "realism," she called *Poseidon* "all splash and no substance." See Christy Lemire, "At the Movies: 'United 93,'" *Chicago Defender*, April 26, 2006, 23; and Christy Lemire, "At the Movies: 'Poseidon,'" *Chicago Defender*, May 11, 2006, 13. Likewise, while the *Village* Voice's review of *United 93* called it a "memorial" that is "respectful," its review of *Poseidon* declared the film vacuous and "brutally obvious." See Dennis Lim, "A Flight to Remember," *Village Voice*, (September 20–26, 2006, 82; and Michael Atkinson, "Just Add Water," *Village Voice*, May 10–16, 2006, C50.

7. Mick LaSalle, "Water, Water Everywhere—to Say Nothing of Fire and Falling Objects," *San Francisco Chronicle*, May 11, 2006, E1.

8. Maitland McDonagh, "Poseidon: Review," *TV Guide*, August 25, 2007, http://www.tvguide.com/movies/poseidon/review/279909; Atkinson, "Just Add Water," C50.

9. Claudia Puig, "Smith Is Powerful as an Urban 'Legend,' but Zombie Factor Saps the Life Away," *USA Today*, December 14, 2007, E5.

10. Desson Thomson, "Not Quite a Living 'Legend,'" *Washington Post*, December 14, 2007, C1; David Edelstein, "And Opening This Week," *New York*, December 17, 2007, 52–53.

11. Wesley Morris, "Where There's a Will . . . There's a Way to Survive. Especially for the Star Whose Magnetism Keeps 'I Am Legend' Well-Populated," *Boston Globe*, December 14, 2007, C1.

12. Kyle Smith, "I Am Blockbuster: Will Smith Can Save the World," *New York Post*, December 30, 2007, 67.

13. Gabriel Snyder, "A 'United' Front?" *Variety*, May 1–7, 2006, 5.

14. Brian Cochrane, "Revival of the Week," *Variety*, May 1–7, 2006, 5. In another uncanny coincidence, just weeks after multiple news outlets reran 9/11 footage to commemorate the seventh anniversary of the attacks, entertainment news sources circulated news that Warner Bros. would develop a prequel to *I Am Legend*. Early

descriptions indicated that this film would focus on Neville in the early days of the KV outbreak. Quoting a representative for Smith, the *New York Post* reported that "it will be about how the disease spreads and the fall of the last great American city. It will also develop the relationship between Will's character and his wife." See Richard Johnson with Paula Froelich, Bill Hoffmann, and Corynne Steindler, "Will I Am 2," *New York Post*, December 15, 2008, 14.

15. Snyder, "A 'United' Front?" 5; Cochrane, "Revival of the Week," 5.

16. Joshua Gunn, "Father Trouble: Staging Sovereignty in Spielberg's War of the Worlds," *Critical Studies in Media Communication* 25, no.1 (March 2008): 21.

17. Sigmund Freud, "Screen Memories," in *Early Psycho-Analytic Publications*, vol. 3 of *The Standard Edition of the Complete Psychological Works of Sigmund Freud*, translated by James Strachey (London: Hogarth Press, 1962), 307.

18. Ibid., 315.

19. Scott Bowles, "Graphic 'Poseidon' Could Upset Audiences," *USA Today*, May 11, 2006, D1.

20. Robert Hariman, "Allegory and Democratic Public Culture in the Postmodern Era," *Philosophy and Rhetoric* 35, no. 4 (2002): 273.

21. Ibid., 290, 272, 287.

22. Ibid., 273.

23. Bonnie Dow, "Criticism and Authority in the Artistic Mode," *Western Journal of Communication* 65, no. 3 (Summer 2001): 339–340.

SELECTED BIBLIOGRAPHY

Bailie, Gil. "Cinema and Crisis: The Elusive Quest for Catharsis." *Image: A Journal of the Arts* 20 (Summer 1998): 17–22.

Bataille, Georges. *The Accursed Share*. Vol. 1. Trans. Robert Hurley. New York: Zone Books, 1991.

———. *The Accursed Share*. Vols. 2–3. Trans. Robert Hurley. New York: Zone Books, 1991.

———. "Concerning the Accounts Given by the Residents of Hiroshima." In *Trauma: Explorations in Memory*, ed. Cathy Caruth, 221–235. Baltimore, Md.: Johns Hopkins University Press, 1995.

———. *Erotism: Death and Sensuality*. Trans. Mary Dalwood. San Francisco: City Lights Books, 1986.

———. *Guilty*. Venice, Calif.: Lapis Press, 1988.

———. *Inner Experience*. Trans. Leslie Anne Boldt. Albany: SUNY Press, 1988.

———. *Literature and Evil*. Trans. Alastair Hamilton. New York: Marion Boyars, 2001.

———. *My Mother/Madame Edwarda/The Dead Man*. Trans. Austryn Wainhouse. New York: Marion Boyars, 1995.

———. *Story of the Eye*. Trans. Joachim Neugroschel. San Francisco: City Lights Books, 1987.

———. *Tears of Eros*. Trans. Peter Connor. San Francisco: City Lights Books, 1989.

———. *Theory of Religion*. Trans. Robert Hurley. New York: Zone Books, 1992.

———. *Visions of Excess, Selected Writings, 1927–1939*. Trans. Allan Stoekl, Carl R. Lovitt, and Donald M. Leslie, Jr. Minneapolis: University of Minnesota Press, 1985.

Benjamin, Walter. *Illuminations*. Ed. Hannah Arendt, trans. Harry Zohn. New York: Schocken Books, 1968.

Biesecker, Barbara. "Remembering World War II: The Rhetoric and Politics of National Commemoration at the Turn of the 21st Century." *Quarterly Journal of Speech* 88, no. 4 (November 2002): 393–409.

Boldt-Irons, Leslie Anne. *On Bataille: Critical Essays*. Albany: SUNY Press, 1985.

———. "Sacrifice and Violence in Bataille's Erotic Fiction: Reflections from/upon the Mise-en-Abîme." In *Bataille: Writing the Sacred*, ed. Carolyn Bailey Gill, 91–104. New York: Routledge, 1995.

Boutler, Jonathan. "The Negative Way of Trauma: Georges Bataille's *Story of the Eye*." *Cultural Critique* 46 (Autumn 2000): 153–178.

Brown, Laura S. "Not Outside the Range: One Feminist Perspective on Trauma." In *Trauma: Explorations in Memory*, ed. Cathy Caruth, 100–112. Baltimore, Md.: Johns Hopkins University Press, 1995.

Caruth, Cathy, ed. *Trauma: Explorations in Memory*. Baltimore, Md.: Johns Hopkins University Press, 1995.

———. *Unclaimed Experience: Trauma, Narrative, and History*. Baltimore, Md.: Johns Hopkins University Press, 1996.

Dean, Carolyn. "Introduction." *Diacritics* 26, no. 2 (1996): 3–5.

———. *The Self and Its Pleasures: Bataille, Lacan, and the History of the Decentered Subject*. Ithaca, N.Y.: Cornell University Press, 1992.

Engelhardt, Tom. *The End of Victory Culture: Cold War America and the Disillusioning of a Generation*. Amherst: University of Massachusetts Press, 1995.

Erikson, Kai. *Everything in Its Path: Destruction of Community in the Buffalo Creek Flood*. New York: Simon and Schuster, 1976.

———. "Notes on Trauma and Community." In *Trauma: Explorations in Memory*, ed. Cathy Caruth, 183–199. Baltimore, Md.: Johns Hopkins University Press, 1995.

Farrell, Kirby. "The Berserk Style in American Culture." *Cultural Critique* 46 (Fall 2000): 179–209.

———. *Post-Traumatic Culture: Injury and Interpretation in the Nineties*. Baltimore, Md.: Johns Hopkins University Press, 1998.

Figley, Charles, ed. *Mapping Trauma and Its Wake: Autobiographic Essays by Pioneer Trauma Scholars*. New York: Routledge, 2006.

Foster, Hal. *The Return of the Real: The Avant-Garde at the End of the Century*. Cambridge, Mass.: MIT Press, 1996.

Freud, Sigmund. "Screen Memories." In *Early Psycho-Analytic Publications*, vol. 3 of *The Standard Edition of the Complete Psychological Works of Sigmund Freud*. Trans. James Strachey, 301–322. London: Hogarth Press, 1962.

Hariman, Robert. "Allegory and Democratic Public Culture in the Postmodern Era." *Philosophy and Rhetoric* 35, no. 4 (2002): 267–296.

Hariman, Robert, and John Lucaites. *No Caption Needed: Iconic Photography, Public Culture, and Liberal Democracy*. Chicago: University of Chicago Press, 2007.

Herman, Judith. *Trauma and Recovery: The Aftermath of Violence—From Domestic Abuse to Political Terror*. New York: Basic Books, 1992.

Hollywood, Amy. *Sensible Ecstasy: Mysticism, Sexual Difference, and the Demands of History*. Chicago: University of Chicago Press, 2002.

Jay, Nancy. *Throughout Your Generations Forever: Sacrifice, Religion, and Paternity*. Chicago: University of Chicago Press, 1992.

Kaufman, Eleanor. "Falling from the Sky: Trauma in Perec's 'W' and Caruth's 'Unclaimed Experience.'" *Diacritics* 28, no. 4 (Winter 1998): 44–53.

Jeffords, Susan. *Hard Bodies: Hollywood Masculinity in the Reagan Era*. New Brunswick, N.J.: Rutgers University Press, 1994.

———. *The Remasculinization of America: Gender and the Vietnam War*. Bloomington: Indiana University Press, 1989.

Kaplan, E. Ann. *Trauma Culture: The Politics of Terror and Loss in Media and Literature*. New Brunswick, N.J.: Rutgers University Press, 2005.

LaCapra, Dominick. *Writing History, Writing Trauma*. Baltimore, Md.: Johns Hopkins University Press, 2001.

Landy, Marcia. "'America Under Attack': Pearl Harbor, 9/11, and History of the Media." In *Film and Television After 9/11*, ed. Wheeler Winston Dixon, 79–100. Carbondale: Southern Illinois University Press, 2004.

Laub, Dori. "Truth and Testimony: The Process and the Struggle." In *Trauma: Explorations in Memory*, ed. Cathy Caruth, 61–75. Baltimore, Md.: Johns Hopkins University Press, 1995.

Leys, Ruth. *Trauma: A Genealogy*. Chicago: University of Chicago Press, 2000.

Lifton, Robert Jay. *Home from the War: Learning from Vietnam Veterans*. Boston: Beacon Press, 1973.

Lowenstein, Adam. *Shocking Representation: Historical Trauma, National Cinema, and the Modern Horror Film*. New York: Columbia University Press, 2005.

Luckhurst, Roger. *The Trauma Question*. New York and London: Routledge, 2008.

Malin, Brenton J. *American Masculinity under Clinton: Popular Media and the Nineties "Crisis of Masculinity."* New York: Peter Lang, 2005.

Marvin, Carolyn, and David Ingle. *Blood Sacrifice and the Nation: Totem Rituals and the American Flag*. Cambridge: Cambridge University Press, 1998.

McLuhan, Marshall. *War and Peace in the Global Village*. Ann Arbor: University of Michigan Press, 1968.

Mowitt, John. "Trauma Envy." *Cultural Critique* 46 (Fall 2000): 272–297.

Radstone, Susannah. "The War of the Fathers: Trauma, Fantasy, and September 11." In *Trauma At Home: After 9/11*, ed. Judith Greenberg, 117–123. Lincoln: University of Nebraska Press, 2003.

Read, Jacinda. *The New Avengers: Feminism, Femininity, and the Rape-Revenge Cycle*. Manchester: Manchester University Press, 2000.

Robinson, Sally. *Marked Men: White Masculinity in Crisis*. New York: Columbia University Press, 2000.

Savran, David. *Taking It Like a Man: White Masculinity, Masochism, and Contemporary American Culture*. Princeton, N.J.: Princeton University Press, 2001.

Scott, Joan. "Experience." In *Feminists Theorize the Political*, ed. Judith Butler and Joan W. Scott, 22–40. New York and London: Routledge, 1992.

Seltzer, Mark. *Serial Killers: Death and Life in America's Wound Culture*. New York and London: Routledge, 1998.

Shaviro, Steven. *The Cinematic Body*. Minneapolis: University of Minnesota Press, 1993.

Shay, Jonathan. *Achilles in Vietnam: Combat Trauma and the Undoing of Character*. New York: Scribner, 1994.

Stevens, Maurice. "Ephemeral Traces: Enigmatic Signification, Race, and the Sciences of Memory." In *Memory, Haunting, Discourse*, ed. Maria Holgren Troy and Elisabeth Wennö, 265–269. Karlstad, Sweden: Karlstad University Press, 2005.

Sturken, Marita. *Tangled Memories: The Vietnam War, the AIDS Epidemic, and the Politics of Remembering*. Berkeley: University of California Press, 1997.

Turim, Maureen. *Flashbacks in Film: Memory & History*. New York: Routledge, 1989.

———. "The Trauma of History: Flashbacks upon Flashbacks." *Screen* 42, no. 2 (Summer 2001): 205–210.

Turner, Victor. *Dramas, Fields, and Metaphors: Symbolic Action in Human Society*. Ithaca, N.Y.: Cornell University Press, 1974.

Van der Kolk, Bessel A., and Alexander McFarlane. "The Black Hole of Trauma." In *Traumatic Stress: The Effects of Overwhelming Experience on Mind, Body, and Society*, ed. Bessel A. Van der Kolk, Alexander McFarlane, and Lars Weisaeth, 3–23. New York: Guilford Press, 1996.
Walker, Janet. "Trauma Cinema: False Memories and True Experience." *Screen* 42, no. 2 (Summer 2001): 211–216.

INDEX

ABOUT THE AUTHOR

CLAIRE SISCO KING is an assistant professor in the Department of Communication Studies at Vanderbilt University. She also teaches in the Film Studies Program. Her work has been published in such journals as *Text and Performance Quarterly*, *Quarterly Journal of Speech*, *Communication and Critical Cultural Studies*, *Critical Studies in Media Communication*, and *Western Journal of Communication*.